Voices of Activists and Academics

Praise for this book

'The need to involve children and youth in making the decisions that have a critical impact on their lives and wellbeing has never been greater. This inspirational book brings to a wide audience the voices, views and visions of children, and those who work with and support them, through research and interventions in a diverse range of contexts. Putting children and youth at the centre, it makes an important contribution to attaining child and youth rights and intergenerational justice.'

Professor Peter Taylor, Acting Director, Institute of Development Studies (IDS)

'The participation rights of children has been one of the most popular and yet controversial in child rights discourse since the UN Convention on the Rights of the Child 1989. This book addresses one of the most contentious elements in child participation – the adult-child relationship – drawn from over 30 years of participation ideas and practices from around the world. Based on experiential wisdom and lessons learnt in engaging with children, the chapters in this book redefine and reimage how meaningful adult-child dialogue and partnership can lead to the sustainable participation of children and young people and reshape the landscape of protecting and promoting children's rights and wellbeing. For those who are interested and engaged in this field, this book is a valuable resource to promote inter-generational dialogue and partnerships between adults and children towards achieving human rights for all children in the world today.'

Victor P. Karunan, Visiting Professor in Social Policy, Thammasat University; Development Studies, Chulalongkorn University, and Human Rights and Peace Studies, Mahidol University, Bangkok, Thailand

Voices of Activists and Academics

Working with Children in Communities

Edited by
Vicky Johnson, Tessa Lewin and Andy West

Practical
ACTION
PUBLISHING

Practical Action Publishing Ltd
25 Albert Street, Rugby,
Warwickshire, CV21 2SD, UK
www.practicalactionpublishing.com

A catalogue record for this book is available from the British Library.
A catalogue record for this book has been requested from the Library of Congress.

ISBN 978-1-78853-388-1 Paperback
ISBN 978-1-78853-389-8 Hardback
ISBN 978-1-78853-390-4 Electronic book

Citation: Johnson, V., Lewin, T., and West, W. (2024) *Voices of Activists and Academics: Working with Children in Communities*, Rugby, UK: Practical Action Publishing http://doi.org/10.3362/9781788533904

Since 1974, Practical Action Publishing has published and disseminated books and information in support of international development work throughout the world.

Practical Action Publishing is a trading name of Practical Action Publishing Ltd (Company Reg. No. 1159018), the wholly owned publishing company of Practical Action. Practical Action Publishing trades only in support of its parent charity objectives and any profits are covenanted back to Practical Action (Charity Reg. No. 247257, Group VAT Registration No. 880 9924 76).

Cover photo shows: Youth focused research in Nepal with the YOUR World Research team
Cover photo credit: Vicky Johnson
Cover design by Katarzyna Markowska, Practical Action Publishing
Typeset by vPrompt eServices, India

Contents

Acknowledgements

This book is inspired by the dedication of people across global contexts who have worked with children in communities to improve their lives, many of whom started out as youth activists. The authors of the chapters and many who have not been included in this book have informed our own very different pathways in activism and academia as we try to achieve a vision where conditions are improved to attain child and youth rights and intergenerational justice. Thank you to all of you we have met along the way and we include children and adults of all ages who have informed our thinking.

We would particularly like to thank our funders for allowing us the flexibility to re-scope the field of child rights. Young people, activists, and academics have contributed different types of knowledge and experiences and there has been a growing sense that we form a community of practice that will continue beyond this book and the other outputs from the Rejuvenate programme.

We thank all the contributors to this book – who have done so much to contribute to the field, and who generously gave us their time in agreeing to be part of this project.

Thank you to Michael Gibbons, Maureen Greenwood-Basken, and Anna Windsor, who supported this work.

Thank you to the fantastic Rejuvenate team at the Institute of Development Studies – Mariah Cannon, Alice Webb, and Amy Cowlard.

Vicky: thanks to my boys who are an ongoing source of inspiration for me in my life. Also, colleagues across the Global North and South, who I have worked with in universities, practice and as partners, who have become and remained friends for life. My friends, Morag and Craig, from the Highlands have also continued to remind me of the importance of the connection between continued learning, self-reflection and direct action.

Tessa: thank you to Caroline, Kipp, Lily, and Erin for being in my corner.

Andy: thank you to Helen, as always, and in memory of colleagues, mentors, and friends, Jude Howell, Lewis Hill, and Bob Benewick, who left while this was being written up.

Contributor biographies

Anannia Admassu

Anannia has a PhD in Applied Social Sciences from the University of Brighton in the UK. He has over 25 years of work experience in government, faith-based, and non-governmental organizations with extensive exposure to community work, particularly with children, women, and marginalized members of the community. He is the Founder and Executive Director of CHADET-ETHIOPIA, a child-focused civil society organization that works with marginalized children. CHADET is a founding member of the Child Research Practice Forum and obtained an institutional award from the Ethiopian Society of Sociologists, Social Workers and Anthropologists for its contribution to alleviating the challenges faced by disadvantaged children in Ethiopia. Anannia's area of research interest lies in child protection, children's education, children's participation, violence against children, and children's migration. Anannia's recent research focused on childhood and youth studies, intergenerational relationships and globalization. Recently, he led the establishment of Ethiopian Child Rights Advocacy Network.

Chernor Bah

Chernor Bah is currently the Minister of Information and Civic Education for the Republic of Sierra Leone (appointed in August 2023). As a teenager, he founded Sierra Leone's Children's Parliament, to centre youth voices in post-war reconstruction efforts. He went on to lead youth-related initiatives across three continents for organizations like the United Nations Population Fund (UNFPA), Catholic Relief Services, and Nike Foundation/Girl Effect. From 2007 to 2008, he served as a Special Youth Fellow at the United Nations. In 2008 and 2009, he led the UNFPA's first post-war youth programme in Liberia. In 2012, Bah was appointed by the United Nations Secretary-General as the Youth Representative on the High-Level Steering Committee for the Secretary-General's Global Education First Initiative. He was the co-founder and Executive Director of Purposeful Productions.

Harriot Beazley

Harriot is a social and cultural geographer and community development practitioner, with over 20 years of experience conducting participatory research in Southeast Asia and the Pacific. She is currently an Associate

Professor in Human Geography at the University of the Sunshine Coast, Australia. Her research is focused on the geographies of children and young people and children and young people's participation, with interconnected interests in child protection, gender, social inclusion, and migration in Southeast Asia, especially Indonesia. Harriot has consulted as a technical adviser to AusA (Australian Aid), the Australian Centre for International Agricultural Research (ACIAR), the Australian Department of Foreign Affairs and Trade (DFAT), United Nations Children's Fund (UNICEF), the UK Department for Environment, Food & Rural Affairs (Defra), Save the Children, and the International Organization for Migration (IOM). She is Co-Editor for the Journal *Children's Geographies*, and Co-convenor of the Geographies of Children and Young People's Study Group with the Institute of Australian Geographers.

Jonathan Blagbrough

Jonathan Blagbrough has 30 years' experience of working with exploited children, specializing in child domestic work. He has undertaken research and worked with a range of local civil society organizations, international agencies, and grant-makers on global and local child protection issues, including Anti-Slavery International, and as Co-Director of Children Unite. Jonathan's doctoral research explored relations between child domestic workers and the children of employing families in Tanzania. In addition to programme management work at Family for Every Child and independent consultancy, he has recently worked alongside the University of London's School of Hygiene & Tropical Medicine on research ethics with children and youth.

Eric Braxton

Eric Braxton is a Philadelphia-based organizer and activist who has spent most of his life supporting young people as a driving force for social justice. He was the founding director of the Philadelphia Student Union and spent 10 years as the Executive Director of the Funders' Collaborative on Youth Organizing. He has lived his entire life in West Philadelphia where he now lives with his wife and son and can often be found making music and rooting for the Sixers.

Beniamino Cislaghi

Ben is a courageous thinker and doer who brings innovation across sectors and disciplines. He has collaborated with several NGOs (Oxfam, Tostan, Save, Care, Plan), UN organizations (UNICEF, International Labour Organization (ILO), World Health Organization (WHO)), and universities (including the London School of Hygiene & Tropical Medicine, Stanford, Columbia, Hopkins, and Makerere) where he was globally recognized for his work on gender equality and social justice. These past professional experiences have fuelled his interest to find new, compassionate, imaginative alternatives for mutual global collaboration, envisioning with others mutually beneficial ways of collaborating.

Tom Cockburn

Professor Tom Cockburn is currently Associate Head of the Department of History, Geography and Social Sciences at Edge Hill, after working at the University of Bradford and Manchester Metropolitan University. Over the past 30 years he has undertaken research into children and young people with various charities and government organizations. He has published on a wide variety of issues concerning children and young people. His single authored book for Palgrave Macmillan entitled *Rethinking Children's Citizenship: Theory, Rights and Interdependence* explored theories of children's citizenship.

Swatee Deepak

Swatee works with private and public foundations in strategy development and design, with individuals and families of wealth on their redistribution strategies. She was previously Director of the With and For Girls Collective, the world's only participatory fund by and for adolescent girls, and was Director of Stars Foundation, a private philanthropic foundation focused on funding children and young people around the world. She is a founding member of several collectives working across philanthropy and social justice movements including Closer Than You Think and Shake the Table and is a Board Co-Chair of the Global Fund for Children and EMpower – The Emerging Markets Foundation. Swatee is a Practitioner in Residence for the Marshall Institute at the London School of Economics and Political Science and has co-founded a global arts- and music-based social enterprise, record label, and glamping business and is an investor in sustainable fashion businesses.

Blair Glencorse

Blair Glencorse is Co-CEO of the Accountability Lab – which makes governance work for people around the world. Blair and his team have done everything from building large-scale socially conscious music campaigns in Nigeria; to monitoring and improving public services in Pakistan; to running a global TV show called Integrity Icon to 'name and fame' honest government officials. Blair is also the Co-Chair of the Open Government Partnership and the Co-Chair of the C20 Anti-Corruption Working Group, advising the G20 on issues of anti-corruption on behalf of global civil society. Blair speaks and writes regularly on issues of open governance, citizen participation, and governance.

Karl Hanson

Karl Hanson is Director of the Centre for Children's Rights Studies and Full Professor at the Faculty of Law at the University of Geneva in Switzerland. He obtained his doctorate in law in 2004 from Ghent University, Belgium. His publications and main research interests are in the field of interdisciplinary children's rights studies and include theorizations on children's rights and childhood studies, working children and child labour norms and policies, international children's rights law, and juvenile justice. He teaches at the University of Geneva in the Master interdisciplinaire en droits de l'enfant (MIDE) and in the Master of Advanced Studies in Children's Rights (MCR). He also teaches children's rights at the Faculties of Law of the University of Geneva and of the University of Zurich. Karl Hanson is Chair of the Children's Rights European Academic Network (CREAN) and co-editor of the journal *Childhood*.

Roger Hart

Much of Roger's work has focused on children's relationship with the environment and its relevance to environmental planning and design. For his PhD dissertation, published as *Children's Experience of Place*, he worked closely with all of the children in one New England town over two years to document their exploration and use of the world beyond their homes. He then went on to develop theory on the potentials of children's democratic participation. This was carried out alongside participatory community research, planning, and design projects in New York City with the doctoral student members of the Children's Environments Research Group at the Graduate School of the City University of New York. This was complemented by similar work overseas in collaboration with international development agencies. He is currently completing a longitudinal account of how children's relationship with the environment has changed through revisits to the town of his original research in the 1970s.

Edda Ivan-Smith

Edda Ivan-Smith has worked for over 30 years on social exclusion with a focus on gender and age issues in Africa, Asia, and Europe, for NGOs, and both the private and public sectors. Prior to her retirement in 2003 she worked for nine years for the World Bank in Nigeria, Afghanistan, and Senegal as a Senior Social Development Specialist where she worked with governments and local communities on developing more socially inclusive and sustainable projects funded by the World Bank.

Vicky Johnson

Professor Vicky worked for national and international charities for over 20 years before becoming a lecturer and researcher at the universities in Brighton and London. She joined the University of the Highlands and Islands in 2020 to lead

UHI's Centre for Living Sustainability, which focuses on sustainability, culture, equity, and social justice, and aims to give voice to the most marginalized and encourage dialogue between communities and decision-makers. Professor Johnson's books include *Listening to Small Voices*, research on children's contribution to fragile environments, *Stepping Forward*, a synthesis of how to include children and young people in international development, *Going Beyond Voice*, examining young people's participation across global contexts, and *Youth and Positive Uncertainty*, about negotiating life in post-conflict and fragile environments in Ethiopia and Nepal (UK Research and Innovation-funded research). Her research crosses themes of child and youth rights, intergenerational and social justice, and nature and people in community-driven research across the Highlands and Islands of Scotland and Internationally.

Tenaya Jones

Tenaya was the Self-Determination Advocate at the Young Women's Freedom Center, a non-profit organization in San Francisco committed to decriminalizing and de-carcerating women and girls of colour.

Fassil W. Marriam Kidane

Fassil has worked with children and youth issues, community development, and social justice since the early 1990s in Ethiopia and East Africa. He specializes in child and youth rights, human rights, and organizational learning. He holds a BA Degree in Social Work and a Master's degree in Organizational Leadership.

Fassil is founder and Executive Director of the Children's Rights and Violence Prevention Fund (CRVPF), a regional intermediary organization that focuses on children's and youth rights and social justice issues. CRVPF developed partnerships with 210 local NGOs and community organizations and provides grants and capacity development support. Many of these organizations are led by young people in Uganda, Tanzania, Kenya, and Ethiopia. CRVPF's focus is building community movements that support children's and young people's issues. Fassil believes in the strength and commitments of local community organizations mostly led by young people to address children's and youth issues in a sustainable manner.

Tessa Lewin

Dr Lewin is a Senior Research Fellow in the Participation, Inclusion and Social Change cluster at the Institute of Development Studies, where she co-convened the MA in Gender and Development from 2019 to 2023. She has 25+ years' experience using creative, participatory, and visual methodologies, alongside other qualitative methods for research, teaching, and research communication in community and development contexts. Her research focuses on gender politics, sexuality, visual activism, and child rights. Her doctoral research investigated the nature of queer visual activism in South Africa. She is well known for her work as a creative facilitator, often with children and young people, and has worked on projects involving digital storytelling, photovoice, radio drama, animation, and participatory video. She led the communications work for Pathways of Women's Empowerment (2007–2012), during which she established the Real World documentary film scheme.

Phil Mizen

Phil Mizen is Professor of Sociology and Dean of Aston Graduate School, Aston University, Birmingham, United Kingdom. Phil is currently a Coordinator for the European Sociological Association's Research Network, The Sociology of Children and Childhood, and a Fellow of the Royal Society of Arts. He is an expert on child labour/work, children in the informal sector and informal settlements, youth labour, unemployment, welfare to work, and precarious employment. For many years he has been researching the working lives of street children and children living in the informal sector in Ghana, with his friend, colleague, and collaborator Professor Yaw Opus-Kusi.

Olga Nieuwenhuys

Olga Nieuwenhuys is a Dutch anthropologist who, from the late 1970s, has researched extensively the lives of working children in the Global South. The main aim of her work has been to reposition debates on child labour and children's economic value from a child-centred, postcolonial, and materialist perspective. Understanding working children's lifeworlds, she argues, helps illuminate that these children know their own worth and their rights. To be successful, interventions or actions in support of children who suffer injustices must take this knowledge seriously. To clarify this position, she has worked in the past decades with Karl Hanson on reconceptualizing children's rights and developing the 'living rights' theory. She is the author of *Children's lifeworlds, Gender, welfare and labour in the developing world* (1996 and 2001) and co-editor, with Karl Hanson, of *Reconceptualizing Children's Rights in International Development: Living Rights, Social Justice, Translations* (2013).

Jessica Nowlan

Jessica Nowlan was the Executive Director of the Young Women's Freedom Center and co-founder of the Sister Warriors Freedom Coalition. She is deeply committed to the liberation and freedom of women and girls and has spent the majority of her career working to develop and implement innovative programming and strategies based on the principles that those most impacted must be at the forefront of decision-making about their own lives. In 2019–2021 she was named a Leading Edge Fellow for her work. Prior to her current role, she worked for several years as a social entrepreneur and as a consultant to organizations working with women and girls and at the intersections of violence, poverty, racial justice, incarceration/re-entry, and workforce development.

Yaw Ofosu-Kusi

Yaw Ofosu-Kusi is a Professor of Social Studies with a PhD in Applied Social Studies from the University of Warwick, UK. Among other responsibilities, he was dean of School of Arts and Social Science of the University of Energy and Natural Resources, Sunyani (2018–2022), and the Faculty of Social Science of the University of Education, Winneba (2015–2017), both in Ghana. He also directed the Council for the Development of Social Science Research in Africa's (CODESRIA) Annual Child and Youth Studies Institute (2011); DAAD Guest Professor at the University of Flensburg (now Europa-Universitat Flensburg), Germany (2013/2014), and over the years taught courses and gave public lectures on African Childhoods in Ghana and Europe.

His research has primarily focused on children's mobility, labour, and street life in the context of the urban informal economy of Ghana. He recently participated in a British Academy-funded collaborative research spanning Africa, Europe, and Asia that culminated in the volume, *The Politics of Children's Rights and Representation* (edited by Sandin et al. 2023). Other works are *The Challenge of African Potentials: Conviviality, Informality and Futurity* (co-edited with Motoji 2020) under the African Potentials Project of the University of Kyoto, Japan; *Children, Childhood and the Future: Cross-cultural Perspectives* (co-edited with Kleeberg-Niepage et al. 2020), and in 2017 *Children's Agency and Development in African Societies*, as a product of the 2011 Child and Youth Studies Institute at CODESRIA.

Claire O'Kane

Claire O'Kane is an international child rights practitioner and researcher with 30 years of experience working with children and young people in diverse contexts. She is a qualified social worker with a Master's in Applied Social Studies, and a postgraduate diploma in social research and evaluation from UK universities. She is a senior associate with Proteknôn and a freelance consultant. Claire is a passionate believer in the power of child and youth agency, children's collective organizing and intergenerational collaborations for justice and rights. She is an author of more than 60 publications on children's rights, participation, and protection.

Ken Justus Ondoro

Ken Ondoro is a distinguished researcher, social and behaviour change communication expert, trainer, and speaker. As the Founder and Managing Director of African Research and Development, a prominent consultancy firm headquartered in Kenya, he boasts extensive experience and field contacts in Sierra Leone, India, Mozambique, Uganda, Tanzania, Zambia, Eswatini, Bangladesh, Rwanda, and Somalia. Ken's professional focus lies at the intersection of research and child-focused community interventions. Renowned for his leadership in designing and implementing community-led child protection approaches within development and humanitarian contexts, Ondoro is a dedicated researcher with a passion for tackling complex social issues. With a robust academic background and extensive research expertise, he employs a rigorous analytical approach, utilizing diverse methodologies and data analysis techniques in qualitative and quantitative studies. Ondoro's aptitude in synthesizing and communicating research showcases his lifelong dedication to using evidence-based decision-making to drive positive social change in the field of child protection.

Lakshitha Saji Prelis

Director, Children & Youth Programs, Search for Common Ground and Co-Chair, Global Coalition on Youth, Peace and Security, Prelis has supported intergenerational peacebuilding efforts in over 35 countries. He co-founded the Global Coalition on Youth, Peace, and Security resulting in successful advocacy for the landmark UN Security Council Resolutions 2250, 2419, and 2535. Now he is co-leading, with the UN, African Union (AU), and EU, efforts to strengthen institutional commitments to national strategies on youth, peace, and security and create a strategic roadmap for youth-inclusive peace processes. Before joining Search for Common Ground, he co-founded and directed the Peacebuilding & Development Institute at the American University in Washington, DC. He regularly advises governments, intergovernmental bodies, and civil society, and is a respected speaker and moderator. Prelis holds a Master's degree in International Peace & Conflict Resolution, and received the distinguished Luxembourg Peace Prize for his outstanding achievements in peace support.

Kavita Ratna

Kavita Ratna is presently a Director of The Concerned for Working Children (CWC; www.concernedforworkingchildren.org), which has been thrice nominated for the Nobel Peace Prize for its excellence in child participation practice. She has been engaged with child rights advocacy since 1990. She facilitates children's participation, especially of working and highly vulnerable young people in India – at local and national levels – and regionally and internationally. She holds numerous national and international portfolios and has been a resource person for diverse international development organizations. Among them, she has provided technical expertise to the Commonwealth and UNICEF Regional Office for South Asia (ROSA) in adolescent and youth participation in governance and is one of the authors of the publication *Claiming Citizenship* (2022), jointly published by UNICEF ROSA and CWC. She has a special interest in developmental communications and has directed and scripted several films, videos, and media products as part of her professional engagement.

Irene Rizzini

Irene Rizzini is Professor at the Pontifical Catholic University of Rio de Janeiro, Brazil (PUC-Rio) and Director of The International Center for Research and Policy on Childhood (CIESPI). Professor Rizzini has published extensively on topics related to human rights and public policies, focusing on children and young people, in their family and community contexts. She has conducted studies on children in institutions, living and working on the streets, and young people's activism and their right to participation.

Shubhendra Man Shrestha

Shubhendra has worked for several international and local NGOs in Nepal on childhood and youth programmes. He worked for ActionAid Nepal, and participated in YOUR World Research (2016–2019) based in Ethiopia and Nepal. He has also conducted research on youth resilience in an earthquake-affected Himalayan region, in the years following the severe 2015 earthquake that struck to the north-west of Kathmandu.

Gabriela Trevisan

Gabriela has a PhD in Child Studies, specialty in Sociology of Childhood, from the University of Minho and a Master's degree in Sociology of Childhood and a degree in Sociology of Organizations from the same institution. She completed a postgraduate degree in Educational Sciences at the Faculty of Psychology and Education Sciences of the University of Porto where she worked with young people from Ginasiano on research into artistic expression and community intervention. From 2001 to 2019 she was an Adjunct Professor at the School of Education Paula Frassinetti (degree in Social Education and Master's in Community Intervention). Since 2019, she has been a member of ProChild CoLAB. She is a member of the European Sociological Association's Research Network 04. She has participated in different national and international publications. Her research and intervention interests focus on the sociology of childhood, child citizenship and children's political action, child poverty, and public policies and children/territory/cities.

Mike Wessells

Michael Wessells, PhD, is Professor Emeritus of the Program on Forced Migration and Health at Columbia University. A long-time psychosocial and child protection practitioner, he co-chaired the global task force that produced the Inter-Agency Standing Committee (IASC) Guidelines on Mental Health and Psychosocial Support in Emergency Settings. The author of *Child soldiers: From violence to protection* (Harvard University Press), he has conducted extensive research on the holistic impacts of war and forced migration and on community-based supports for people affected by armed conflict and other violence. Currently, he leads multi-country action research on community-led child protection, and he supports interagency work to integrate mental health and psychosocial support with peacebuilding. He regularly advises UN agencies, governments, and donors on issues of child protection, psychosocial support, and peacebuilding.

Andy West

Andy has worked with children, young people, and related issues, practices, and policies since the early 1980s, principally in Asia and the UK, but also in the Middle East, Africa, and the Pacific. His main work focused on marginalized children and youth. Apart from direct work with children and young people, including supporting their own research, he has been involved with communities, NGOs, international NGOs (INGOs), UN organizations, and local and national governments, on development of practice, policy, and research particularly on child/youth perspectives, rights, protection, and participation. He ran an award-winning advice and counselling youth centre, co-founded local organizations and campaigns, conducted research, and taught in UK universities before living and working mainly in East and Southeast Asia for over 15 years. More recent research includes Ethiopia, Nepal, China, and the Himalayas. Publications include books, articles, and reports concerning children and young people, and other interests including colonial history, museum collections, and material culture.

Acronyms

AU	African Union
CAS	Catholic Action for Street Children
CBO	Community-based organization
CERG	Children's Environments Research Group
CIESPI	International Center for Research and Policy on Childhood
CRSA	Child Rights Situation Analysis
CRVPF	Children's Rights and Violence Prevention Fund (East Africa)
CSW	UN Commission on the Status of Women
DFID	UK Department for International Development (now the Foreign, Commonwealth & Development Office)
EU	European Union
FCYO	The Funders' Collaborative on Youth Organizing
FGC	Female genital cutting
FGM	Female genital mutilation
ILO	International Labour Organization
INGO	International non-governmental organization
IPA	International Play Association
M&E	Monitoring and evaluation
MOOC	Massive open online course
NGO	Non-governmental organization
PRA	Participatory Rural Appraisal or Participatory Rapid Appraisal
SDGs	Sustainable Development Goals
UNCRC	United Nations Convention on the Rights of the Child, adopted 1989
YWFC	Young Women's Freedom Center (United States)

Foreword

This lovely and challenging book asks us to reconsider many of our assumptions about our work and our world. And it is about time! The 'us' and the 'our' referred to in this first sentence are of course we *adults* in the field of social work with and for children. And this book gently, but insistently asks, 'whose world is it, anyway?'

If we pause here to reconsider, in the spirit of this book, we can ask: 'What if we reconsidered the very idea of "our world" itself?' … NOT as something that *we* [adult book readers and social workers and social scientists] own [as in 'our']; and not something *we* [adult book readers and social workers and social scientists] are the centre of …

This book is a beautiful, multi-voiced, extended exercise in reconsidering how the world might be thought of and experienced in a very different way: as a shared biosphere, a space in which 8 billion diverse humans coexist, with varied relationship webs, pursuing a wide variety of goals and impulses and imaginings.

From this vantage point, we can ask why the lived experience of only some humans should serve as the centre of our attention and the basis for claiming that one group – adults – are the rightful apex of a structure of social control. This book is a set of chapters describing various efforts to overcome that default wiring and the systemic structures that derive from this view.

This book also encourages us to consider the possibilities of reimagining the strangely rigid and controlling ways in which adults assume things about children, socially control them as a rule, and rarely engage with and listen to children as fellow travellers on the journey of life, when in fact weighing down young humans with this early dose of anti-social experience is not in anyone's interest. 'Why not do this differently?' this book asks, and 'How might we if we chose to?' The idea is to stretch way beyond the concept of 'child participation' [in an adult world], to a world including all of us humans.

And the final chapters of this book hint at an even deeper question: 'How would the world be different – for children, families, communities, the human family, and the living planet – if we did reorganize how we live and work around the simple notion that children and youth, like adults, are people, and their perspectives add new richness to human wisdom and capacity?' The underlying principles that slowly come into view in this book are not a nostalgic superficial gesture back to a romantic notion of pre-industrial indigenous communalism, but rather an appreciation that all humans across the lifespan have insights to offer, self-interests worthy of consideration, and enrichments of our social life together that we all and our biosphere can benefit from. Each chapter shows us interesting ways we can and should engage the youngest humans in meaningful conversations and consultations that can reshape the landscape of the redemptive social work we are concerned to do. For this I am grateful to all the authors and editors and commend this book to a wide readership.

Michael Gibbons
March 2024

INTRODUCTION
Scaffolding child and youth rights

Vicky Johnson, Tessa Lewin, and Andy West

Purpose and background

This book seeks to draw lessons from academics and activists in the field of child and youth rights in community-driven interventions and research. It draws on a series of detailed interviews from field experts across diverse global contexts.

This material originates from *Rejuvenate*, a partnership programme co-led by the Institute for Development Studies and the University of the Highlands and Islands, and connecting field practitioners and academics from across global contexts. The initial intention of the programme was to map participatory work in the field of child and youth rights since the introduction of the UN Convention on the Rights of the Child (UNCRC). A collection of literature was selected, and interviews were held with field experts, some of whom are included in this book. The literature, and the projects and people it referenced, formed the basis of an ongoing (and growing) 'living archive' and a working paper (Johnson et al., 2020). These began a process of dialogue and deliberation about the inclusion of children and young people into global discourses on social justice and sustainability, against the backdrop of the historical lack of substantive inclusion of children and young people in research and intervention processes over the past three decades.

The onset of Covid at the end of 2019 and the subsequent pandemic impacted on many social groups, and especially on children and young people. In parts of central Africa, for example, where schools closed, children were sent to work, both at home and outside (personal communication, INGO research). Girls and young women in particular experienced violence, including sexual violence; some boys and young men were taken into gangs; and there were reported increases in teenage pregnancy (ibid.). Local organizations subsequently reported that children's situations did not change with the ending of the pandemic, and it was difficult to return them to school (ibid.).

Children and young people in so-called developed countries also experienced problems as, for example, highlighted for the UK by the Children's Commissioner. In evidence to an inquiry, the UK Commissioner was reported as saying there was no one around speaking up for children's best interests (Sodha, 2023). The notion of 'speaking up for children' stands out: the idea or practice of children and young people being consulted, not addressed in news reports. Similar to experiences in parts of Africa (as reported through INGO research, personal communication), children in the UK were reported as having lost their connection to school and not returning on a regular basis once the pandemic was over (Skopeliti, 2023).

In moments of crisis the problems and inequalities experienced by oppressed and powerless groups are exacerbated: previous crises, such as humanitarian emergencies, have demonstrated both how children and young people are impacted and the importance of their participation (West and Theis, 2007). And contributors to this volume highlight experiences of the necessity of engaging children and young people during the Ebola crisis (see for example, Deepak, Chapter 4 and Glencorse, Chapter 21). Yet, as these news reports indicate, the global pandemic once again showed how their views and circumstances were generally marginalized.

How did we get to this stage? Not only in the UK but around the world, given the focus on children's and young people's participation by development agencies and non-government organizations, university departments and others, over the previous three decades. These shortfalls experienced by children and young people suggest that accounts of the development of participatory practice outlined throughout this book are important. They indicate the state of work on the eve of the pandemic, and the problems identified at that time. They also remind us that learning gained can be taken up now, given the impact of the pandemic, in responding to changing circumstances and that there is an urgency to taking up children's and young people's participation in a systematic, open, accountable, and meaningful way across all sectors, if we are to realize their rights. Learning from the past three decades is crucial in order to identify key issues and innovative practice.

Throughout the 1990s, following the UNCRC, there was both lively debate and exciting progress on children's rights and participation largely from the third or non-governmental sector. This was supported from the late 1990s by academics' engagement in interdisciplinary social studies on childhood, youth, and international development. In order to move from the protection of children to a more inclusive understanding of their lives and roles in society, there was growing academic attention paid to how to include young people in research and intervention, and how to listen to (and act on) their contributions. Intergenerational power dynamics, and the underlying social norms that privilege adult perspectives, still often eclipse the importance of gaining insights from children and young people. This book seeks to profile a set of voices that have worked to promote and privilege the inclusion of children and young people in their work and social change, in the hopes that they will motivate and inspire others with an interest in doing so, and to support and rejuvenate this field.

Participation as a contested term

Following the UNCRC, participation became a central, if contested, component of child and youth work. There were, however, critiques around its meaning, and concerns that it had become focused on the 'tools' of practice and on the delivery of defined organizational programme components, or donor funding requirements. Underlying questions of power were often sidestepped. At the same time, the use and popularization of participation practice in development work was subject to similar critique, for example in the 1999 'tyranny of participation' conference and subsequent book of the same title (Cooke and Kothari, 2001). Concerns in development work also arose from the ambiguity of the term, and that its practice had become routine and hollow, and later responses also aimed to recover participation as empowerment and as emancipatory strategy. Previous forums in which practitioners and academics met in extended international workshops to discuss contested terms and the 'how to' in children's and young people's participation are discussed in works such as *Stepping Forward* (Johnson et al., 1998) and *Steps to Engaging Young Children in Research* (Johnson et al., 2014).

Efforts to promote the UNCRC in policy and practice generally included promotion of 'participation' although especially in the decade after 1989 the term was rarely defined, nor its practice potential explored in child rights training workshops. An early commentator on the development of the UNCRC discussed those rights under the heading 'Empowerment Rights': the term participation not appearing in his index (LeBlanc, 1995). As the contributions to this book show, the term, or rather the word 'participation', remains contested, in particular around what it means, how it is used, and in what context. An underlying concern is whether the use of the term 'participation' is still valid, or whether it has been surpassed by more recent research and conceptualization around, for example, the notion of children's agency, or issues of intergenerational relationships and partnerships. Such issues emerged from the start of this period, as the contributions to this book highlight from the perspectives of practice, experience, and example. The emergence of such issues in participation and its terminology within child rights since the UNCRC inception sparked our interest in speaking to contributors about various arenas of practice and innovation. These include: community engagement in child protection, navigating power relationships and other issues in child and youth-led work, intergenerational approaches and research, establishing spaces for children and youth, and engaging marginalized groups.

This book pays attention to the question of terminology. Its contested definitions mean that 'participation' has many different meanings to policymakers, practitioners, and young people, with consequent variations in practice. Questions are therefore asked about how terms translate into the realities of work with children in communities and what facilitates more inclusive processes that support the agency of young people to contribute to decision-making and action that affects their lives.

Articles in the UNCRC stipulate that 'States Parties shall assure to the child who is capable of forming his or her own views the right to express those views freely in all matters affecting the child' (Article 12, not in full), and 'The child shall have the right to freedom of expression' (Article 13, not in full). The subsequent labelling of these and others as forming 'rights to participation', meant that the term 'participation' became privileged over any alternatives regarding children's rights to their involvement in decisions affecting their lives, and was seen to need promotion.

The widespread early ratification of the UNCRC, making it the most successful UN convention, with its proviso that states must incorporate its provisions into legislation, meant that the inevitable 'awareness raising' and training on its contents for government and NGO staff had to be pursued rapidly. Short, simple messages, and contents in easy to read, abbreviated form, were produced and are still circulated. Participation was central to these efforts. In parts of the world the UNCRC became promoted as 'the 3Ps': Protection, Provision, Participation; in other places a quadruple formulation was used, of Survival, Development, Protection, and Participation. In both cases, participation was last in the list and usually the final part of any accompanying training. It was the most difficult of the concepts not only to communicate, but to gain any consensus on. The difficulties might be summarized as: 'Yes, children should survive, yes, they should be protected, yes they should have provisions such as education and health for their development; yes they can participate in football, sewing, art classes ...; oh, what do *you* mean by participation then? Certainly not. 'Despite the resistance from many to an interpretation that encouraged children to make decisions and take action, participation remained central to promotion of the UNCRC, seen as an underlying principle and specifically articulated through certain articles, especially Article 12.

In child and youth rights work, the term participation prevailed despite ambiguities. Practice principles and standards were developed in the early 2000s, and eventually the term 'participation', practice standards and principles became formally adopted through General Comment number 12 of the Committee on the Rights of the Child in 2009. This General Comment focused on the right of the child to be heard, and Article 12 (expressing views) in particular, but also laid out the implementation of the right to be heard in a range of different settings, ranging from family and alternative care, through health and education, play work, to immigration, asylum, and emergency situations, nationally and internationally. The General Comment acknowledged how practice had emerged under the conceptualization of 'participation' and *had* evolved in recent years. Thus, although concerned with the right of the child to be heard, the General Comment includes some 38 uses of the term 'participation', nine 'participate', and four 'participatory'.

By the time of the General Comment in 2009 the work and practice of participation had been taken up with children and young people in a variety of arenas, including academia, advocacy, and policy work, and particularly through development practice. But the slippery nature of the word and underlying concepts, difficulties in translation across languages, discussions over meaning and the growth of practice, disillusion, and even anger over tokenistic and decorative efforts, left open the question of whether the term was and is still valid; that it is still useful to describe and articulate rights practice that aims for self-determination, decision-making, and action. Or does it muddy the waters?

This book

This book is about the state of children's and young people's participation in the context of 30 years of children's rights articulated through the UNCRC, and the perceptions, ideas, practice, and experience of over 25 practitioners in a range of settings. The material is drawn from research undertaken for the Rejuvenate project 30 years after the UNCRC was adopted, focused on the state of substantive participation in child rights work, and including interviews with practitioners around the world, supplemented by the experience and practice of the editors over the past 40 years (see selected references for guides to further reading). The process of research interrogated the meanings and usefulness of the term participation itself.

Our focus on personal experience, examples of practice, and the highlighting of conditions for its success, as well as key issues and contradictions emerging in the field, stems from the commitment shown by our contributors throughout their practice to making use of the UNCRC and to work with and for children and young people. They consider the practical and ethical complexities inherent in different approaches and methods, including the problems of intergenerational involvement, and in holistic engagement. They consider also the various priorities and issues connected to donor funding as well as practice dilemmas, in particular who participates and how, what sort of participation is approved, and what power dynamics are involved. The personal accounts situate many of our contributors as activists for children and young people, who are committed to ensuring equity and diversity, as well as participation and rights.

In particular in their role as activists, but implicitly in all projects, child rights practitioners are centrally concerned with issues of power. Most obviously because of their age, but also in relation to many other intersecting status and identities, children lack social as well as physical power in relationships with adults and institutions, and often also in relation to other children. Their lack of power means that their views, problems, and circumstances, and their ideas and solutions, are often ignored, or not taken seriously or addressed. Hence the emergence of what is commonly referred to as 'participation' practice.

Contributors raise a number of issues that have emerged over the years since the term participation became popular following the inception of the UNCRC in 1989, and its subsequent ratification around the world. The research for the book was conducted and interviews took place before the Covid-19 pandemic, an event which demonstrated yet again how children and young people are not consulted or involved, even in periods of great uncertainty and crisis which will have particular effects on their future. Although the timing of interviews means that academics and activists spoke of their lifelong experiences before this global phenomenon, we have realized that many of the same considerations are relevant post-pandemic. We acknowledge that the period of, structures of, response to, and effects of the pandemic give greater impetus and importance to the need to understand both methods of engaging with children and young people and why this has not achieved the status so many practitioners and promoters of child rights have clearly intended. The requirement to listen to children and young people and support their agency is as relevant in recovery and after as it ever has been.

This is a book about action and experiences. It is based on practice and reflection on practice, and learning from this across disciplines, and although contributing practitioners are based in academia as well as non-government and other field organizations, this is not intended as 'academic' text. Many contributors look at how they started out in projects, finding there was a lack of resources, a scarcity of guides, and often not much interest in children's views and decision-making. While a growing literature exists around methodologies, practice, research findings, childhood and youth, including ethnographies, to feel a compulsion to read and digest it all would seem to suggest new practitioners are incapable of starting out for themselves. Clearly the problems and dilemmas of the past need attention, but also a main tenet of practice, as evidenced throughout this book, is the need to recognize change, and the importance of looking at, understanding, and responding to the particular context, time, and space: each is different and so projects cannot be 'replicated' if they are to take account of and respond to the particular context.

Dilemmas highlighted here show a range of issues, approaches, ideas, and conundrums, but there will always be new circumstances, particularly in the light of new technology, but also new conflicts, and other perhaps currently unimaginable circumstances. The past is not a template but serves as an important guide in the main learning around ethical practical approaches and accountability, and in taking on intergenerational justice.

How the material was gathered

Those included in this book have both depth and breadth of experience as academics and practitioners. The narratives captured in the chapters are based on interviews with activists and academics who are innovators in supporting the 'voices' of children and youth so that their participation can better inform decision-making about issues affecting their lives. Most of the authors are not children and youth – they are those who work with them and for them, as facilitators and enablers. There is also a chapter written by youth activists in the US who were interviewees in our original Rejuvenate research. More interviews and writing from youth activists will be important going forwards. Many of the adult interviewees were previously youth activists and have remained dedicated to the inclusion of children and youth in processes of social change. Some have worked on broader community development and issues of sustainability, in which they recognize the value of including innovative ideas from young people. Our selection here is in no way comprehensive and of course there are some important thinkers and practitioners missing. But we feel confident that this collection serves as an important and useful contribution to a field in which there is so much more work to be done.

The interviews that form the basis of each chapter varied from 30 to 90 minutes (depending on the availability of the interviewees). Interviews were conducted immediately before the Covid-19 pandemic, between April and October 2019. Interviewees were selected to provide a range of perspectives from varied communities of practice, covering different global contexts and different periods of time in the continuing development of the field of child and youth rights. The interviews with academics and activists who have been in the field for longer are helpful in providing historical perspectives from which to reflect on progress and problems in the substantive inclusion of children and young people in research and intervention work. Those younger, or fresher to the field, provide both perspectives on the continuation of innovative and inclusive approaches, and also more recent ideas about how to provide children and young people with the spaces they need to become confident and competent in community work and as social actors.

The process of shifting from oral discussions to book chapters began with recordings of the interviews, and subsequent production of transcripts. In order to make best use of the material, and convert from listening to a readable text, it was decided to retain the oral sense, the spoken word, as far as possible. Also, by removing the questions, which were often either discursive or abbreviated, the speech flows more naturally. We use subheadings instead, which often indicate the content of questions (for example, when interviewees were asked about examples of successful projects, unsuccessful or problematic projects or issues). Each interview followed its own course, and so although some basic, similar structure is evident throughout, the flow of each chapter follows the interests, experiences, and issues raised by the interviewee. Each interview starts with an outline of the background of the interviewee and their core relevant experiences before moving on to making use of that experience in discussing the development of innovative work and contemporary issues in children's participation. Many interviewees discussed terminology, and questioned how we think about, discuss, and define rights and participation.

The edited transcripts were reviewed by the interviewee contributors to this book, to check their perspectives had been recorded accurately, to make clarifications and corrections, and to add references. They were asked to maintain the 'speech style' and not overburden the text with references, since this book is largely based on personal experience and perspectives. In some cases, contributors made considerable changes to flesh out their views, and to take account of changes that had taken place in the interval between interview and editing of the transcript. These have largely successfully maintained the speech style, which we maintained, along with the basis in personal experience, to make the book as accessible as possible, bearing in mind that 'heavy academic style' can be off-putting. A couple of chapters have moved further from speech style as the contributors wanted to take this opportunity to say more than they had about experience and issues.

Ethical approval for this study was gained through the Institute of Development Studies (IDS) at the University of Sussex, and informed consent forms and information sheets designed for the purposes of the research were provided to each interviewee. As part of this, interviews were taped, transcribed, edited, and sent to field experts for their further editing and approval. These comprise the mini chapters in each section as follows.

Layout of the book

The book is organized in six sections: first, this introduction; then four themes that include the monographs from field experts; and finally a conclusion based on the contributions and interviews that raises challenges and opportunities across the field. Although contributors have been allocated to a particular theme, many could feature across the whole range. All contributors are committed to involving children and young people from all sectors and backgrounds in the processes of inclusive social change and have given significant thought to the complexities and ethics this involves.

This *Introduction* (Johnson, Lewin, and West) aims to situate the sections that follow it, and the interviews within them, as part of the Rejuvenate programme. We regard this work as a timely contribution intended to re-energize child and youth rights advocates working both within academia and as practitioners.

The first theme, *Historical and international context*, features academics that contribute experience from varied institutional contexts including: academia, UN organizations and policy settings (including the UNCRC and World Bank), funding bodies (including philanthropic funders), international and national non-governmental organizations, and grassroots and youth-led organizations. Contributions in the form of monographs or sub-chapters attributed to individuals include the following field experts: Roger Hart, Edda Ivan-Smith, Swatee Deepak, Ken Justus Ondoro, Jonathan Blagbrough, and Tom Cockburn.

The second theme, *Practice from regional contexts*, focuses on the importance of taking context into account in putting into practice child and youth rights on the ground. This section includes shorter monographs that provide experience from different parts of the world including various countries across Europe, Africa, Asia, Latin America, North America, and Australia. The contributors from this theme include: Anannia Admassu, Fassil W. Marriam Kidane, Yaw Ofosu-Kusi with Phil Mizen, Shubhendra Man Shrestha, Harriot Beazley, Irene Rizzini, Jessica Nowlan and Tenaya Jones, and Gabriela Trevisan.

The third theme, *Youth activism into thinking*, contributes experiences from field experts who have started their lives as youth activists and taken their experiences into academia, policy, and practice. This demonstrates the importance of supporting the inclusion of young ideas into decision-making, but also highlights how much a notion of activism is often a core element in practice. These contributors include Karl Hanson, Lakshitha Saji Prelis, Blair Glencorse, Eric Braxton, and Chernor Bah.

The fourth theme, *Thinking forward*, focuses on the challenges and opportunities of working with children and young people, and provides input into the future of the field of child and youth rights. It issues a call to action to help readers reflect on what support is needed for the meaningful participation of children and young people in social justice work. Contributors for this theme include Beniamino Cislaghi, Mike Wessells, Olga Nieuwenhuys, Claire O'Kane, and Kavita Ratna.

Our *Conclusion* (West, Johnson, and Lewin) draws out major learnings and findings from practices linked to contexts across countries and continents. It outlines paths of development in child and youth participation practice since the 1990s and highlights a range of issues and contradictions inherent in work to support child and youth rights activists, practitioners, and academics, as well as new opportunities and innovations.

References

Cooke, B. and Kothari, U. (eds) (2001) *Participation: The new tyranny?* London: Zed Books.

Johnson, V., Ivan-Smith, E., Gordon, G., Pridmore, P. and Scott, P. (eds) (1998) *Stepping Forward: Children and young people's participation in the development process*. London: Intermediate Technology Publications.

Johnson, V., Hart, R. and Colwell, J. (eds) (2014) *Steps to Engaging Young Children in Research: The guide and the toolkit*. The Hague: Bernard van Leer Foundation.

Johnson, V., Lewin, T. and Cannon, M. (2020) *Learning from a Living Archive: Rejuvenating child and youth rights and participation*. REJUVENATE Working Paper 1. Brighton: Institute of Development Studies. https://doi.org/10.19088/REJUVENATE.2020.001

LeBlanc, L.J. (1995) *The Convention on the Rights of the Child: United Nations lawmaking on human rights*. Lincoln: University of Nebraska Press.

Skopeliti, C. (2023) '"It broke the link": how the pandemic disrupted children's relationship with school', *The Guardian*, 24 March 2023. https://www.theguardian.com/society/2023/mar/24/it-broke-the-link-how-the-pandemic-disrupted-childrens-relationship-with-school

Sodha, S. (2023) 'Empty classroom seats reveal "long shadow" of Covid chaos on Britain's children'. *The Observer*, 22 October 2023 https://www.theguardian.com/commentisfree/2023/oct/22/empty-classroom-seats-reveal-long-shadow-of-covid-chaos-on-children

West, A. and Theis, J. (2007) *The Participation of Children and Young People in Emergencies*. Bangkok: UNICEF.

PART ONE

Historical and international context

CHAPTER 1

Historical and international context: an introduction

Although the modern history of children's rights extends back a century, and children's social participation beyond that, the content of this section focuses on the period immediately preceding, and the period since, the 1989 United Nations Convention on the Rights of the Child (UNCRC). The Convention's predecessors include the Declaration of the Rights of the Child adopted by the League of Nations in 1924 and the UN in 1959. Children were involved in making decisions and taking collective action long before that, on matters of concern to themselves, and in community affairs. One notable example being the school strikes held in September 1911 across Britain, apparently originating in Hull in the north of England. Children were striking against violence by teachers, long hours, and for holidays and pay. This collective action was mirrored internationally a century later in the school strikes for climate change.

As indicated earlier, the focus of the historical context for this book is on the years leading up to and after the 1989 UNCRC, a convention which has particular origins in the 1979 International Year of the Child, and earlier debates on rights for children in the 1960s and 1970s, at least in Europe. The focus here, as throughout the book, is on practical experience and example, and in drawing out principles, points, and debates from these. The key underlying issues include the terminology of participation, in its contested meaning, but also how the concept translates in terms of language and practice, and cross-cultural issues of interpretation and performance. International concerns emerge through this, and in practice through global and regional gatherings and forums of children and young people, raising issues of language, who is involved, and who is selected. Further international issues revolve around citizenship, and what this status and concept means for engagement, especially in terms of age. Throughout, there is always the practical question of method and practice: how is participation done, by whom, to whom, with whom, and for whom?

In Part One the six chapters focus on the broad context for children's participation in research, environmental planning, project implementation, community development, funding issues, and child protection in communities, including issues of slavery and domestic work, and the question of citizenship. They look at a range of interventions, especially child- and youth-led approaches, particularly of girls, across a variety of sectors, from government and community to the private sector. As noted in the Introduction, most of the interviews that form the basis of the chapters were conducted in 2019; the elapse of time (and the Covid pandemic) has meant that the circumstances for some interventions and the work of organizations have changed (particularly noted in Chapters 4 and 5; the importance of the pandemic context is outlined briefly in Chapter 1). This reminds us how children's participation is not static, and attention must be paid to time and place as well as who is involved.

Roger Hart (Chapter 2) provides examples of involving children in environmental planning, design, and research from his work from the 1970s, and the development of a newsletter and a reworking of Arnstein's (1969) citizen ladder into a ladder of children's participation. He looks at subsequent work, gathering examples of children's everyday participation in household and community life around the world, based on his recognition that children's learning and development does not match their stereotype as passive recipients of education. His work includes projects with street children and child labour movements, as well as children's clubs, and work in schools.

The historical and international context is broadened further through the work of Edda Ivan-Smith, who was involved in the seminal 1992 project 'listening to smaller voices', engaging children in rural Nepal. Here she looks at issues in project implementation, capacities, and community-driven development and questions of context from the perspective of a large international agency like the World Bank. She looks at the politics of stakeholder engagement, empowerment, and the use of indicators in measurement, including the notion of gender 'tagging' and its potential applicability to children and young people in monitoring and evaluation.

Moving to a different funding sector and a perspective based in the Global South, Swatee Deepak discusses the development and management of projects both involving and for adolescent girls in Africa over the past 20 years, from the perspective of philanthropic organizations. She focuses on issues in collaborative funding, the involvement of girls in selecting organizations to fund and promote, indicators, funding issues, capacity building, and reporting across what has become an increasingly large project and organization based in the Global South.

Ken Justus Ondoro addresses another organization based in Africa, and focused on community and child- and youth-led child protection interventions and methodologies using four pillars of action, and operating within the overall framework of the UNCRC. He looks at examples of practice in East Africa, noting conditions for successful projects and barriers, particularly poverty, in child- and youth-led approaches. He comments on advocacy issues with governments, priorities for funding, and gaps in evidence particularly for community-led work in terms of issues for donors.

In two shorter pieces, contributors discuss examples of approaches to engaging children and young people in Africa and the UK. Jonathan Blagbrough looks at the development of 'advisory committees' of girls and young women and boys, and the regular meetings held as a way of getting the voices of domestic workers raised and heard. This larger project, concerned with issues of slavery, ran across South American, South Asia, and Africa.

Tom Cockburn looks at examples of community-based work with children and young people in northern England. He looks particularly at how the issue, question, and conceptualization of citizenship can serve as an encompassing framework in which to examine and analyse children's and young people's situation, rights, participation, power, and engagement.

All of the contributors here, as in other parts of the book, raise and discuss issues around the language and terminology of key concepts that have evolved through practice and policy work articulating the UNCRC, as well as through academic analysis and popular, public perception. Throughout the book are thoughts on the usefulness of terms such as participation and agency, particularly from the perspectives of different types of institutions, such as non-governmental organizations, donors and philanthropic organizations, and the public. Other concerns emerge from the discussions, such as who represents children in these spaces or if and how they represent them, if children make decisions themselves, or in partnerships with adults. Also discussed are issues of interdependency, and generation; and the spaces and environments in which children and youth can participate and engage, and how such places, spaces, agency, and engagement are sustained, including within the frame of citizenship.

Reference

Arnstein, S. (1969) 'A ladder of citizen participation', *Journal of the American Planning Association* 35(4): 216–224.

CHAPTER 2

From understanding children's experience of environments to finding ways to help them participate in changing them

Roger Hart

Background

I'm going to get slightly mixed up with dates, but it might help to explain that I went to the States to just broaden my education by working on a PhD in Geography before returning to the UK to take up a job that was waiting for me. I began working with children within my first few weeks at the Graduate School in Massachusetts and this quickly began to change everything for me. I switched from my plan to study the growth of informal settlements in Latin America, to being asked to work with children on their geographic learning. With funds from a large new grant from the Federal Government to investigate children's geographic learning, my professors had purchased a plane and I was asked to pilot it and begin shooting aerial photographs. These photographs were needed to investigate whether they could be used effectively as maps to improve young children's geographic learning. I began by using very large versions of aerial photographs of the local neighbourhood laid out on the floor in a nearby school classroom with children aged seven to eight. I discovered that the children of this age were excited by this and quickly began to work with one another to identify places and use toy vehicles to travel through this photographic representation of their city. I found this first experience of working with children most enjoyable and very soon concluded that my career from here on needed to involve work with children!

After more exploratory work with children, I designed a Master's thesis to instigate how well aerial photography served teachers and children for geographic learning in classrooms. Because I was being advised by an educational psychologist, I used an experimental research design with the teachers and children of nine 3rd grade classes (8–9-year-olds). Three of the classes used maps to study the local geography of their community, city, and state. Three other classes used aerial photographs, and the third group of three classes used aerial photographs supplemented with a flight over their neighbourhood and city.

The aerial photographs proved to be a superb tool for teaching mapping and geography compared to regular abstract maps. A flying experience proved to be an unnecessary supplement to the learning potentials of using aerial photographs alone (there's a joke about the 'ceiling effect' here!). I never published this work, beyond making a few monograph copies of the thesis because, even though the teachers and children of the nine classes enjoyed the experience, I was not proud of having used a strict experimental research design for this work. I concluded from watching the classrooms that my research design made the children passive in their curriculum, although this is of course what tends to happen in schools generally. It was a missed opportunity, for if I had asked the teachers to say to the children something like: 'Let's look at these photographs that Mr Hart has taken from above your school and beyond and here are some coloured pencils. What would you like to do with them?', I believe that the children would have comfortably worked on them as maps; colouring in and naming places that were meaningful to them and making their own key. Their learning journey would have thereby been based on their own everyday experiences and knowledge in their neighbourhoods and the teacher could have powerfully built upon that. I suppose that was my first realization of the central importance of children's own participation in a setting where adults commonly, though well-mindedly, have too much control.

After this experience, I looked at all that had been written on the development of children's understanding of their spatial world from around the world (Hart and Moore 1973). Then, for my PhD dissertation research, my psychology professors encouraged me to conduct research in a controlled environment to learn about how children explored and mentally mapped their world. I began to think how to design this research, but I was again not comfortable with the controlled research design orientation of my advisers. Then, one day in the library, I came across a book called *Baboon Ecology* (Altmann and Altmann, 1973). In this inspiring book, I discovered that we knew more about the everyday spatial range of baboons and how they mentally mapped the world than we did about children. It was all that I needed to rebel against mainstream psychology and to design my own naturalistic, ecological study with children.

This PhD dissertation was the inverse of what I had done for my Master's thesis. I found a town that was small enough for me to get to know all the children well and that had a very supportive elementary school for me to work with. I explained to all the parents and school teachers why my research on how children explored and learned about environment could be valuable. I told them and their children that I wanted to understand what places they liked and did not, where they went and with whom, what they did in these places, and why they did not go to other places.

In terms of why I did it, I gave them two explanations. First, because it could be valuable knowledge for environmental educators in their thinking about how to teach children about the local environment. Second, because it would also help planners and designers to understand how to create more appropriate environments for children. It became quickly clear to me that few people in the town could understand why learning about how children spontaneously explored the environment could be relevant to education, but they did seem to understand my planning and design argument. I think that the story they, and their children, started telling each other was that Roger is here to do this work so he could improve the planning and design of places outside of this town because we have here an ideal setting for children! That was not my story, but it was good that they accepted me warmly!

The children understood that to do this research I needed to work closely with them. The research strategy was a combination of interviews and mapping activities with the children in the school, walking interviews with them through the town and then follow-up participant observation with them as I regularly ranged all over the town. They understood and were comfortable with my doing this work. For example, one group of seven children aged 8 to 11, living on Main Street, made me always take my shoes off. I asked why and they said that that is how they liked to play. I explained that where I come from in England, children wouldn't be allowed to do that. They told me that this is how we do it here, and you'd better take your shoes off, because you said you wanted to understand how we play. After that I regularly took my shoes off. In these kinds of ways, my research became increasingly participatory, so that when I finally left the town after over two years, it was difficult parting for both me and for many of the children and parents. To my surprise the dissertation was published as a book (Hart, 1979). I attribute this to the fact that I walked away from doing a kind of research that was common and accepted and chose instead to conduct a close, naturalistic study with children, which was highly original at that time.

Another key moment in my awareness of the importance of children's participation in planning and decision-making was when I began to teach at the Graduate Centre of the City University of New York in 1975. I started to conduct more ecological research with children in their environments, thinking that I was going to be able to have an influence on the urban planning process in cities. I realized quickly, however, that planning in America is not really planning – it's development, and that planners were unlikely to listen to me.

Fortunately, I was soon asked to help in planning by local community organizations in New York and I started to collaborate with them in open space planning in the South Bronx and Harlem. I knew the best way to find out how children used space was to work with children, but I had never thought of them, until that time, being directly involved in the official planning and design processes. I had by now formed the Children's Environments Research Group [CERG] with doctoral students at the Graduate Centre and, as one of our research domains, we started working with groups of parents and children on community planning and design. We seemed to be inventing everything for there was so little at that time that I could find about participatory methods for working with children. We did many participatory projects, through the 1980s and 1990s in low-income neighbourhoods of New York City, including schoolyard redesign, play environments on top of buildings, spaces for young children in community gardens, and an open space planning project for a South Bronx neighbourhood. We were constantly learning about how to involve children and youth of a wide age range and to make sure that girls were as equally involved as boys.

In 1976 I was invited to speak at the first Habitat Conference in Vancouver and also to organize and run a children's conference. I teamed up with volunteer students, and we had a school in the suburbs of Vancouver. They gave me a spacious gym to involve 36 children, although all of them were from well-off families, mostly diplomats. It was a valuable experience for me as well as for them. I explained to them that because we were trying to understand human settlements, I was going to give them the chance to build one. So, they built a gigantic 'squatter settlement' in this building and we followed its growth for two weeks. If I'd had research assistants with me, I would have made sure to document this process, but all I have are one or two photographs of it.

The squatter settlement plan worked well. The only rule we had was that whenever somebody felt that there was an issue about planning or a conflict or something they wanted to raise, they should tell one another that there needs to be a meeting. At these times, they all stopped work and came together. This became a spontaneous, organic process. I remember that at one of the first sessions a meeting was called because girls were upset that boys were building windows in their cardboard houses that overlooked their homes and invaded their privacy. So, privacy quickly came into our dialogues about habitat planning and design and they all had a rich discussion about it before going back to work again. All of these experiences fed gradually into my realization about the importance of children's participation in many domains that were typically solely in the orbit of adults.

Making sense of children's participation

I am a long-term enthusiastic member of the International Play Association (IPA). Its members are largely playworkers and people really engaged in supporting genuine free play, but there are a few people like me in other professions, including planning, design, and research. The United Nations Educational, Scientific and Cultural Organization (UNESCO) declared 1979 the International Year of the Child and IPA decided to encourage projects related to this designation. The IPA board decided that children's participation in the development of play would be something that we could do for IPA. We had a newsletter called *Childhood City* that I was editing with Robin Moore and Leanne Rivlin. It was produced four times a year and was a predecessor to the *Children's Environments* journal.[1]

Childhood City was just a newsletter. We did a series of three issues on the theme of children's participation. For the first volume of that newsletter in 1979 I introduced the 'ladder of participation' concept developed by Sherry Arnstein. I had found it useful, but I critiqued it and transformed it for its relevance to children. My close colleague and Co-Director of CERG', Selim Iltus, quickly drew a clean copy of my scribbles, in one shot, without correcting it. Many people have asked me since, what does it mean that some steps of the ladder are tied with ropes and others with nails? I have to explain that they are not a meaningful part of the concept; just Selim being playful!

One day in 1982 I received a phone call from Mary Racelis, the person who had taken on an important championing initiative at UNICEF (United Nations Children's Fund). She was surprised when she realized that as the innovative champion of participatory development in UNICEF, she hadn't thought of also involving children. When she placed an order with me for 350 copies of each of our newsletters on participation to send out to all of the national offices of UNICEF, I said: *'What! The circulation of our publication is only 200 people!'* I told her that I couldn't send her the newsletters out because they were primarily about US projects and that I would be ashamed to show the world that we had no accounts from less developed countries. She then asked me, 'Where would you go to learn more?' And I said, 'I think Sri Lanka first because I'd heard that they had an innovative national participatory community movement that involves children'.

On my return from an impressive tour of Sri Lanka with the director of the programme, Vinya Ariyaratne, I explained to UNICEF that 'I can't write this up, because I don't understand it'. What they were doing with the Sarvodaya Movement was very participatory but children in all the villages were all doing very similar projects. The children were involved in building water wells with adults, and then they would regularly clean them, decorate them, and monitor them. They were proud of that work and genuinely involved but they were not projects where children had some involvement in initiating or designing them. I wasn't critical of the result, but it was so different from the meaning of participation in the West, where the emphasis was on shared decision-making. I think I wrote about that in my first UNICEF book on children's participation, but very carefully. I didn't want to step on any toes because the truth is that I didn't know then, and still don't understand well, what participation means in Asian countries. I just know that what I often saw when I subsequently visited that continent was a more collective way children had of working together on projects. They seemed to quite naturally defer to one another, not because they had been specifically trained in any particular group processes, but because within their culture they spontaneously acted in ways that were more interdependent than the more autonomous, individual-istic orientation I knew of in the USA and Europe.

So, the way that I dealt with it subsequently, whenever I was invited to lecture anywhere in Asia, I would explain that I could not lecture about partic-ipation, because that would imply that I know what that means in your culture. However, because I wanted to try to understand the differences, I learned to say, yes, and turned the lectures into dialogues, more like workshops. I discovered that even when there were well over a hundred people in the 'audience', it was possible for the event to be interactive and for all of us to learn.

Children's participation: From tokenism to citizenship

A few years later, in 1991, I was working as a consultant with the Urban Child Programme of the UNICEF International Child Development Centre in Florence, Italy. As part of its research programme on street and working children, they arranged for me to travel to visit the Philippines, Brazil, Kenya, and India, to visit preventive programmes for children at risk of becoming street children. I discovered that, for a number of countries, children's participation in decision-making was becoming fundamental to their approaches to improving children's rights. As a result of my learning from all of these consultations, I was commissioned by James Himes, the director of the Centre, to write a small book about children's participation (Hart, 1992]. This small book and the graphic expression of a ladder of children's participation has had a remarkable effect in promoting others to think about and discuss some of the challenging and culturally variable issues involved in understanding adult–child relationships. Unfortunately, though, instead of seeing my ladder as a beginning vocabulary for promoting critical reflection on the issue, it has been seen by many people as something that should be universally used to evaluate if children are being involved correctly in any setting or culture. So I have therefore written a follow-up paper that seems to be having a useful effect in encouraging people to step back a little to critically reflect upon the ladder (Hart, 2008).

Children's participation in sustainable development

In 1996 I was commissioned by Deepak Bajracharya in the small, newly established Environment Section of UNICEF HQ in New York to write a book for them on children's participation in environmental projects. The Declaration from the United Nations Conference on Environment and Development held in Rio de Janeiro in 1992 had introduced the concept of sustainable development as a critical new vision of development, so we decided to title the book *Children's Participation in Sustainable Development*. Unfortunately, someone in charge of publications in UNICEF changed the title at the last minute because they felt that the term sustainable development was not known by the public! So, I quickly came up with a very long title, but it doesn't clearly articulate this intended view of achieving development while also sustaining the environment (see Hart, 1997).

With material sent to me from UNICEF offices throughout the world, I attempted to put together a book that could make some modest contribution to articulating how children might participate in ways that were in line with this important new societal concept. Unfortunately, most of the projects that were sent to me from overseas were just like the ones that I was familiar with myself from North America and Europe. They appropriately involved children in local actions on the environment but the focus of these projects and the questions being asked all seemed to come from adults. Certainly, adults working with children on local environmental initiatives should be free to suggest issues to work on but to rely entirely on that is not an effective way to foster the development of a citizenry that feels they have the right and the responsibility to act on issues that they feel are important. I had learned from my own participatory work with children in New York City that there were some very effective ways to achieve this degree of ownership by children of the research and action process, so we decided that I should also travel to find examples of this from less developed countries.

With recommendations from the field staff of national offices of UNICEF in Latin America and their collaborating NGOs, I identified programmes in the region that promised to be of value. The first programme that I visited for the book was in Ecuador: El Programa del Muchacho Trabajador (PMT), the National Program for Street and Working Children. It was a perfect introduction for my new exploration of the ways that children can effectively participate in projects to improve the environment. It was a local to national level children's participation programme that was similar in structure to the programme that I had visited in Manila for the previous UNICEF book. The PMT programme, headquartered in the capital, Quito, had many units located in the three major geographic regions of the country: the Amazon, the Andes, and the Pacific. Street working children throughout the country got to vote upon what the particular children's rights focus would be for each year. Fortunately for me, the year that I went to see them the children had chosen to work on the theme of the environmental rights of children.

What was special about 'El Programa' was that children were organized into small groups called 'Espacios Alternativo', which meant that they were not in a church, and they were not in the school but in an alternative space. There were hundreds of these local spaces that were their own, created for them to be able to plan and to act upon their rights. A team of brilliant animators designed a guide for the volunteer adult facilitators in each group. For example, early in the children's process of identifying environmental issues, they were encouraged to interview their elders on what were some of the big environmental changes that had occurred since they were children. Each Espacio Alternativo had local workshops where the children designed and ran projects every year. They shared their projects with peers at the town or city level conferences and then, through elected representative children, they presented them for discussion at regional and national level conferences. I visited the children's groups in each of these different regions and heard their accounts of some of the valuable human rights-based environmental projects that were so important to them. One example that, through their search and communication efforts, they were able to move on to the agenda of a municipality was the dangers of vehicle pollution, something that the street working children were particularly aware of.

The challenges of children's representation

The street children's projects that I visited for UNICEF in the Philippines and in Brazil at the beginning of the 1990s were deeply participatory. I believe that they got special attention because after the formal national recognition of children's rights with the CRC, the actors were beginning to be seen as citizens with rights and were often characterized in the media as pioneers in democratic change. The CRC had arrived and you could feel it, and children and their advocates would consistently talk about it that way. It appeared that it was now easier to talk about kids having a voice through the front pages of newspapers than it was to say that poor people were going to speak about their rights. Both countries had recently been under dictatorships when the CRC was launched in 1989.

In Brazil, hundreds of street children were driven by bus from every corner of the country to be in the plaza in front of the parliament when they were debating the UN Convention. The children brought something like 2 or 3 million signatures from street working children from all over the country. The next day the senators came out and invited three of the child leaders into their session. The three walked up the steps and all the others followed! They walked into congress, and I suppose the security folks didn't know what to do. So, for every politician, there were two children! Then the three young people gave speeches, and at the end, congress voted that the entire CRC should be written into the constitution. This project was not about the kind of partici-pation that I'm discussing in this interview of course; it was 'social mobili-zation' organized by NGOs with UNICEF. Nevertheless, social mobilization can sometimes be a powerful first way to introduce children to the idea that they are citizens with the right to have a voice about their rights. The CRC was also quickly built into the agendas of the organizations and agencies working with street working children in the Philippines.

The reason why I found child labour groups so interesting was because they were sustained groups where adult advocates gave children the chance to establish structures and processes which were meaningful to them and enabled children to run them. In contrast, I visited some peacebuilding projects with children in Latin America that were thought of as children's projects, but I was disappointed to discover that their meetings were typically run entirely by adults. The children did some excellent peace-related projects in their communities, but it seemed like a missed opportunity that the children were not involved in running the meetings; they were more like a continuation of school.

Like in Brazil, the national movement of working children in the Philippines was large in scale but it also operated through small, highly participatory, groups of children. While I was visiting in the 1990s, these local groups worked in creative ways, relying especially on theatre, to identify what they thought were the most important human rights issues to act upon. Elected represen-tatives from each of these groups would then carry the ideas of the group to a city level conference of children to identify what they thought should be developed for city-wide action. Representatives were then elected from the city groups to a national conference. The children's debates and voting on their rights issues then resulted in children electing representatives to deliver their concerns to the national government.

In 1997, I was invited by Redd Barna [Save the Children Norway] and Save the Children USA to work with colleagues in Nepal to investigate how children clubs in the nation were developing as democratic groups (see Hart and Rajbhandary, 2003). I was very impressed by what I saw in the different regions of the country. The groups of children in each village gathered voluntarily and were self-organized and managed with just a little basic training in alternative participatory democratic structures and processes. As a result, they were able to function as free-standing groups in many villages throughout the country and could manage their own projects. In some ways, they mirrored the women's groups that had been formed some years earlier. Children could now be approached by development agencies as members of a self-determining group. Without such groups, any outside developmental agency is limited to asking children to conduct projects that they want to see happen. Instead of this, the self-managing children's rights groups offer a chance for children themselves to generate, and act upon, their own priorities for change. When adults in some of the villages saw how well the children were working together, they invited children's clubs to send representatives to the official Village Development Committee meetings.

Moving towards intergenerational community governance

Ideally, we should be trying to find ways for a genuine partnership between children and all members of a community for community-based change on human rights for all. A few years ago, I wrote a paper with two colleagues called 'Beyond Projects', which basically makes the argument that there should not only be opportunities for children to participate in building projects that fulfil human rights but also sustained opportunities for all people within communities to work together, across generations, for human rights (Hart et al., 2014).

I'm happy to say that one author, not part of our CERG', has in recent years been able to conduct a wonderfully close look at what *The Peruvian Movement of Working Children* has been able to achieve with their sustained intergenerational, 'Protaganismo' approach (Taft, 2019). We share enthusiasm for development of this kind of intergenerational community governance within the CERG'. But our own contribution has been to attempt to provide some modest support for groups that are no way near as advanced as the one Taft has been documenting. We had the goal of providing some simple tools to help communities have intergenerational dialogues on important dimensions of community life.

We began by developing the tools for use in the beginning phase of the 'Child Friendly City' movement. My colleagues, Pamela Wridt and Sruthi Atmakur, through their international work, have since discovered that our participatory, intergenerational, child-friendly assessment and planning tools are also valuable across a wider range of scales and types of environments than just cities. We therefore began to call the tools a *Child Friendly Places [CFP] toolkit.*

The pictorial survey instruments enable people of a wide range of ages and abilities to score key indicators of neighbourhood quality that relate to their well-being; and then enable them to compare those indicators across groups of children of different ages and gender, with parents and grandparents and with other actors in their community. Since 2008, CERG has worked with multiple partner organizations around the world to produce the CFP resource kit that empowers children, adolescents, families, educators, service providers, and decision-makers to assess their local environments using child-friendly indicators.

The results from this process have been of great value in planning and designing changes related to the health and well-being of children, young people, and adults. For example, my colleagues in CERG had considerable success in applying this idea of fostering local groups of children to be involved in decision-making following a national emergency situation in Haiti. After a very destructive hurricane, children were brought together in local groups, alongside adult participants, for training in the use of the participatory environmental assessment tools to guide the re-building of their schools. In another adaptation of the tools, CERG collaborated with Plan International's *Because I Am A Girl – Urban Programme* to produce *Young Citizens Score Cards* to improve the well-being of many children, young people, and adults around the world with a particular focus on 'safety and protection'.

Note

1. *Children's Environments* is now called *Children, Youth and Environments* and is no longer produced by our Children's Environments Research Group.

References

Altmann, S.A. and Altmann, J. (1973) *Baboon Ecology: African Field Research.* Chicago: University of Chicago Press.

Hart, R.A. and Moore, G.T. (1973) 'The development of spatial cognition: a review', in R.M. Downs and D. Stea (eds), *Image & Environment: Cognitive mapping and spatial behavior*, pp. 246–288. Aldine Transaction.

Hart, R.A. (1979) *Children's Experience of Place: A developmental study.* New York: Irvington Publishers.

Hart, R.A. (1987) 'Children's participation in planning and design', in C.S. Weinstein and T.G. David (eds), *Spaces for Children*, pp. 217–239. New York: Plenum Press. https://doi.org/10.1007/978-1-4684-5227-3_10

Hart, R.A. (1992) *Children's Participation: From tokenism to citizenship.* UNICEF Innocenti Essays No. 4. Florence, Italy: UNICEF/International Child Development Centre (also published by NGOs in many other languages).

Hart, R. (with Espinosa, M.F., Iltus, S. and Lorenzo, R.) (1997) *Children's Participation: The theory and practice of involving young citizens in community development and environmental care*. New York: UNICEF and London: Earthscan (also available in many other languages).

Hart, R.A. and Rajbhandary, J. (2003) 'Using participatory methods to further the democratic goals of children's organizations', *New Directions for Evaluation* 98: 61–75.

Hart, R.A. (2008) 'Stepping back from "The ladder": Reflections on a model of participatory work with children', in B. Jensen and A. Reid (eds), *Participation and Learning: Developing perspectives on education and the environment, health and sustainability*. Newbury Park, California: Sage.

Hart, R., Fisher, S. and Kimiagar, B. (2014) 'Beyond projects: involving children in community governance as a fundamental strategy for facing climate change', in *The Challenges of Climate Change: Children on the front line*. Florence: UNICEF Innocenti Research Centre. https://www.unicef.or.jp/osirase/back2014/pdf/140730.pdf.

Proshansky, H.M., Ittelson, W.H. and Rivlin, L.G. (eds) (1976) *Environmental Psychology: People and their physical settings*, 2nd edn. New York: Holt, Rinehart and Winston.

Taft, J. (2019) 'Continually redefining *Protagonismo*: The Peruvian movement of working children and political change, 1976–2015', *Latin American Perspectives* 228 46(5): 90–110.

CHAPTER 3

What you miss by missing out: different gender and age perceptions and experiences

Edda Ivan-Smith

> *We did this interview in 2019. Since then there have been some changes: Edda retired from the World Bank in December 2023; in Afghanistan, the political events of 15 August 2021 triggered a complex economic crisis and the Bank no longer has the full programme of work of 2019. In close coordination with the international community, development partners, and the Afghanistan Resilience Trust Fund (ARTF) donors, the World Bank is unlocking ARTF funds to support the Afghan people and deliver critical health, education, and livelihoods support.*

Background

Many years ago I worked on the books *Listening to Smaller Voices* (Johnson et al., 1995) and *Stepping Forward* (Johnson et al., 1998). I have always had an interest in participation and inclusion, particularly how there are stumbling blocks for sectors of the community, be it children, women or different ethnic groups, to achieve development objectives within development organizations via governments, via NGOs. What I find strange now, a lot of those issues that we were talking about in terms of accountability and proving the impact in certain groups in the early 1990s, in terms of participation, in the sense of having women, young people, and children having some stake in development, those questions have not been addressed. These questions are still being asked 20, 25 years later.

Community-driven development and public perception

I have been at the World Bank for five years.[1] As you know, it is a very large organization and works in a very different way to NGOs. I would say one of the things that is really exciting and interesting in terms of approach is particularly in areas where we have security issues, like Afghanistan or so-called conflict-affected countries: for safety reasons, we can't just go out to monitor how projects are progressing. We put the community in the front seat, in terms of monitoring. So, with third parties, local NGOs, ask, what do you think are the indicators that will prove that this project is successful or not? There are some issues; it's not perfect because there is always the risk of elite capture where of course you have the brightest or the most articulate people who take it upon themselves to monitor. You have to start somewhere.

We have a whole branch of programmes called community-driven development (CDD is the World Bank acronym). Those of us who've worked on gender issues or disability or youth and children are trying, I don't want to say 'to smuggle' because it sounds like something illegitimate, but trying to use that context to start looking more closely at youth and adults and gender issues. One of the issues, and I think it's shared by a lot of people like me at the Bank, is that traditionally, youth have been seen in the context of being victims. We have a lot of health projects, with maternal mortality and under-fives, and education projects; in parts of West Africa there are issues of rehabilitation of child soldiers.

I understand that, if you are USAID or DFID [former UK Department for International Development, now the Foreign, Commonwealth & Development Office], you are accountable to parliament. The public understands education, the public understands health. They do not necessarily or easily understand empowerment, they do not understand participation, particularly if they think their taxes are being paid to that. We had a very good example. We had a good project in Tanzania, which was about empowering young girls, particularly those that were pregnant and returning to school. DFID was one of the contributors. We had a trust fund. DFID was called to account by parliament, they said, what do you mean in empowerment? What do you mean by participation? Where is the well or where is the school? The kind of tangible expression of my tax money. So, I do sympathize with that.

What we are trying to do in the World Bank, and as I said, we are not entirely successful, usually depends on the region and the history of the region. I think the first thing we have to do is to look at what we are missing by not looking at different groups. There is a very good project that just started in West Africa, in Nigeria. We had to call it something different because it was about women's economic empowerment and the Government of Nigeria did not like it, so it was called something else like economic development. But the Nigerian Government has come out with a report that said that a large part of the slow development of Nigeria's economy is because women's businesses and women's economic access to assets was not being met. That was hindering this potential powerhouse. So, it was self-interest. Very often that is what you have to go for. Suddenly the government thought, we've got millions of these entrepreneurial women, who for cultural or educational reasons cannot get loans. This would be often very young women as well; they would often be considered as youth, 16 to 25 years old. Because they can't inherit land, they have no collateral when they go to the bank to get agricultural tools. You and

I might think that they needed to be empowered, but the government might say they needed to be given tools because Nigeria's economic development is appalling compared to what it had and what it is.

So, we are trying to do more research on what is missing by having this, I suppose I will say, social accountability, in terms of what people and the community want, rather than us just saying, we are going to have a project on youth and children because we think we should. Empowerment is such an emotive word. Even participation is.

Women, children, youth, disability: missing groups

In Afghanistan, for obvious reasons, the capacity of the government is very low, but they are extremely enthusiastic, very responsive. For example, we have a huge programme on gender-based violence and sexual harassment, which at first would surprise you given the context. What we found, not only in Afghanistan but in other parts of the world, our projects won't work in their optimal because we were missing out on a group of people. What we found working on *Listening to Smaller Voices* is that economically children and young people contribute a lot. Whatever you think of child labour, that is the reality. Therefore, they should have some kind of say on how those projects are run or develop. I think that is slowly getting to different people in the World Bank. It is culturally a huge shift for us because of our history and what we are. We are not an NGO. We do work with a lot of NGOs.

We have two big objectives, if you go to the World Bank website, to eliminate absolute poverty, and to increase shared benefits. In that is implied everybody who is being marginalized. We still have this story of health projects and education projects; children and women are seen within that, and we have the same problem with disability. Not all women are vulnerable, and not all vulnerable people are women or children as we know. So, we are beginning to unpack that, but it is a difficult habit to break.

We had a project in Nigeria where we try to develop the capacity of a water user association around irrigation projects. It involved children and youth to some extent, but I can't say that was the focus. There was a scope for that, and we tried to involve nomadic people, who have not been involved before. We were trying to involve the local and state government and hold them to account. Very often it was done by mobile phones because the literacy rate was low, particularly among women. In northern Nigeria, it is quite a traditional society, where women are not allowed beyond the home. We had to think about ways they could participate without having to go outside. We had the same issue in Afghanistan.

A lot of the research the Bank has done has been about monitoring and evaluation; we are quite good at that. In terms of shifting to a more youth focus and gender-focused programmes, research might be the way we start because we know about indicators. We know about monitoring. We know about evaluation and impact. We have quite a vigorous evaluation of our projects when they end. That goes into a system. We just started what is called a gender tagging. So, every project now has at least two indicators that will track closing the gender gap in that particular project. You could have children and youth tagging.

The other big thing is disability. We had a commitment to disability. 'World Bank what are you doing?' And embarrassingly, we had to say: well, not much. We now have a disability advisor to the Bank. One of the things that I love, which I think resonates with our experiences with children and young people, is, as the advisor said, 'we have to move from this welfare approach to disability'.

I was working on a project in Nigeria. A mainstreaming agricultural project. We had a stakeholders meeting. (Just to go back a little bit. Whenever you are preparing a project for the Bank, you have to prepare and present it to the World Bank board. They approve it or not. There are certain things you have to have done before the board. One of them is large stakeholder engagement.)

So, we had this stakeholder engagement. There was a huge number of people from disability organizations. One woman, a wheelchair user, said: 'I am a farmer and I love farming, but I never get to hear about agricultural projects. I only get to hear about welfare projects or how can I get a pension. I am 45 years old. I come from a family of farmers, but I am never told about farming projects'. That really lit up for me. I was retelling this to our Disability Advisor and she said, yes, of course, there are welfare issues but there are people who are disabled who are farmers. Some people are disabled who do irrigation. That is slow in the Bank. Slower perhaps than NGOs are.

We are beginning to tag for different aspects of intersectionality. A new sort of set of safeguards, called environmental and social framework, puts a big focus on inclusion and that would include disability. The Bank at corporate, headquarters level in Washington is putting a lot of emphasis on disability. Our projects are now being more closely scrutinized about that. Again, not in terms of welfare.

It doesn't mean you leave the welfare behind. Somewhere like Afghanistan, I don't have the figures to hand, where you have a whole cadre of what would be the working population who are disabled. Men and women who were breadwinners and now they cannot be. But they could be. They might be wheelchair users, and they might be blind, but they can still be productive, and that is not happening. That means that you have a whole generation of people who are just being written off. That is something that we really have to take on board in the Bank and we're not doing that.

Indicators

In terms of indicators, at the moment what we have are quite quantitative. Again, that is because we are the World Development Bank, so people want to see what they are getting for their money basically. Qualitative indicators need many more skills, and I don't really think that we have those skills in enough numbers to make those indicators.

When the community is doing the monitoring they might develop some of their own indicators. Certainly, in Afghanistan, they have been trained in that. They might be very simple, for example, if it is a health project, last year, three of my four children were really ill or I had to take them to the hospital. This year, I only have to take them twice. At least, linking these indicators to things that communities could see, and not some arbitrary academic things that have been developed in Washington. No, my children have been so much better since the water resource is cleaner or I don't have to borrow as much money, now I am involved in this community credit project.

They are very simple, but we still don't have a good understanding of gender-sensitive indicators. One of my roles when we get project proposals, and we prepare for the board or monitoring projects after they have been approved, is to input this social inclusion perspective. Very often they have something on gender disaggregation or gender-sensitive indicators. Now, I was writing youth and age. And people were asking: what do you mean by age? I said: what do you mean by gender? It means women and men. Exactly. You can also have young and old, and they say: 'it is a lot of work'. And it is not a lot of work.

In terms of the 'gender and generation' terminology, because we also have issues, particularly in South Asia and parts of West Africa, with widows, who are very marginalized and sometimes abused as a community, 'age' is just easier than generation. Also, because how do you define a generation? I like it because I think gender and generation indicate more of a cultural clash than gender and age, but I think if we were going to start making people understand we use age. We have to walk before we can run. I'm trying to sell that concept to my colleague who is a water engineer. He is going to look at me and say: what do you mean by generation. I have just got my head around gender-sensitive indicators and now you are trying to confuse me. What do you mean? And I would have to think about what I mean.

Participation terminology

The Bank uses agency a lot, but we have a lot of academics. I think participation is a bit redundant. Engagement; one of our key words now is citizenship engagement. We all quite like it. It was previously consultation which means nothing, which means that you are showing just a piece of paper with the sign, Consultation.

But engagement feels active. Having a choice to engage or not. Needing to have that information. Informed consent. It is sort of like the local council, they send you lots of stuff about your building sites, for example. I chose sometimes not to engage in that, but I know where that information is on the website. And I am very grateful for it. So, I know that I can go to the town hall on Thursday evening if I object to a new building, but actually I want to meet you at the pub instead at that time. But I know it is there, and I think that is very, very important for me. I think that is the whole thing about engagement.

Engagement I like; and it sounds more equal. It does not sound like the Bank is telling the community to participate because that is part of our programme. It gives both responsibilities.

I am generalizing horribly. There has been a tendency to objectify the community. We will have participation because that is what it says in my brief. And you don't know which the indigenous ways of engagement are. You don't know what the ethnic tensions are. You cannot just do that. Engagement, I think, it is a much safer word.

Perceptions in the community

In the community-driven approach we say 'integrated development'. We have quite a few youths and not children; I don't think we really have anything targeted or involving anyone under 15, 16 unless it is a health or education project.

When I worked in an INGO, I was in Ethiopia talking to this father who was the chief of the village; you always have to go to the head obviously even if you want to later on talk to the women or children. He was saying how difficult it was being a farmer. They had several famines. It was difficult for him to borrow money. I said, what about your family? He said, what about them? I said, you have seven children, and you have a brother-in-law. And he said: they are useless, they don't help me at all. They are useless.

In the meantime, there were all these people running around us, looking very busy while I was talking to him. I said: what do they do? He said: they are useless. He just spends the time looking after the cattle. She just cooks the food. He just sells. He was basically listing all these crucial economic roles that these seven children and his wife, and his sister and his brother-in-law did. And that is not seen as contributing. I thought that was crucial and I think that is the argument that we have with people who think in that way. I said: they are already participating. These children are already contributing to this household income. So, it is not necessarily that you have to say: we feel that children need to get involved. They are involved but it should be counted.

The perception: Children don't do anything. Women don't do anything. It is going backwards. We have that lovely 24-hour clock of what men do, what women do, what children do, what granny does. There is your argument to make it visible. But particularly if you are doing it in the Bank, given our history, it would have to be accompanied by a step before that. How do you do very basic research about what different community members do? It could be as simple as that, 24 hours; we are not talking about having to do a PhD in sociology. People have been increasingly asking me about PRA [participatory rural appraisal] because we realized that the tools that we had are quite clunky, because we are trying to get closer to communities on what they do and what works. The tools we have at the moment, a lot of them, are not sufficient. We have been talking about reaching the most marginalized people; reaching people who are illiterate, who don't speak the national language. All the barriers we have talked about in the past. We have got to do something more than just doing questionnaires or focus group discussions which are quite intimidating.

Terminology and tagging age and disability

In the Bank we use gender-sensitive. That means being responsive to the changes in the dynamics between men and women. My problem with the terminology 'focus' is that, just taking the gender example again, gender focus, people might think that just relates to health projects, because women look after children. We want to reduce maternal mortality, and it actually does not reflect how their lives are.

The terminology child and youth-inclusive; again I don't know if it catches, maybe nothing does, the reality of their lives. This is why I like sensitive because that also could be something that is driven by children or driven by women or driven by people who are disabled.

The terminology 'sensitive' might be old fashioned but that is what we use in the Bank. I don't think it is the new state-of-the-art word, but remember we started 70 years ago. In a way, that is where we are going ahead. We are doing a lot of stuff for LGBTQI communities and that is interesting.

For me, taking again the example of my water engineer or my mine specialist, I don't know if 'child focus' would mean anything to them. I think it is a powerful word.

I think that tagging is a good start. With the gender tagging at the Bank, that has started getting people to think. Beforehand, we used to have a checkbox thing: are women involved? Which does not mean anything. They are cooking the meals. Gender tagging, you first of all have to develop really good indicators. Then, say how you are going to get the information for these indicators. You have to do some work. Then, you have to update every six months.

Then, when you've updated it, you have to see if it is going well, and if it is not going well, what do you need to do about it? It is not anymore about 50 per cent of women who came to the meeting. So, a lot of project managers hate it for obvious reasons because it is a lot more work, but it is a much more effective way of measuring what we are doing in terms of gender.

I see no reason whatsoever why they cannot do that with age and disability. That is something that I really want to start pushing in the Bank and I have talked to the people who have to develop or design the gender tagging to look at their process or methodology and how then we can adapt that to age and disability.

Community capacity building

We always tend to forget communities in terms of capacity building. People have to engage in participation and particularly in countries recovering from conflict or war and a very oppressive regime, where engaging can get you killed, at one end of the spectrum. There has to be capacity building to understand why you are doing it because quite understandably they could be very suspicious. Also, 'you are wasting my time. I have to do my farming. What is in it for me?' Although we don't have to forget that element of capacity building, that is important for governments, for local partners, but the focus should be on the group; whether it is the women, or whoever is your target community. Maybe not call it community, maybe not call it capacity building, because that also could be quite loaded. Something about preparing, or laying the groundwork. When you have to do a research project, a dissertation, there are things you have to do. You have to do your literature review; all of these steps before you start your dissertation. It should be the same when we are introducing an approach or a methodology. That is what needs funding because it is not often difficult getting the project funded. This is when things go wrong. You don't have the time and money to do preparation. The right preparation takes time and costs money.

Developing research and consultancy capacity

We have tried to develop centres of excellence and link with local think tanks and universities. We are beginning to do this in Afghanistan. One reason is that we found it is very difficult to get consultants to work with governments to develop the kinds of documents that we need. So, we thought it is not only about building capacity of government, but it is actually about building capacity of consultants, academia; we are not getting people going to universities, studying the right sort of things so that they emerge with the skills they need to support the government. So, you have to have multiple approaches.

For example, you might have a very good department of sociology or anthropology, but that does not mean they know about child-sensitive or gender-sensitive indicators. I am sure that is true in parts of the so-called developed world as in parts of Afghanistan and India. I think that is slightly shifting the definition and scope of those departments. For example, the Bank is very keen on this issue of social inclusion, not only because it is the right thing to do but we realize that projects are failing because we are missing out a whole group of people. You would think that a professor of sociology, anthropology or cultural anthropology would be tuned to that, but not necessarily. That might be because of the culture of the university. People don't see that understanding that kind of thing is going to give you work. If we start development saying, what we need is people doing a, b, and c, what we need is partners, consultants or think tanks and graduate students who have this sensitivity;

it takes a long time, it is not going to happen in 12 months, but you have to start somewhere.

Frameworks

I keep using the gender experience and that we've come a long way with gender analysis although we still have a long way to go. I think that how it started getting people thinking is that women, like all other people, live very complex lives. They are not just interested in maternal mortality. They are interested in the money they are going to get for their crops. They are interested in developing their children, in having a better quality of life. Suddenly, development planners and managers realized that you cannot just get them in the health project.

Equally, you cannot just get children in education. When you have an education project, you might have to take account of their responsibilities, because they might be the main breadwinners. So, what do you do? Stop working and the whole family goes into poverty? Obviously, they have to be in safe and healthy environments. So, thinking outside the box and not tagging; not tagging children per se but tagging roles and who does what.

Not tagging children just for the sake of tagging children. Trying to get rid of those assumptions. The same way that you try to get rid of these assumptions about women, for example, that all they did is have babies and that is why we had them in health projects because they just have babies. You really need to revisit that methodology.

The SDGs [Sustainable Development Goals] are really important. They are more useful to us as practitioners than the Millennium Development Goals. This new environmental social framework that we have developed owes a lot to the SDGs. They work on a human rights level in local governments, so you can talk to governments and to people and they understand it means to have the right to clean water and the environment. But you can scale it down and talk to your community under the mango tree. They understand the relevance.

I still find people saying: youth and children? They understand education programmes, not youth. Catherine Panter-Brick (see Worthman and Panter-Brick, 2008, fieldwork done in 1993) subverts some of the assumptions about children. She did a very interesting study on street children in Nepal. She is a biological anthropologist. She did this stress test from saliva samples. She found that street children that run away from their rural homes were less stressed than children within families. Why? She said because the children that escaped and that survived were the cleverest ones, because they can survive in the streets. They have escaped from whatever abuse. But also, to survive in the streets, I could not do that. You have to have your wits about you. She suddenly turned around this whole victim thing. She said that they developed families with other children. They are quite organized. For me, that was mind-blowing.

Note

1.   Edda Ivan-Smith worked at the World Bank from 2014 to 2023.

References

Johnson, V., Hill, J. and Ivan-Smith, E. (1995) *Listening to Smaller Voices* London: ActionAid.

Johnson, V., Ivan-Smith, E., Gordon, G., Pridmore, P. and Scott, P. (eds) (1998) *Stepping Forward: Children and young people's participation in the development process*. London: IT Publications.

Worthman, C.M. and Panter-Brick, C. (2008) 'Homeless street children in Nepal: use of allostatic load to assess the burden of childhood adversity'. *Development and Psychopathology* 20(1): 233–255. http://dx.doi.org/10.1017/S0954579408000114

CHAPTER 4

Working with and for girls

Swatee Deepak

> *We did this interview in September 2019. Since then there have been several changes: Swatee left Purposeful in March 2020, and now works as a philanthropic consultant; Stars Foundation is now closed, after 19 years of operation; With and For Girls is housed at Purposeful and has had a strategic review.*

Background

Stars is a private foundation. We fund children's and young people's organizations starting with early childhood development, through primary, secondary school, livelihood support, child protection work, SRHR (sexual and reproductive health and rights), etc. A broad range across the spectrum of children and young people.

In 2014, the Girl Summit launched by DFID showed across all SDGs [Sustainable Development Goals] indicators that adolescent girls were in the worst position in access to health care, education, frequency of violence, whatever. The World Bank published research on how little aid funding was directly to adolescent girls, 0.02 cents of every dollar in official, not private, philanthropic, flows. They asked, how are you responding to this? What kind of pledges are you going to make?

We saw across all our young people and children portfolio a really strong gender component, but not necessarily skills or expertise in the organization. We reached out to partners. We had been doing award programmes to recognize children and young people, focusing on local organizations and giving them recognition for work they have been doing. We wanted to do a girls' award; the initial four organizations became eight, to create a new girls programme. What should it look like? What would we be focusing on?

What came out was that the award should not just have a Global South focus, but be completely global, because there is not one country where the indicators were better for girls than boys. Secondly, we decided to lift up programmes led by adolescent girls: a global girl-centred or girl-led award. Girls have been leading programmes for a long time but are completely unseen within development, women's funds, and philanthropy. Obviously,

FRIDA – The Young Feminist Fund,[1] had been on a similar trajectory before the programme was launched, but it was in its infancy when the Stars collective was formed in 2014.

Our focus was 'let's fund globally, girl-led organizations', and by 'girl-led' we wanted to push for a cultural shift within the sector. Focus on girl-centred approaches, recognizing strong, established groups globally that were locally led and owned but working on multiple issues in the community, not specifically girl- or gender-related, but programmes really focused on girls. Organizations with girls as part of their decision-making, strategic development, budget allocation, and with a role in governance and management practices.

At the time Plan International UK was doing a lot of work on girls in youth participation, they had a youth advisory board helping drive a lot of their programmes. What also came out was that if we are saying girls don't have a seat at the table and this award is about recognizing the amazingness that happens when girls are leading, then we should also use a participatory lens to select who wins the award.

Since 2014, we have had three rounds of the award. Then, in parallel, Stars changed; in 2014, our funder put into motion a big set of strategic changes. There was that kind of bold naivety when we started the collective; we only wanted to launch the award for one year and see what happened. We did not have a strategic plan or a budget that was multi-year. There was so much momentum building that we left the strategy to build afterwards; that succeeded.

We knew the *With and For Girls* programme would need to move out of Stars as the incubator. Stars co-founded and co-created the programme with partners, but a team actually ran it, did the selection, the diligence, got the money out of the door, managed the award winners. That was the team within the Stars Foundation, not built within the collective. Last year [2018], we identified that Stars could not incubate this anymore, we needed to move.

We defined criteria for a new home for *With and For Girls* and invited organizations to submit proposals to run the collective. All 10 collective funder partners at the time scored in the RFP [request for proposal]. We had sections of the RFP where we allowed adolescent girls from our regions also to score. I ran that process, and worked with the girls to understand the framing, criteria set, and asked for criteria they would like to see, and helped define the RFP process so they would get information, but not be overloaded with things like business models and financial plans.

We did diligence; in a sense our board needed to make a merger decision. We picked Purposeful, a relatively new organization that had been going for two and a half years.[2] We recognized that if we wanted to support grassroots movements led by girls, they needed resources beyond funding.

Purposeful had begun as a hub to support a nascent and organic adolescent girl-led movement in Sierra Leone. A lot of factors informed its development – it is post-conflict; Ebola was obviously a huge health crisis that had closed schools for 12–18 months; and rates of gender-based violence against girls went up in a community that is very impoverished. Rates of pregnancy went up. There is an archaic law in Sierra Leone that prevents pregnant girls and teenage mothers going back to school.

A movement of girls demanding their rights in Sierra Leone started, and needed a lot of support. Not just funding, but safe spaces to enable individual girls in very rural areas who were maybe illiterate, but could use the phone, so they could organize some friends, and they created a lot of momentum from that.

So Purposeful became a new home for *With and For Girls*. The partners and adolescent girls were excited by the prospect of a development paradigm that is Global South-led. Our headquarters is in Sierra Leone, informed by the grassroots; it is there for girls with a deep commitment, with a strategy, not likely to change focus into something else, like a philanthropic entity might. We did a big merger, the team that was at Stars came across into Purposeful and we have been based there since the beginning of the year [2019].

Indicators

We had looked at the fact that the feminist philanthropic sector had not been nurturing and culturing the grassroots where movements were starting, and was instead focusing on the 'shining leaves'. A FRIDA report showed that girl-led movements have been in existence as long as any social movements, but were denied a place within traditional philanthropy, because of patriarchy, age, and Global North–South dynamics.

Our first indicator for success is: is the organization local? We have definitions of local; for instance, with an organization set up by a Peace Corps volunteer we would ask if it is now completely local and ensure that the volunteer has no involvement in governance. Things that worry us are when that person is heavily involved, or evaluating programmes from America, when it is supposed to be in a Global South country. That definitely is not locally led from our perspective. But there are variations, where the person is away, or just runs the fundraising, or where development is done by a local team and girls are part of that: that is still (for us) locally led.

The second is girl-led, when girls are wholly leading the organization. We define girls as age 10 to 19 but go up to 27. The reason is a lot of groups we have been funding are also LGBTQI-led. Girlhood and what we defined as girlhood significantly changes within the LGBTQI population and a lot do not enter girlhood until their early 20s, because limiting factors prevented them from becoming girls when other people are biologically becoming girls. I say all of this in quotation marks, because if you know anything about being intersex, gender is not just socially constructed, it is also biologically constructed. Research published this year on funding for LGBTQI youth has shown the model that we take as being girl-led has actually allowed more flow to local organizations supporting LGBTQI populations in a way targeted funding sometimes has not.

A girl-centred organization, for us, is even a local organization that speaks on things like livelihoods or community development, where programmes are really focused on girls, and girls are designing and making governance decisions about programmes – strategic, or programmatic, or financial decisions. It could be girls on an advisory committee that influence support, or girls on the board themselves, etc.

Making awards

Traditionally, we had an award for organizations with a turnover between US$100,000 and $50,000, and a smaller award for turnovers down to $20,000. After an external evaluation last year, a lot of referral partners were saying: we have amazing organizations that meet your criteria, but not your income brackets, but are girl-led or girl-centred. We created a new 'emergent award', organizations with income between $20,000 and $5,000.

We've always supported organizations that are unregistered, but previously asked they supply a fiscal sponsor we can do due diligence on. This year with the emergent award, we are not knocking them out if they don't have a predefined fiscal sponsor. The collective will find them a fiscal sponsor, and some partners themselves can act as fiscal sponsors. So, there is an ability to support the organization. Organizations get nominated through referrals; we then do due diligence and eligibility checks against our criteria, checking that organizations are: locally led, either girl-led or girl-centred, and that their income level is appropriate.

Once those are verified, the organizations can respond if they are interested in being part of the awards process; at the time the organization might not know they have been nominated, so we check, and if they are OK to meet the deadlines, then we conduct due diligence on the finances and risks that the board is interested in.

Then, we put a shortlist together. We cut the world into five panel regions: Europe and Central Asia; Middle East and North Africa; sub-Saharan Africa; Asia-Pacific; and the Americas and Caribbean. Now 11 funders are part of the collective, and all put forward people to score those panels. The process runs in English, French, Spanish, Russian, and Arabic. We made sure panellists speak those languages of the region, to be as fair as possible to the local organization. Asking them to review something in English is going to knock out people who do not write well.

In our first stage panel we discuss whether this organization is girl-led or girl-centred, the programmatic side, and any due diligence issues; maybe finances, governance structure, and if we need more information. We first assess whether organizations are fundable and we're able to risk manage them.

We shortlist 10 organizations and ask previous award winners whether they would host adolescent girls who do the participatory grant-making panel for their region. If an organization says yes and agrees the terms of reference, we give a grant of $5,000 and a counterpart within our team for setting up the panel: documents, training materials, support, interpreters or translators, and helping them to get girls on the panel to understand the context for adolescent girls in those countries. We help facilitate that process, but the local organization defines when the panel takes place in October.

The panel has to be adolescent girls between 10 and 19, but the organization defines any other things. We ask for different, broader viewpoints; that comes out anyway, these award winners are already working with girls in those communities from different caste or socioeconomic backgrounds, who are disabled, not literate, etc. We ask for a minimum of five girls in the panel and have had up to 12 girls in the past.

In the Asia-Pacific panel, for example, you get 8 or 10 girls from Nepal, and they receive a shortlist of organizations from Pakistan, India, Japan, Hong Kong or the Philippines. The training for them is to try to understand the factors inherent in spaces where the organization works. The organization is asked to submit a visual application for the girls that can be film, pictures, spoken word, a poster, a poem, or something. The girls schedule one-to-one interviews that will last two to three hours, with each shortlisted organization, over two to four days. They have interpreters online, the grant is there to support with internet provision. Obviously, we still have technical problems. Who does not?

They set questions themselves and define who they want to speak to. I think there is a huge difference between what happens in regular philanthropy and what happens in our version. There are organizations where you are totally guided by what is written. Someone who writes well comes across powerfully and ticks all your boxes and this one looks really good. Some that don't give that compelling version of the work they do, go down in estimation, but still go through to the panels. Sometimes I have loved an organization and hoped that the girls picked it, and the others. Who knows? The girls might find something that we did not.

What the girls do, where I think that flip happens, they often say, for instance: 'we want to do an interview with your organization, but we have three hours and we want two hours just with other girls. We want an hour with management or trustees'. No adult is allowed to be a part other than technically, helping things like internet problems or interpretation. Girls often want to talk to other girls, and quickly identify whether the organization is truly girl-led or girl-centred in a way we cannot. The girls do interviews, deliberate for a day or two and pick the winners in each category. Through that process they give us indicators that we are really supporting organizations that are girl-led and girl-centred.

Due diligence happens in parallel to the girls' panels. There could be safeguarding, corruption, or governance issues flagged. We always say to the girls, if none of those factors come up, whatever you decide will be realized by the collective. They know the organization might not end up winning, related to other risks we are responsible for. Managing as a collective, none of those issues have been unresolvable, we have always funded organizations the girls chose. Issues have been minor enough to manage or we added some condition to the award that gives a conditionality that allows risk management and mitigation to happen.

We invite a representative from each winner to come to London for a week for a ceremony, to meet one another, do group activities, and girls from each panel come to London to give the awards. A lot of winners feel the award is different because finances are attached; they win awards in countries or even internationally, but that is recognition, not resources. The second thing is they feel more validated because girls picked them; it is about girl-led and girl-centred organizations; and it is a collective of some best-known names in philanthropy. That gives a different sense of recognition.

Strategic objectives

We have four strategic objectives as a collective. The first is about increasing recognition and resources to girl-led and girl-centred groups through the award itself.

The second objective is around implementing a positive shift in philanthropy towards more unrestricted funding to locally led, and grassroots girl-led and girl-centred groups. We have indicators for that. The money that moves through the collective is a tracker, the funders increasing the flow of funding through the collective. We have a partnership with 68 organizations with whom we share due diligence data. We track how much additional funding gets to winners because of the award and we do events around influencing philanthropy itself. We supported 12 adolescent girls to go to the human rights funders meeting in Mexico City last year. They ran the closing plenary session on how now is the time to fund girl-led movements; they created pledges for funders. Our role was facilitating visas, keeping them safe, bringing them together, supporting logistics and interpretation, and making sure everyone had an equal voice.

This goes to a reflection, that when you think about girl-led or youth-led within the development community, there is a certain cardboard cut-out of what that young person must look like. They are often articulate in English, usually very confident, able-bodied, able to hold the room, project themselves, and so on. Our collective is trying to show that leadership of girls does not necessarily show up that way. That there are girls that cannot speak in English, are not that articulate, are extremely shy, don't want to own or run the room, but still deserve to be listened to. A lot of our role is about utilizing our power as a collective of known philanthropic voices to call our peers to listen and not come with preconceived notions on what they expect girls to deliver, youth leaders to say and not say, and who among the girls are to be taken more seriously than others.

The third objective is supporting capacity development of girl-led and girl-centred organizations. The fourth is supporting collaboration between girl-led and girl-centred groups around the world.

Self-care and capacity building

On capacity development we have often offered additional cash that organizations could utilize for training or consultants, etc. Those models shifted after feedback from winners. They said for them to increase capacity, they were burning out and need self-care support instead. So, we started a self-care fund. Our evaluation shows self-care and coaching to executive leadership, or leaders of the organization has a tremendous impact in them being able to absorb other capacity developments, whether training or additional resources. It almost acts like a key that unlocks the capacity to bring those other resources.

We were making opportunities around influencing philanthropy, furthering our goals as a collective, but weren't necessarily tuning into what girls wanted and resources they needed to influence spaces important to them. We made a visibility fund. Essentially a lot is for national travel; a lot of winners are based in very rural locations and they might not get 10 girls to the capital for a week to protest, or organize groups, or go to regional or international conferences like CSW [Commission on the Status of Women] or Women Deliver. We have done that alongside offering legal support and funding, but also access to immigration lawyers that can help them navigate. It is increasingly difficult to guarantee people can travel, because of the world at the moment. It is trying to get girls access to at least what young people at NGOs have access to, which is those big teams that help with those sponsorship letters, etc.

Reporting

In an ideal world, we wouldn't ask for reporting but we are tax registered, we only get charity status if we meet the demands of the charity commission and our partners have to meet theirs. You need a mechanism for knowing the funding was charitably spent. When you are working with smaller groups you cannot do that unless there is a report. It is a simple budget form that has three questions that tells us on what they spend the funding. They are not tied to the spending, they can change it. We ask them to define how they want the funding.

Girls say we don't know how to manage that amount of money, we want $2,500 every month to help manage cash flow for the first time. The financial report is a dialogue between award manager and organization and open to change. For a lot of smaller groups it is easier to do that. Larger groups used to working with other funders get scared to change their budget they send us, because they are like: we did not do this because this, this and this, and we ended up not moving on this. The team do a lot to say 'it is totally fine, we understand things change. Just talk me through it, and I will make the changes and then send them to you and if you are OK with that being where you are, we can just check back in.'

The questions we ask are: since the fund was dispensed, what would you like to tell us about work you have done for girls? The second question is: do you want to flag any issues in the sector, in your country or internationally or regionally that is affecting the work? The third is an undefined report, basically open-ended, and helps us know what is going on with girls around the world.

Even though we are a collective it is hard to know what issues are happening in Mali, Moldova, El Salvador or Chechnya. The relationship with organizations is really valuable to get an understanding of what is happening for girls and what is becoming difficult. A lot of reports flagged closing space issues and roll backs for gender, where governments are imposing additional regulations, removing registrations for organizations, closing bank accounts or where the organization is getting intimidated. A lot have been subjected to social media trolling, some have been followed home or got really bad threats on staff members, or on the community, especially LGBTQI groups working in Chechnya for instance. The reports are used for us to take a pulse on this, and information we feed to funders or civil society which is trying to track closing space. The girls' pledges went into the special rapporteurs' reports, and we flag human rights issues girls are facing. These reports are not just to further our collective missions or tick the charity commission box here in the UK but inform the sector and help us understand factors that would allow philanthropy to support girl-led and girl-centred groups in the best way possible.

The question of language and participation

In terms of situating ourselves we code-switch all the time. At the moment we sit in children's and young people's philanthropy, feminist philanthropy and there are different frames and languages that will get us were we need to be to turn more money into girl-led and girl-centred approaches.

We change the way we narrate what we are doing. In feminist and progressive philanthropic spaces, we talk more about the girl-led approach and participatory grant-making, because those terms are well understood and established. On the other side, it is still hard even in those spaces because girls are still being taken out of that equation. There is evidence suggesting that while women's funds hold the bulk of girl-led organizing, they still don't necessarily take a girl lens in the work they are doing. That is the angle we come from; the message is that girls funding is not just this cute girl power, buzz word thing, but these girls are living these realities. They have this strong voice, they have been organizing a long time, and they have been left out as a movement. The space needs to be aware, open, and broaden for girl-led action to come out.

Conversely, in some spaces there is much more on taking that participation angle. Why? What are the reasons girls or young people should be participating? What does that mean for them? How it informs the way philanthropy is working, changing or moving; these are more conservative spaces.

We are working on an AGM session about the intersections of violence against women and violence against children. Those are two sectors of funders and practice, even though there are so many interlinkages, and gender norms are at the core of escalating violence for both. The sectors have set very far apart from each other and they are funded in parallel ways, which has created schisms. Research shows that one has been very grassroots owned, mainly women's and girls' and feminist spaces coming from the movement up, as opposed to child protection and violence against children, a very top-down approach.

We used the right of the child and the rights-based approach, but we would never say feminist because there are conservative funders in this space who shut up the moment you say that. You have to narrate in a way that gets the message recognition and to where it deserves to go, and furthers the field. It is easier to get off your moral high horse to make that happen, because it is for the better. I would say that there is a lot of conservatism within children and young people spaces.

The way we are framing the conversation on participation: how do we move from a space where trustees take all the decisions about grant-making? What does that mean in terms of the way you manage risk? How is that narrated and what does the structure look like from a governance perspective? It is more focused on trying to get decision-making away from your trustees. It does not focus on why participation or girls' voices are important. Even if that is an undercurrent of the conversation it is not a dominating factor; it is about we know that the people that sit on boards are not representative of the communities we seek to serve.

Unfortunately, many foundations, public, private or corporate, have structures that give recognition to those types of skills in a governance setting that we as practitioners know is not right; not one that leads to better decisions, informed and understood for what the sector needs to move forward.

While we might not be seen as experts by our own boards, working and redefining what an expert is moved accountability from trustees to experts. Then we could redefine experts to be girls, and define why girls would be the experts, because they are experts on their own lives. If this award is about recognizing girl-led and girl-centred approaches it is because we want to recognize girls are denied the space at any decision-making table. Yet we know they have deep knowledge in the things that affect their lives, so they should have a say in our grant-making process as well as the recognition that we give to other organizations demonstrating that approach.

There are progressive philanthropic entities looking at ways to shift power in the sector. The way participation and participatory grant-making are mechanisms by which a philanthropic entity is able to shift power internally and sharing that learning with the field helps us to see how to create dialogues and conversations than can help shift the whole sector together.

Barriers

There are barriers preventing funders from doing this work. One is the governance structures of foundations. A lot want to do participatory grant-making, understand the benefits of it. I think it is how you shift your board and power holders because I do want our sector to change. A lot of our peers agree and want to do this, but whether those messages get into the hands of and resonate with board members, is a problem that stifles a lot of movement in our sector.

There are not a lot of risk-taking boards that understand those benefits in a way that they feel the risks are being managed and mitigated. Because with corporate foundations' groups, a lot of it is about sharing how we went on that journey at Stars, not about learning in three-day board meetings; there were lots of steps in between to feel assured about risk. Since boards are not representative of the community and may not understand the value of a programme on one issue in rural Nepal, and another in Colombia, we told them, we know you guys are super busy, and three days is a lot for you to review all the award applications. Let's bring panels with regional experts at UNICEF, multilateral, and bilateral: you guys will still be the final ratifiers of this decision, but the award gets the added association with those other entities that you know. We went from that definition of regional experts, to then being able to be in a place where girls could be redefined as a regional expert.

Notes

1. See website https://youngfeministfund.org/ accessed 30 September 2022. 'FRIDA provides young feminist organizers with the resources they need to amplify their voices and bring attention to the social justice issues they care about. We enable the support, flexibility and networks to sustain young feminist visions.'
2. See website https://wearepurposeful.org/ accessed 30 September 2022. Purposeful is 'an Africa-rooted global hub for girls' organising and activism'.

CHAPTER 5
Holistic child protection

Ken Justus Ondoro

Background

I was a researcher, more involved in teacher training and competence research. About eight years ago I was engaged in an ethnographic study on community-based child protection systems in Kenya, in three counties. I was the lead national researcher that produced a really informative report to the child protection sector in Kenya. It got organizations, institutions, including government, to focus more on how to put the community at the centre of every child protection intervention. For the last eight years we have been doing that with the University of Columbia group here in Kenya.

African research and development

I formed my own entity, *African Research and Development*, to look at child protection interventions through four pillars.

The first pillar is family and community, where we advocate for community-based child protection strengthening systems. We support organizations in ensuring what they call community-based, community-led, child-led, and youth-led are actually practically so. Because we saw organizations talking about they are that, but when you look at what they are doing it is not that.

The second pillar is policy and governance. Whichever group you have, community-based, community-led, child-led, if you do not link to policy, governance, and government so lessons and approaches can influence policy and practices through existing formal systems, then, you might barely achieve sustainability. We look at governance in two levels. One, within government structure; two, within organizations working with community, because we have been directed to organizations saying they were doing community-led approaches, but if you look their systems are more top-down. Most of the time you find it is community-led on paper, but top-down in practice.

The third pillar looks at safeguarding, because we have child protection practitioners and organizations unconsciously perpetrating some form of harm to children. We also had some development actors exploiting children in one way or another. So, we ensure they have safeguarding policies about how they interact with the community and with children and youth; systems to address safeguarding issues.

The fourth pillar, learning institutions, was informed with studies we have been involved with in Kenya. There is a lot of abuse reported in the media, and children are being abused within learning institutions. Last year, we had the highest number of children abused within learning institutions. There was a school where almost half the girls sitting for final examinations were pregnant and the pregnancies were linked to teachers of the school.

We look at all of these components. If an organization is not working in all these pillars, then the intervention should seek to be linked to another organization or government that tends to address these other pillars, so that you have a holistic approach to child protection.

Methodologies

We have been using ethnographic methods. Mostly when you are mapping community-based systems, the qualitative approach is best. We have used children's tools, like body mapping and trace mapping, to engage children in identifying areas where they feel safe within the community. The body mapping allows you to hear children's perceptions about what happens to themselves and their bodies and that way you get to learn if children have interacted with any form of abuse or exploitation.

Participant observation we do a lot to see how children interact with adults and how children are treated in specific contexts. We have built from the initial qualitative research into a household survey which is more quantitative. We have conducted extensive training in capacity building community-led and child-led approaches in Kenya, Uganda, and Tanzania.

Framework

The framework for us is mainly the four pillars within UNCRC. We understand traditional approaches used to support children to realize those rights; through studies we have done, we realized that even though some approaches may be effective, others are not effective in supporting children to realize their dreams.

The approach we are trying is situating the community at the centre of every intervention, trying to obtain the same goal, ensuring children realize their dreams, goals, and rights, but using an empowering approach. Not coming into the community and telling them what to do *per se* as most programmes do. In essence, trying to find out what resources the community has, levering them, and empowering the community to take the lead in ensuring children realize those dreams.

In Uganda, we work a lot with Fassil W. Marriam Kidane who runs the Children's Rights and Violence Prevention Fund (CRVPF). He tries to employ a bottom-up approach in all the organizations he supports in Uganda, and ensures every organization understands and employs community-led approaches in their intervention.

In Kenya, there is a small organization called *Kesho Kenya*. *Kesho* is a Swahili word for tomorrow. It has endeavoured to employ community-led approaches and resources in child protection programming. Recently it got bigger funding, and is now implementing a more top-down approach within the school setting. It had a very smart way of working with groups that community members had formed themselves, levering resources the groups had. They were meeting women, men, children and young girls in those groups. They were not talking about child rights but engaging the community to identify the bad things they thought happen to children in particular contexts and how the community can organize and play a key role in protecting children.

Another organization supported an ethnographic study on a county in Kenya on a community-based child protection system for infants and young children, 0 to 5 years. After the study, we involved community members ranking the child protection issues for infants and young children, and coming up with ways of addressing the issues they identified. We pulled out when our contract ended. But I have heard they proceeded to implement exactly what the community members identified and have been facilitating the community to take the lead in addressing issues that affect children 0 to 5 years.

Most organizations working with children currently talk about being community-led. Very few talk about child participation, and little about strengthening informal child protection. In practice they do the normal top-down approaches that they are used to.

Successful intervention

This is one successful project we implemented in partnership with the Columbia group for children in adversity. After doing the ethnographic study, we engage community members to pick one harm they identified during the ethnographic phase and come up with ways of addressing that child protection concern. After we complete the study we carry out feedback sessions with community members to address some of the issues coming out in the report.

We had a study in a county on the coast of Kenya. We recruited a community facilitator, not from the same community but the same culture, who spoke the same language. More than 10 child protection concerns were identified in the ethnographic phase. His work was to facilitate the community to settle on one particular concern and come up with activities to address that. The process took about one year. Community members decided to address sexual harms, through activities that included football, theatre, and drama for youth.

Adults were concerned about issues of parenting, but did not call it parenting. They said parents complained that children today know a lot with regards to sex compared to them, and parents need support on how to engage and talk with children in matters of sex. Parents identified a teacher who was already doing what they wanted to learn, but on a voluntary basis. Youth organized football sessions where they talked about issues of life skills, sex, education. They also came up with their own drama skills, and messages to highlight through performances using theatre groups.

After the facilitator left, we left the community on their own to do the activities they said they would do. The activities identified by children and youth are still active today compared to those identified by parents. In fact, youth scaled up, because now they are inviting neighbouring villages not only to come and play football but also to talk about issues affecting them, issues of life skills, sex, education, abstinence.

You might be thinking several projects run by NGOs are similar. The uniqueness of this intervention was that youth came up with their own messages to put across in terms of life skills; they identified issues affecting them and what they liked to learn. Most importantly they identified resources within their community they thought would help them learn what they wanted. They organized themselves and formed a football club. They engaged community members and parents contributing money to enable them to buy balls and organize tournaments where they talk about the issues mentioned.

I used to go maybe once every three months, to see how community members are progressing. We have not done an evaluation, so I cannot authoritatively say this has had a positive impact. But mid-term visits showed [change] in child well-being, in children not engaging in sex, and children who had been engaging in sex concentrating more on food, or influenced by peers to adopt other positive behaviours. Interestingly we also had reports of improved performance in schools, especially for children involved in these activities. That is one of the best community-led approaches that I can talk about at the moment.

Children participating in drama activities range from 9 to 17 years. Younger children had their own football games for entertainment; mostly they participated in drama. One established theatre group in that village facilitated children forming their own theatre groups and performing about issues. Teenagers had their own groups, from 12 to 17 years; the average age was 15 years.

Let me be frank: this intervention was not easy. The process took so long for community members to take up and run. When we went to the community, there was a lot of talk about what are you doing for us? What have you brought us? You are coming all the way from the capital city, so you are coming with a lot of money or paid a lot of money. What is in it for us?

It took more than six months in continuous community conversations to tell them: one, we are here to learn from you; two, we would not like to engage in traditional NGOs ways – come with the project, then leave when done. We encourage the community to see problems as their own problem, children as their own children, and children reported to be sexually abused, defiled, and dropping out of school, as their own children.

We also engaged in conversations to try to make community members reflect on investing in their own children. We used examples of successful individuals from this very poor village, whose parents were not rich, to emphasize taking children to school, working hard to pay school fees, and supporting them to go through education. One key example was a government minister from the same community, also some younger women and men perceived to be successful. We engaged them to talk to their own community, encourage them to support their children, create time and resources to ensure their children would not be abused and were growing in an environment to reach their full potential. Coming to the point where community members are willing to make time, and use their own resources to do the activities they proposed, took a very, very long time.

Unsuccessful interventions

Two examples of failed projects I have seen. A community-based project we went to evaluate. The project documents wrote: engaging the community to identify issues they would like to address; engaging community leaders and capacity building; engaging girls and boys to actively participate in not only identifying but also taking action whenever there are issues they feel are affecting them.

We found the project did not engage the community. They went in partnership with another community-based organization (CBO) already doing the same. They used more or less the same population the other CBO has been working with. They recruited a few parents who were taken to the town, booked into a two-star, three-star hotel, and trained in child rights. Remember, these were parents that have never left rural villages and were taken to fancy hotels. They recruited young girls who had never left their rural village, took them to this hotel, trained them, and then boys, and then village elders. When these people came back to the community, instead of advocating for the rights of children, they talked on how the organization has a lot of money, but instead of giving money to support children, they take them to fancy big hotels, pay a lot of money and give nothing.

The project was also targeting teenage mothers out of school and in school; when they were taken to fancy hotels, girls who did not have children felt that the qualification to be taken to fancy hotels by this NGO, was to get a child. To every young girl the perception was, if you have a child out of wedlock, you are better positioned to get support from this NGO. When we did interviews it was very difficult to write that report, because what we found was not pleasing at all.

Another example is in Sierra county. This project supports young mothers through paying school fees and providing daily needs in schools. It was a good concept, but what happened again was issues of perception. The project did not engage the larger community, just a section who are young mothers. They were treated differently from other girls. More or less similar to before, they were taken to town shopping, had new uniforms, everything they needed. School fees were paid so they were not sent away from school. Other girls in the community who did not have children perceived it as having a child as a young girl is a way to get NGO support.

Conditions for success

It is difficult, but when I visit most communities in Africa what I get is, for lack of a better term, a community that is already polluted by NGOs, in a sense that what is called child-led or youth-led is a group of youth within that community who have been facilitated by organizations to form that group and receive an incentive to be part of the group until the project comes to an end. In most communities you will find groups such as a child parliament or child something where children come to share their views. But once the project doesn't exist, those groups also cease to exist.

Let me talk about what being sincere and open to the community, and coming down to the community's level has done for the intervention I described along the coast. At our first entrance to the community, we told them: we do not have resources to give, we will not pay your children's school fees, we won't give you food. We are interested in learning about children, their everyday lives and their well-being; to discuss with you, learn from you what you can do to protect your own children.

We never went with a big branded vehicle, we did not wear fancy clothing; we tried to fit in as much as we could. At every meeting we would not sit above them, we did not have a special seat for us and then the community would sit down. We would sit and discuss at the same level. Throughout that process the community members saw us as part of their community. Because we spent a very long time, had a 'simple life', tried to fit in, community members were able to identify with us. It was not us taking a project into the community, it was a discussion to see what the community could do to protect children from the issues that they identified. There was no one coming to lecture them on child rights, abuse, and government policies. It was the other way around, community members educating us on their issues and how they would like to address those. Giving youth space to also identify issues and challenges and deciding on what they want, for me, is one of the reasons why they are carrying on with their activities today.

The second thing that promotes youth-led and community-led approaches is working with already existing structures; finding smaller pockets of systems such as community groups, maybe a group of parents who engage with children in certain activities, a group of elders doing something to protect children, or a group of women. Working with those groups as opposed creating new systems within the community. When you map work with existing groups, you can introduce topics you would like them to discuss or engage in, within their normal running and operating processes. The most difficult part is coming in and forming these groups and then time for child-led approaches.

One prominent practice in Kenya is the children's parliament, or children's agenda. In every part of Kenya, they recruit children who are eloquent, can speak out, and who are transported to the capital, booked into a hotel, and trained on child rights.

I would not sample a number of children to engage in children's rights. I would try to make it a community intervention. However much you empower a child in terms of building knowledge and capacity, if you don't create a conducive environment from the immediate family to the larger community, this child will be vulnerable, taking into consideration their age, physical toughness, and all that; they might still be prone to certain abuses. But if you do it in a way that empowers the child and builds the immediate family and community as a whole, then you create that safe space for the child.

The approach and notion of youth-led has been used by so many people to attract resources, it is a controversial term in Kenya. Youth groups have been used and exploited by the political class for a long time; most youth initiatives formed and facilitated by external forces tend to go through this exploitation. On the contrary, youth groups or youth-led initiatives that started on their own have stood the test of time. Most, I am not saying all, continued to exist; we even have youth-led groups whose members graduated to adulthood, but who recruited other youth to join and continue running the same activities, with the same goals the group had initially.

One example is a youth group in a refugee camp, in Mombasa, in a slum called Bangladesh Slum. The group was formed by boys and girls who wanted to fight issues of defilement, because of the prevalence of defilement of that slum. They came together, and started a campaign through theatre groups. Almost every weekend they staged plays in a central place, and passed messages to adults and children. They started visiting schools, talking to younger children and performing, sensitizing them on their rights, telling about safe rules to follow going home, which youths to avoid, which areas, because there was a lot of sexual abuse in areas where they were brewing the traditional brew. They would inform them to avoid these areas or when you see suspicious men, what you can do is run back to schools or to the neighbour. It was not about child rights, but they used contextual knowledge to try to make children safe. They were passing messages, but instead of using traditional posters, guides, and materials, because they did not have resources, they were doing writing, graffiti on the wall. Later on, organizations noticed this group and started working with them and supporting them. The group still exists, but the initial formation was not by any external funding or idea. It was formed by youth from that particular context and I think that is why the group is still in operation doing the same activities.

Barriers

The other barrier is poverty, a major challenge in community-led approaches. When you work with very poor settings they ask: yes, we are willing to create time to protect our children, but weigh that against food. Their priority is not safety of children but putting food on their table. In the slums where we worked, mothers were encouraging their young girls to engage in prostitution to support themselves and their families. We met very young girls who were very knowledgeable about their rights, about the existence of systems of child protection and how to access them, about issues of exploitation, mostly sexual exploitation. But these girls were being exploited sexually, engaging in sex just to get sanitary towels. Just for that alone.

As much as you are trying to work with systems that are there, you realize that in poor areas certain practices and beliefs also emerge, like witchcraft. You find that certain indigenous systems that were very supportive to children have been eroded, because of change from traditional to modern.

Another challenge is the child protection sector has not embraced the idea of giving space for the community to take the lead or co-lead projects. Child protection interventions have more or less similar points of view; that community members are perpetrators of violence against children; or that bad things happened, and the community does not have capacity to address such issues. So you approach the community as already guilty, already sick; what you are going to do is provide medication for that sickness. But approach it the other way around: they have limited information and capacity to initiate and support interventions that are community-led or child-led.

Organizations are still not prepared to give space for the community. The staff don't understand what community-led or child-led is about, they are conditioned to the organizational system, to taking the lead, to quantifiable reports within a specific timeline. So, you find sometimes the barrier is the organization trying to implement community-led or child-led approaches.

Advocacy

We had several workshops with the Government of Kenya, to try to influence policy. The government is now embracing community-based approaches. It has been a very slow process to influence policy, and government, because in the Department of Children Services the people we started working with, when we were doing the ethnographic study, have all since been transferred. They are new people in the office, so, you walk in and the first question they ask is: who are you? The way the government system works here is that there are structures and systems but most things depend on the individuals occupying offices. We had a very supportive team when we started, but all the team members have since been transferred. One breakthrough in 2016 was the government adopted a community-based approach as part of the workplan for that financial year, and even allocated resources.

Evidence gaps

Donors need to show impact, and quantitative reports speak louder than qualitative ones in terms of reach and targets. The challenge we had with community-led, child-led, youth-led is to develop a monitoring, evaluation, accountability, and learning framework. It is still in process. We are trying to make it able to show evidence of this approach, in the same manner that you show evidence of other top-down approaches. That is a gap. The other gap is not many strategies out there talk about community-led, its effectiveness. To put more directly, there is little evidence for community-led approaches and so we have also been working on that. Combined together, if the sector is able to develop these two, these are the tools we can use to attract funding from larger donors.

Evidence is the gap. If you are funding a child labour project, an FGM [female genital mutilation] project, children out of school project, it is very easy to implement, very easy to come up with indicators, very easy to evaluate. The community-led approach needs more work, more qualitative [evidence], and then you can develop quantitative out of that. Sometimes, when you are starting you don't have the full indicators that you will be tracking and so you develop some indicators along the way. But then, when it comes to evaluations, how do you compare with the baseline? We will be strongly advocating for baselines and evaluation being done in an experimental way.

Using experimental design where you have the intervention group and the group not receiving the intervention, seems to be expensive for most NGOs. The intervention that we did on community-led approach includes an experimental design, so we have a control group and an intervention group.

Key priorities for funding

The priority is community-based projects. The bigger challenge is with the formal system, organizations, NGOs, and government. So, one set of funding goes to training and capacity building the formal system to embrace a more community-led approach. Once organizations are ready to embrace and have the skills and ability to create space for organizations and children to take the lead, then we move into the community.

The funding has to be structured in a way that allows time to engage and make the community move from the NGO mindset, 'we have reported funding and tangible stuff', to this other side, where they see problems affecting children as their own and feel they have responsibilities as caregivers, relatives, or just community members to take the lead in addressing those issues. Making children realize they have power and that also it is within them to protect themselves.

I see funding going into two streams. If I am doing a top-down approach I can do that within one year; a baseline, roll out activities, find ways of engaging the community. I can measure after one year and for sure you will see some changes. For the community-led project, the same project will take two or three years. The reason is that you will also learn in the process and create room to prepare the community psychologically so ownership starts at the inception phase not at the end of the project. Most of us in the sector, towards the end of the project start talking about community ownership back to maybe government taking some roles that have been taken by the NGOs. Ownership right at the start of the project needs a longer time.

Mutual relationships

From my experience, interventions in the community are a relationship issue, as opposed to a staff, project, or NGO issue. So, approach it in terms of building a positive relationship between the people involved in the project with the community. Out of that relationship, human beings would be able to make sacrifices and create time for you. That relationship must be mutual. The community should not feel that you are exploiting them by using their time for your benefit.

How do you create that mutually beneficial relationship? One, being sincere and telling the community we are able to do a, b, and c, but not x, y, and z. Two, you find that some organizations are structured so that staff are seen to hold a certain amount of power in the community and community members feel they are part of the government system, and some fear gets in. But you also find some organizations where a project manager goes to the community and people see him not as the project manager but as John or Ken. You have to have a balance between the two. You have to try to come to the level of the community where you speak the same language, discuss the same issues, be sincere about the timeframe, what the project will do, what role staff will play. Also tell them how you would like them to be engaged, and ask whether they will be able to create time to be engaged in project activities.

I see development interventions, whether in humanitarian contexts or in stable communities, as a relationship between project and community that has to be mutually beneficial. The benefit to the community might not be tangible, in the form of money or food rations that some NGOs provide. It can be that the community feels their children's well-being will improve by them participating. If you are able to convince adults, children, and youth they will benefit from participating on that project from the child protection point of view, for sure I know people would have an interest in being part of that.

If community members are able to say, that is our project, we made the changes, we were able to overcome these challenges, and support our children to do a, b, and c, for me, that is ownership and sustainability. As opposed to saying it was a UNICEF, INGO project, they did everything.

The other successful aspect of a project is when I see positive changes in the community. An example: when I started the intervention along the coast, I never thought I was young then, I did not have grey hair like now, I never thought community members would embrace and run with it. When I did visitations in the community and came to learn that young girls and boys were walking as far as 10 km to go and play football, seek education for life skills, do theatre performances, reach out to other children in the community. That really motivated me. That remains the biggest success to me, disregarding what the evaluation will bring out. These children walked 10 km. It is a very,

very poor village, it is a very arid village, they walk barefoot, play barefoot. And you see them happy, you see them smiling, they share their experiences with you, and you look at them and feel like shedding tears. For me, that has been the success specific to this intervention. I never knew the community had capacity and time to do that. Most importantly, I never knew the community could be so motivated to carry on with the activities.

CHAPTER 6

Understanding domestic work and children organizing

Jonathan Blagbrough

Background

I began working on children's work issues with NGOs about 20 years ago. I began with a focus on child domestic work as well as some other children's work issues. Currently, I am looking at exploring relations between child domestic workers and the children of employers in Tanzania, but also at trajectories and pathways of girls and young women from child domestic work into something else.

Approaches

I will start with something close to what I am doing at the moment. One of the approaches that we decided to take around slavery with our partners about 10 years ago; it was to implement a small grant scheme that focused on groups of girls and young women who were working as domestic workers. This was not just to ensure that their voices were being heard, but also that they have been listened to in terms of programme development. A lot of things came out, a lot of different ways of doing it came from it as well. We were working with partners in Peru, Costa Rica, India, Nepal, Tanzania, and Togo.

What happened, particularly in Tanzania, was that I came with this idea, which I probably stole from somewhere else, of what we called advisory committees. Going back to Tanzania recently for fieldwork, I was actually amazed to see it in action. I was taken, as part of the fieldwork, to a meeting of girls and young women and boys who have been attending regular monthly meetings, and who seemed to be co-creating along with the local organization, an approach, of what it was that they wanted to focus on, how the organization that was supporting them should be operating, and things like that. In Tanzania, that was the genesis of the Tanzania Child Domestic Workers Coalition, based in Mwanza. There was a publication that came out, published by Anti-Slavery International, *Small Grants, Big Change* (Blagbrough, 2013), which was trying to write up the experience at that point.

The selection of advisory committee members, a particularly difficult task, was something the local partners decided. They all did it in very different ways, some more participatory than others. What we found was that, in most cases, there was some kind of leadership and structure in place anyway. All the organizations were working on children's participation in some shape or form and a lot of it focused on helping to develop certain young people into leaders, in order to spread advocacy, spread the word to others.

It was mainly children in the advisory committees. It was supposed to be under-18s but in some cases, the organizations had worked with them so they could operate by themselves. In some cases, there was someone from an organization that was acting as a facilitator. Sometimes there were different ways in which the children and young people were being involved. It depended on, or came down to the structure of the organization itself, and the capacity of the staff.

In terms of selection, there were a whole lot of different ways of selecting, but it tended to be within the ranks of the organization. These were all people who were benefiting in some ways. Young people were benefiting in some way. They were connected to the organization in some way.

The idea was actually to put a sustainable structure in place that was not related to a particular project or programme. It was for the organization itself to be able to have systematic input from children and young people into their projects and programmes. That was the idea.

Some of the organizations were already doing this to some degree, but this was a focus on a particular issue – child domestic work. The young people would be a sustainable resource for the organization and be an example of getting involved. In this case, I seem to remember in Costa Rica it was quite strong, but it depended on how the organization operated initially.

Child clubs and youth groups: I have very mixed experiences of those. In some of the evaluation work I have done they are often presented to me in a way in which children and youth participate. It is presented as good practice; it is presented as an example of advocacy, but I don't really see [it]. I think that children and young people who were involved got a lot out of it. However, I am not sure whether they advocated particularly effectively. But then, I have a bit of a bias on the issue of adult advocacy because I think that so much of what is called advocacy is raising awareness.

In Tanzania, I guess it is part of the historical anomaly and other things; they have got a system of street leaders which partly comes from the colonial era. And the organization, the Tanzania Child Domestic Workers Coalition, targets those street leaders who have influence in very small pockets. These adult street leaders can then be encouraged in various ways to take on the mantle of reaching out to others. In some cases, they have been pretty good at helping to facilitate the involvement of young people within those communities as well. They are very much separate from the organization.

I think that is partly because of the way that NGOs often work, particularly NGOs that don't have an awful lot of resources. Things kind of happen based on, 'well, I have a link with these people here who know the street leader, so we will work there'; informal networks, and then someone else, and someone else. So, it is not systematized in terms of parts.

Language and terminology

The term children's participation has become a buzz word used by so many people in so many different ways, meaning so many different things. So, in some respects actually going to someone and saying, I am interested in children's participation, you come with a lot of stuff. I agree we should not use that term participation.

I don't think of the work I have done as community development. But actually, it has been a surprise to me. I have done a bit of work with an INGO and actually, it was quite refreshing to see some of their work and see how it was framed in a community development context. Rather than necessarily saying, this is the work happening in child labour and we have children and participation. I don't know, it seems a bit wider framing. I just like that idea of trying to avoid the current, the buzz word, people still continue to use. But that means very, very different things.

I should simply ask how children are involved in their communities, including schools, formal, informal settings. It is just a way to prompt people to think out of the box a little bit. As a way of them thinking, how are children involved? There are these ways that we have always considered to be children's participation. But informally they do have a role.

There is a negativity that tends to come around in children's participation. The understanding that there is always some deficit or other in the children's lives which is trying to be covered. And actually, thinking of it more as capabilities might be better and might move us away from thinking that participation is how we deal with vulnerability. A positive term might be interdependency.

I am getting quite interested in the notion of movements. One thing that excites me about movements is the fact that adults kind of try to control things, but movements are much more organic than that. I quite like that idea.

One of the things I was really pleased about was the unintended consequences of the small grant scheme, where there is a minimum requirement for administration, and very small amounts of money. There were lots of failures. But in some cases, it did seem to strike a chord. It did seem to allow young people to get together in various ways. To sort of organize together or to come together in their areas. The purpose was not to try to link people internationally and I think that is quite a problem.

But what you want to avoid is people creating, or recreating, structures where you get a leader who is supposed to represent all of these many different experiences. It may start with the best intention, but it does not necessarily work out.

Reference

Blagbrough, J. (2013) *Small Grants, Big Change: Influencing policy and practice for child domestic workers*. London: Anti-Slavery International.

CHAPTER 7

Journey to understand children's participation and citizenship: a personal view

Tom Cockburn

Background

I came to be concerned about children and young people's rights when I graduated in sociology. I was doing a PhD about child rescue and using historical documents. I felt some kind of connection with the voices of children in the past, with photographs and accounts of children by adults who were making decisions about whether to remove them from their families, or remove them from the country through emigration. While I was doing that work there was such an extraordinary connection with children.

Afterwards, my first job was in the Department of Applied Community Studies at Manchester Metropolitan University. Community Studies was considered an old-fashioned field. It had a very bad reputation in terms of imperialist logic; I thought that was partially correct, as there were elements of colonialism in it. But I think that there was something else, and it is interesting that this [European Sociological Association conference] session is around belonging and boundaries – I just thought – we have been here 30 years ago in community studies working on such issues.

Colleagues introduced me to working with children and young people. I started involving myself with community studies involving children. The first major project was the Moss Side Youth Audit, which looked to catch the views of children and young people, for Manchester City Council, about what they wanted from the area. I am sure I was not reinventing the wheel because we wanted children and young people to have a central definition and control over local decisions. We wanted them to be part of the final report. We wanted young people to identify with the research methods that we were using.

There were some life-changing meetings with young people and it was life-changing for me. We worked with an outreach worker from Save the Children. We saw two young lads stripping cars and the outreach workers started engaging with them. I talked to the young people and these young men were interested in participating in the project. They insisted that they did not want to carry out 'qualitative' interviews, as they wanted 'hard facts' because only 'facts' are what would get the council to listen. To cut a long story short, they proved to be absolutely right. That is what governments and policy-makers want. You can provide as many stories as you like, but they will ask: what percentage thought this?

Citizenship

The other journey came from moving to Bradford University where the big issue was around community cohesion: how Asian and White communities can work together. Throughout that, I had an academic interest in socio-logical analyses of citizenship, and problematizing children within those debates. I think citizenship is important. It has as bad a reputation as the word community. It is exclusionary to outsiders and places British citizens as subjects with a burden of responsibilities. However, the concept also opens up our subjectivity, or subjective citizenship. Citizenship is an important concept, because it has these varied elements and can also provide a sense of shared belonging.

Citizenship, for me, is important from the perspective of children. It involves things such as belonging, reciprocity, rights, the expression of rights but also responsibilities, and citizenship of course has very negative aspects to it. It is also different, I think, from when I first started writing about the opening up of the concept of citizenship to others, because now, when we are looking at citizenship, it is expected that young people are part of it; you need to be inclusive about things.

In the first peer review I received, for a draft academic article I wrote in a sociological journal, the reviewers sent two short messages: that children are not citizens and, therefore, this article is meaningless. Both reviewers said that. I persisted and eventually, the journal *Childhood* published what I thought was an important contribution (Cockburn, 1998). What I felt that the models of citizenships don't have, what, I think, is crucial to concepts of citizenship, are our interconnections. We are interdependent. As adults we are interdependent upon children to sustain our societies, we are interdependent on elderly people for their wisdom and bringing us into the world. Why are we having this notion of partial citizenship to some and not others? I think that is why citizenship is a key concept worthy of challenge.

The other part of citizenship that is important I think, and feeds into participation debates, is the UN Convention [UNCRC]. There are limitations of the UN Convention, but the participation element remains important to children. I do accept that participation is not the most important article; health, life, education are more pressing. I also think a neglected component is the right of association. I worked with the Carnegie Trust research about 10 years ago that looked at the importance of the right to freedom of association (Cockburn and Cleaver, 2009).

The reason why I think that the right to associate is important is that certainly in the 1990s and 2000s, laws were passed in this country [UK] that I think specifically identified children and young people as not having the right to associate. The right of children to 'hang around' with their friends outside a shop and other spaces was subverted by 'anti-social behaviour' legislation, including dispersal orders, which were particularly targeting children and young people in public spaces. Yet, the right of children to hang around and associate and communicate with each other is key, it is part of the UNCRC and important for children to learn how to participate with themselves and others. I will give you an astonishing example that followed a piece of work that I did for Bradford City Council. There was a group of girls we asked about what they wanted around transport for young people. They said, we want to be able to be in the train or bus station with our male friends because we feel safe with them, but the security people in the stations moved on these friends and that makes us vulnerable to sexist comments and to all sorts of other dangers from adult men.

Legislation restricting the movement of children was the culmination of a whole series of practices where children and young people were seen as a problem needing to be out of sight in public spaces. There is the classic stuff which I use in my first-year teaching: these are paintings by artists such as Pieter Bruegel that depicted villages in the 16th century that were literally full of children playing and contrast this with photographs of shopping centres anywhere in Britain, where children are virtually absent. Today, children are contained within institutions, where they are controlled, rather than themselves in control. This is not good for their development of citizenship, participation, and association.

Language and terminology: participation and citizenship

My thoughts are that citizenship is a concept that needs to be thought over, reclaimed, and retrieved by young people. There are issues of marginalization, migration, access to identity cards, passports, problems of no border entry, and so on. So, in the real world the concept is real and important. We can academically unpack that. I don't want to belittle that. Refugee rights and how they should have British citizenship and so on. That is an absolutely key important debate, particularly for those young people.

But I think that there are other things in the margins that are also significant for all children. We have 14 million children in the UK at the moment, and children and young people feel, at best, ambivalent about participation. Participatory citizenship for children and young people is limited and narrow. We live in a society in Britain where we are constantly asked our opinions: we are asked to rate our trip on the bus, the delivery of our packages, and so on. That is the world where children are brought up. They are asked about teaching and their experiences of education all the time and yet, we also have the NSS [National Student Survey] results in my department where the students feel that the department does not listen. So, does this mean I don't listen to young people in my charge? It is hard for institutions to be able to conduct a proper dialogic way of responding to feedback.

That seems to tell me that young people, and people in general, feel they are not being listened to. That is the key to understanding children's current citizenship and participation. Asking children and young people in a meaningful way is a very difficult thing and I think that youth workers are very good at listening and acting on children's voices. There have been several papers on how desperate we are to listen to children's voices, establishing authenticity, and so on. What we are really struggling with is the question, do we actually listen to children? The Moss Side Youth Audit project, did the council listen to children? The work in Bradford, did policy-makers listen to what kids were saying about their communities? They did up to a point where children's voices coincided with their own. In fact, there were aspects of children's and young people's voices that we had to edit out, as they contained views we construed as racist or sexist. So, are we representing all young people's voices authentically?

Barry Percy-Smith's work is important in that he focuses attention away from putting responsibilities for participation on children to those of adults and institutions. We need a better understanding of the pressures on those working in bureaucratic organizations. What are the perspectives of professionals, policy-makers, and workers in organizations? Do they just want to get to the end of their working days? And is listening to children being disruptive? We have a culture that sees children and young people as disruptive in any case, and when this is combined with bureaucracies, then, you have a toxic cocktail. So, I think that if you are looking for a 10- or 15-year strategy on participation, we have to turn the light on the institutions. Why aren't they listening? What processes are stopping institutions from acting upon young people's voices or prioritizing young people? There has been some important work done on it. Interviews with policy-makers – the usual political response: 'We like it if we can, but with the resources that we have ...'. A whole variety of responses like that. I think there is a piece of work that needs to unpack some of that. This needs a long-term, mixed-methods approach, that is, of course, expensive and time consuming. But I think this would give us a more rounded viewpoint.

Part of this long-term project must explore the general political cynicism in European countries where adults and children feel they are not being listened to, or that they are 'left behind'. What are the processes of marginalization, the feeling of alienation, the despair that we have in our political structures in Britain and elsewhere? How are we going to engage with that? And engage with people who have power, who can facilitate change? We talk about children's agency in sophisticated ways but, actually, as adults, we don't have complete agency, because there are more powerful people than us who can make things happen. And what is important is how we can make things happen, if we wanted to change something in the community, and the processes needed.

This will involve adopting a *realpolitik*, and discussions on the limitations of where we would like to go.

Learning from the lessons of research and experiences of children's participation is another important area. Projects have asked organizations why they did not deliver what young people were saying, to get that dialogue about organizations becoming listening organizations. It is not just problematizing people who are not listening. I think that you can change attitudes, like the one I alluded to earlier when an article on children's citizenship was rejected. We have been making arguments, 20, 30 years ago about the importance of participation and people saying that children are too immature to participate and be listened to. That is now different, now it is conventionally recognized that professionals have to listen to children.

Cosmopolitanism

Cosmopolitan citizenship and global citizenship are a really interesting set of ideas. Gerard Delanty's work on cosmopolitanism is quite good. What you have with cosmopolitanism is the classic – if you have global citizenship, you must have a global government. Under the current state of the world that would mean that America is the policy enforcer. No, thank you. Having said that, there is a shift in political opinions away from 'class based' politics to one of populism and cosmopolitanism. This can be seen in the Brexit debate in the UK and other forms of populism across the world, that can be contrasted with the cosmopolitanism in urban places, usually cities. The cities of Manchester and Liverpool were hugely Remain voting, as was central London, which included up to 80% of the vote. Then, you go to other places where there is a distrust of globalization and in particular the expression of globalization in migration. These tend to be rural or towns a long way from urban centres. There are therefore some groups of citizens who are open to cosmopolitan ideas, and there are others who are resistant to it. This seems to be the dividing line in politics today and children are somewhat caught up in this, although few, if any, ask children their views. It won't be just in the UK. So, in Hungary citizens in Budapest are quite opposed to Viktor Orbán; residents in Istanbul are opposed to Recep Erdo an. This is seemingly a divide, but both sets of people feel their views are not listened to or taken seriously, and that takes us back to our earlier discussion of the complexities of participation.

The model of citizenship that I have in mind is something that is not just our relationship to the state; important though this is. It is not just the relationship between the individual and state, it is everything else we feel connected to and those things we feel distant from that defines our sense of citizenship. Cosmopolitan citizenship therefore does need to look at the ways our relationship to others shapes our sense of identities and this can't easily be boiled down to neat structures. Indeed, it is our relationship to the world around us that forms our sense of self and this can include architecture, technology, media, and so forth. The post-human perspectives that Spyros

Spyrou and others have worked on demonstrates the complicated ways in which children interact with both human and non-human actors and how this shapes their sense of identity.

There was a conference question once posed: if you had unlimited resources what single research project would you do? Most of us said exactly the same thing, which was, to find a particular space and map the intricacies, the small power dynamics, the silencing, the making possible of children's lives, so we could begin to have a handle on the complex and fascinating worlds of children. I think our discipline of sociology and the sociology of childhood within that discipline has an enthralling and exciting future. Drilling down into the complexities of their lives at a local level and how this interacts with the global is key. As is the way this pans out across the globe, including the majority world. I am looking forward to how this unfolds.

References

Cockburn, T. (1998) 'Children and citizenship in Britain: A case for a socially interdependent model of citizenship', *Childhood: A Global Journal of Child Research*, 5(1) 0907–5682: 99–117.

Cockburn T. and Cleaver, F. (2009) *How Children and Young People Win Friends and Influence Others: Children and young people's association, their opportunities, strategies and obstacles*. A report to inform the inquiry into the Future of Civil Society in the UK and Ireland. Summer 2009. London: Carnegie UK Trust.

PART TWO

Practice from regional contexts

CHAPTER 8
Practice from regional contexts: an introduction

The widespread adoption of the United Nations Convention on the Rights of the Child (UNCRC) around the world from the early 1990s brought with it equally rapid attempts to explain and train government and NGO staff on its content and implications for law and services. The training on the CRC offered by INGOs and UN bodies varied in terms of the way the UNCRC was abbreviated and interpreted for ease of dissemination and learning. For example, in parts of Europe the framework of the 'three Ps' was articulated, describing the core content of the Convention in three segments under 'Protection, Provision and Participation'. In East and Southeast Asia a quadruple segmentation was taken up, under the headings of 'Survival, Development, Protection and Participation'. Notably in both frameworks the notion of participation was placed as the last in the list, and commonly last in any training module, session, and workshop; it was often found to be difficult to communicate, because of the slippery nature of definition, and because a focus on issues of survival, education, and health was easier to explain, explore, gain consensus, and measure.

Part Two provides an overview of regions around the world, and types of project focused on children's rights issues in different countries; it shows the importance of taking into account the local context. In this part, practitioners from Africa, Asia, the Americas, and Europe describe how they got involved in working with children along with some of the key components of practice in their country and region. They identify core issues with the terminology around participation and issues facing children.

As throughout the book, the chapters are based on personal experience, and open with a personal account providing an overview of how the contributor came to be engaged and involved in working with children and young people. The issues, dilemmas, methods, and other points emerge from their practical experience. As noted in the Introduction, most of the interviews that form the basis of the chapters were conducted in 2019; although the elapse of time (and the intervening Covid pandemic) means that the circumstances of projects and organizations will have changed, the underlying practices and issues of 2019 are what provide the basis for future work. This reminds us how children's participation is not static, and that attention must be paid to time and place as well as who is involved.

In Ethiopia Anannia Admassu (Chapter 9) outlines work in communities involving children through CHADET, a child-focused organization that works with children and communities. This includes the role of CPCs (Child Protection Committees), play, strategies in communities to deal with social norms, development of children's participation, and criteria for successful projects. He also describes regional networking.

Based in Uganda, Fassil W. Marriam Kidane (Chapter 10) discusses an approach to funding and supporting smaller organizations around children's rights and violence prevention. He describes national work and collaboration on violence prevention in Uganda, looks at conditions for successful participation, barriers, and challenges.

Yaw Ofosu-Kusi (Chapter 11) looks at the development of his work with street-connected children in Ghana and the context of popular perceptions around their lives. He discusses the notion of child-friendly cities in the country context. He also looks at his collaboration with Phil Mizen and they discuss issues in research, participation, and work with local organizations.

In Nepal, Shubhendra Man Shrestha (Chapter 12) describes the development of children's involvement in the post-conflict peace process, particularly the 'Children as Zones of Peace' programme. He raises issues around gaps, particularly for the most marginalized, and core questions of accountability.

Harriot Beazley, based in Australia but with substantial and long involvement in work in Indonesia, discusses processes of developing research with street-connected children in Yogyakarta (Chapter 13). She looks at issues in identifying appropriate methodologies and ensuring research collaborations operate from the same standpoint.

Based in Brazil, Irene Rizzini (Chapter 14) looks at her involvement in the Child Watch International Research Network, and a range of issues in the development and processes of children's participation in Brazil and regionally. She uses examples from a number of projects she has worked in and connections to Global North–South politics and issues of involving children across the spectrum, from those who are richer and in school to the poorer children, often marginalized and seen as dangerous.

In the USA, Jessica Nowlan and Tenaya Jones (Chapter 15) describe the work of the Young Women's Freedom Center and their own involvement in this organization focused on those who were in detention. They look at the change from being youth-run to youth-centred, and particularly at the problem of adultism and challenging this.

Gabriela Trevisan in Portugal looks at work with school dropouts, young mothers, and poor communities (Chapter 16). She highlights theoretical perspectives, indicators of success, networks, and initiatives. As do some other contributors, she looks at ethical issues in research and practice in poorer communities and contexts.

Apart from the threads running throughout this part of the book on the usefulness of terms such as participation, and issues around practice, the contributors have common concerns about work in communities, the involvement of children, and questions of dealing with social norms. Issues of inequality, poverty, and marginalization emerge as the core context and shaping factors not only for the projects but for the lives of children and young people. These elements combine to shape issues and processes of children's and young people's participation, particularly how social norms and power in communities may limit their opportunities and adult expectations.

Sharing learning and experience is another major concern for practitioners. The regional contexts are clearly important and well-articulated, for example in East Africa through networks, and in South America through the continuation of the local Child Watch International Research Network. But, as with all contributions in this book, personal experience and history is important in people's involvement in and development of their practice; particularly individual commitment to working with children and young people, and underlying ideas of social justice along with rights. The boundaries between practitioners as activists or detached professionals can be difficult to draw in the contexts of inequalities, rights, notions of justice, and questions of what can be done.

CHAPTER 9

Challenges in overcoming social norms and tackling child migration

Anannia Admassu: Ethiopia

Children's participation and community-based child protection committees

I was inspired by addressing the needs of vulnerable children in my country. We developed projects where we can address some of the pressing needs of children, such as street and working children, and children who are orphaned. But what we have realized is that one of the major reasons why people are not supporting children to the desired level in countries like Ethiopia is because they don't know enough about what they need to do with regard to child participation, child protection, and so on. So, in our project we built a component where we can engage communities to understand what they can do for children, and created a platform to have children to sit with adults and tell them what their needs are.

We call it community-based child protection committees (CPC). This is a locally grounded body, composed of parents, teachers, children, and other influential community leaders. They come together, discuss the problems of children in their communities, and mobilize members of the community. To address at least some of the problems, if not all, we have implemented projects on education and health, unless we are able to further engage communities in projects we can sustain. We aim to sustain the response, but also reduce the scale of the problem before it occurs. For example, we were working on child migration in the Amhara regional state. The key issue was how to engage children and support children to stay in their communities; this is the sort of thing we were doing. But at every stage, we were engaging government bodies because we wanted them to take over whatever we had started. So, this would ensure sustainability.

Strategies in communities

Overcoming barriers and social norms in communities is the most challenging part of the exercise because we were dealing with traditions, like child marriage. Communities cannot easily take change as an easy thing. This is about attitudes and practices. We even engage religious leaders, but the communities are hesitant to pick it up in the first instance. It takes time, but you have to be patient enough to keep the pace of dealing with the communities. That has been a challenge.

What I have found more important was trust. Building trust between us and the members of the community. We also need to know who is really most influential, who would really manage to convince and persuade members of the community to cooperate. I know it is not easy, but once they know that you are not giving up (because I am not), I cannot put it in a time frame, because in the context of our country projects last between three to five years. Bringing attitudinal change within such a short period is not an easy thing. So, we make sure that we work with locally grounded community-based organizations in the case of Ethiopia. These are societies that are really active in development as well, but there is really good trust in them and local government in the eyes of the community. So, if they know that you are going to stay in the community, that you are not going for a while, like some of our projects in the countryside, you will achieve better results. We stayed there for 10 years, for example. You can't achieve change in communities where children's voices were not heard before. You cannot simply do this in one or two years and convince the community and bring them to the level where they can listen to the voice of children. Even in the first place, to believe in children's participation. They think that children are children, they don't have the capacity to make decisions and to give their opinion. They wonder how children can give ideas on development and so on. But I have seen it myself in implementing projects, that listening to children's voices will bring significant change. For example, we implemented a huge girls' education project, where the major challenge is attendance of girls, where they may not come to school due to household chores. So we worked in this platform, and in another platform for girls' education known as 'family hub'. The family hub brings together parents, children, teachers, and influential leaders of the community. We discuss that we are not really trying to impose anything on the parents, but to find ways of resolving the problem together. This is how we managed to move things on.

Developing children's participation

The key thing would be providing evidence on how this works. How this works elsewhere in the Global South, or in the context of Ethiopia, even with some variations from one region to another. For example, our youth research has been done in Amhara and Oromia regions, with different cultures and attitudes and so on. What has worked in one part of the country might not work in another, but it is likely that it will be working. If you go to parents and influential leaders in the community and government officials with some evidence, you can demonstrate for them that this is happening; this is what we did based on children's opinion and this has brought change.

I can cite another example. We are providing support, such as scholastic materials, for girls going to school, but we were providing a similar type of support for girls and boys. We give them exercise books and other materials and so on. We did not know that we have to deal differently with girls and boys; it was really a learning exercise. They told us that they have different problems. For example, currently, we are providing sanitary towels for girls, we have set up separate toilets for girls and boys, which was a problem because girls won't come to schools during their menstrual cycle because they don't have a safe space. This has come from the children themselves. We were learning ourselves.

What makes success

I think, as I said, we need more research in identifying, crystalizing the problems of children, but we have to address their other needs as well because it is not just about awareness. If children are not going to school, we need to find a mechanism through which we know the problems, then we have to find ways to address the problems that have emerged in the research exercise. So, whoever is funding the research might not be able to support the project. We are really in need of agencies who would address the rest of the problem, like we did with the YOUR World Research project (see Johnson et al., 2022).

We know that there are problems among the youth and young people. So, now we are trying to make use of the data generated by YOUR World Research, changing it into a project, where it would practically address their needs. Otherwise, communities would lose their interest in cooperating with you. For example, in a project where we have implemented a community-based sanitary project many years ago, in a poor community in one of the worst slums, members of the community challenged us (me and my boss – an American woman) by saying that, 'everybody comes and goes. They see us, ask us about our problems, but they won't come back. So, what would be the advantage of getting involved? Why would we tell you about our problems?' So, I think from a practitioners' point of view, we need other programmes that would be really helping us. We can demonstrate for other funders as well: look, we did this research, these were the findings, based on these findings we developed a programme that would address the needs of the communities. So, this would really make the circle full.

Key elements of a programme

I think that they need a coordination mechanism on how to best do it. They have to compile the data properly, and they have to also be able to document. For example, in the Amhara region, they have what they call the CCC – Community Care Coalition. This Community Care Coalition has been organized at a regional level, all the way down to the lowest government administrative structures. But they lack capacity, such as training, documentation, how to document the issues coming from the community and from children, and so on. What I have observed is that there is a lack of coordination mechanisms between the different stakeholders and platforms. Funders could really help local communities who are striving to create a mechanism to make sure that the support to be given for children continues.

Regional networks

We have experience of working with other child-focused organizations in Eastern Africa, from Kenya, Uganda, Tanzania, and so on. But at times, this gets very loose, unless we create some sort of platform where we can exchange research findings and experiences on the ground and learn from each other. I remember delegates from Eastern Africa were coming to our project in Addis and seeing how we were implementing joint multisectoral projects with other NGOs.

We used to have a platform where we met once a year, where different organizations made presentations on what they have been doing, the challenges, the lessons learned, and ways forward. That kind of platform would really help to exchange new ideas and ground-breaking experience. This can even go further; we would be in a better position to push our government as well to take action towards supporting children.

Other organizations with whom we have linkages include the Population Council because they have also been doing research around children. We still need to maintain our relationship with the Ministries of Women, Children and Youth in my country, but also with other research initiatives, such as Young Lives, which have been involved in doing research among children, and higher learning institutions. In this case, I would be very much interested in involving local universities, regional universities, not only in the capital but other higher learning institutions located near to our operational areas, such as Universities of Gondar and Bahir Dar. If we see the Amhara region, the population is over 20 million. That is where more vulnerable children are. It would really be good if we also engage research institutions as well as higher learning institutions.

One organization to link to is UNICEF. That is one thing, but there is a very good regional organization known as the African Child Policy Forum. They are involved in undertaking research and documenting challenges and good practices concerning the lives of children in Africa. The advantage is if we come up with very good research findings, African Child Policy Forum would be a very good platform for us. It is a high-profile platform.

Theoretical perspectives

We often say in CHADET that we are learning by doing. So, I really appreciate the approach of praxis, introduced by Paolo Freire, shown in his book *The Pedagogy of the Oppressed*. Freire really believes in the potential within the communities. It might take ages and ages if you go through the formal channels, but CHADET especially has very good experience in working with communities. So, everybody will come and see what has happened if you manage to bring meaningful changes in communities. We have to have a place where we demonstrate that this thing is really working. So, people can be convinced.

That is really important, because whatever marvellous research finding that you come up with, everything else would remain in the shadows unless you demonstrate for others that this is working and how you can change the lives of children and communities. This is what I believe in.

References

Admassu, A. (2019) *Conceptualising Childhood: Perceptions and practices of childhood education and migration among the Argobba community in north-eastern Ethiopia,* PhD Dissertation, University of Brighton, UK.

Johnson, V., Admassu, A., Church, A., Healey, J. and Mathema, S. (2019) 'Layered and linking research partnerships: Learning from YOUR World Research in Ethiopia and Nepal', *Exploring Research-Policy Partnerships for Societal Impact, IDS Bulletin* 50(1). https://doi.org/10.19088/1968-2019.107

Johnson, V., Getu, M., Getachew, M., Ahmed, A. and West, A. (2021) 'Trapped bodies, moving minds: Uncertainty and migration among marginalised urban youth in Ethiopia', *Children & Society* 35: 944–959.

Johnson, V. and West, A., with Church, A., Getu, M., Tuladhar, S., Getachew, M., Shrestha, S., Ahmed, A., Neupane, S. and Gosmann, S. (2022) *Youth and Positive Uncertainty: Negotiating life in post-conflict and fragile environments.* Rugby: Practical Action Publishing.

CHAPTER 10
Building successful participation

Fassil W. Marriam Kidane: Uganda, East Africa

Background

I have been working for over 20 years in civil society organizations, and local, regional, and private philanthropy. My professional background is in social work (first degree) with a Master's in Organizational Leadership from the United States.

I was working with Save the Children US for a long time as a programme manager and then I co-founded a local NGO in Ethiopia, called Forum on Street Children-Ethiopia, where I have been the director for seven years.

Then I worked with the Oak Foundation and managed the Eastern African Programme: grant-making for local NGOs, mostly regional and local in East Africa, focusing on Ethiopia, Uganda, and Tanzania. I have been there for almost 12 years.

Children's Rights and Violence Prevention Fund

While I was at Oak, the trustees increased the funding, and we stopped funding local NGOs and CBOs because they were too small to manage by Oak. This prompted Oak to find other means to try to identify intermediary organizations that support smaller organizations in getting funds from the bigger foundations. Oak asked if I was interested in starting this kind of regional intermediary grant-making organization. I have been with Oak for over 12 years. So, that is how the Children's Rights and Violence Prevention Fund (CRVPF; http://www.crvpf.org/) started. Other donors came later.

Our programme focuses on Uganda, Tanzania, Ethiopia, and Kenya, and is currently partnered with 210 community organizations and local NGOs. Because of limited capacities in the outreach of these organizations, we identified a strategic approach we call a 'place-based cluster partnership approach', that encourages three to five CBOs and NGOs to come together to work; they either share the geography area or specialist approach. We have been funding organizations like that for the last seven years.

We have been using the cluster partnership approach process to bring organizations together and give them the grant to work together before they know each other well. However, at a later stage, we established a six-month planning and learning grant. This is for any organization in the cluster to apply for a programme; we give six-month grants with a focus on three areas. One, to provide time and space to get to know each other's work; the directors and the programme officers must know each other's programmes and identify areas of intervention. They must sign a memorandum of understanding that they are committed to working on the joint project. Their roles and responsibilities must be identified. For example, one could be a grant holder and sign an agreement with us but also implement a project with others.

The second area is we encourage a six-month period to do a baseline assessment to identify and listen to children and young people and their families and communities' formal and informal leaders. Currently, CRVPF has three grant-making programmes: Prevention of Violence Against Children (PVAC), Adolescent Girls Power Programme (AGPP), and Youth Capacity Development (YCD). All three programmes are strategically connected; the YCD programme focuses on facilitating safe and dignified employment and self-employment opportunities for young people.

The third focus area is building the organizational capacities of cluster partners. We have developed an organizational self-assessment tool and encourage the cluster partners to self-assess on an individual basis with the support of CRVPF staff or a consultant to identify the strengths and challenges of the organization. The cluster partners will come together and jointly will identify five priority areas for capacity development for CRVPF support. CRVPF, using external consultants, will support partners in the areas of leadership, financial and programme systems building, human resources, and purchasing computers and software that support the organization's development.

Violence prevention programme

The violence prevention programme is linked with UNICEF and part of the INSPIRE package.[1] We are just about to start the programme promoting the INSPIRE package and strategies. We are working with the Ministry of Gender, Labour and Social Development in Uganda to promote it because the Ugandan Government has conducted a national survey on violence against children. The survey recommendation was to implement the seven INSPIRE strategies at a national level to prevent and protect children from violence.

The problem in Uganda is that many government organizations, local NGOs, and civil society actors are not aware of the INSPIRE package. This is the situation; can we pilot the seven strategies in six districts where our existing partners are operating using different methods: media, campaigns, workshops, seminars, training, at schools, at community, and at the government level? Before doing that, we conducted a baseline assessment to know the knowledge and experience of those who are targeted for the training and promotional work. Then, we started that programme and at the end of six months, we are going to evaluate it again to see if the promotional work makes a difference if people are aware of the seven strategies.

Nationally we are also working with the Ministry of Gender to promote the seven strategies at different levels. For example, we are working with a social organization in Uganda to train partners and members on the seven strategies. Before doing that, we interviewed them to get background on what they know about the strategies. After the training, we will wait a bit and then do the same post-interview and see if they are applying the training.

Some of our partners are just starting. They just got the fund a month back; it is an initial programme. This is one project where we are involved in linking local activities to regional, national, and global initiatives to contribute to the global violence prevention movement.

We collaborated with Raising Voices in Uganda, which has done a very good job of violence prevention in schools. There were six partners, local NGOs, in six districts. We requested a nationally recognized evidence-based manual, so they can work with our partners at the local level, to support them. Raising Voices supported the implementation of the school programme manual. They are reaching more than 100 schools. We always have a cluster approach, usually, two or five coming together to work in a local area.

We have a project in western Uganda where four organizations and one media organization came together to implement violence prevention work. Our strategy is to focus on three areas because our violence prevention programme is focusing on the prevention of violence, not on the protection side. On the prevention side, we have three intervention strategies: one is parenting, with parents; the second is looking at spousal relationships; and the third is addressing household poverty. These three work at the household level.

We believe we can reduce violence because we work on parenting and on spousal relationships, improving gender relationships, and improving household income. By implementing these three integrated components, we believe we can make a difference at the household level because all the research and surveys show that violence is taking place at the household and family levels. That is why we are targeting families.

Second, we are targeting communities through a media campaign, by working with youth and women's associations at a community level. The third one is working in schools. Family, community, and schools are the three pillars of our work on violence prevention.

Adolescent programmes

A new adolescent programme started with almost 31 partners in the region. The partners are adolescent girls' groups, local NGOs, and women's groups. The clusters in each country conduct the baseline assessment in their areas to identify the critical issues that hinder adolescent girls' power, decision-making, and choice. Now, we are doing a power analysis looking at adolescent girls' power, on their bodies, finance, and on adolescent girls' confidence.

This is like research conducted by our partners, supported by our national consultant and regional office. Our partners are interviewing and working with adolescent girls. Partners are mostly local NGOs. In Nairobi we have one cluster of three organizations; in Kilifi the coastal area, one cluster; in Uganda, four clusters; in Ethiopia, two clusters.

CRVPF provided a six-month planning and learning grant, and after six months of a listening and planning process, we brought the 31 partners and some adolescent girls from Kenya and Tanzania for one four-day learning and sharing workshop. During the meeting the partners and the adolescent girls shared their six months of experience and especially adolescent girls shared their life solutions. Based on the four days of meeting common intervention areas were identified to support adolescent girls in the region.

Conditions for successful participation

If you look at it, if you start from the initial participation of partners, through the planning grant process, they must discuss, work together, and be in direct support. The planning and learning grant also assists partners to have better information about children, adolescent girls, families, and formal and informal community leaders since they listened to their concerns during the situational and power analysis period. They will also be more accountable to the children, adolescent girls, and other stakeholders in the community. Our staff will be there, but this is a process of collaboration and learning from each other. After six months are completed, we encourage them to develop a proposal for a long-term grant. That process helps them. In the four-year strategic plan CRVPF plan to build community movements that support children and adolescent girls safely. We believe most of the community organizations and local NGO leaders will be part of the community movement.

Building process

With the adolescent girls' programmes, adolescent girls are involved. We encourage girls to be active, to be trained, and then we interview other adolescent girls. That process is very important, and we encourage participatory activities. Partners have a high level of involvement in the participatory consultation process. When they are doing their power analysis, they engage other girls and train them, and these partners are recruited from adolescent girls. In fact, in Tanzania, three of our partners are adolescent girls who are legally registered.

We encourage a high level of participatory activities and consultation because in our original organization, initially, we wanted to create a community movement. That is our ultimate objective, creating a movement that supports children's development, resilience, and participation, providing adolescent girls with space and decision-making. To create that kind of movement, I don't think a top-down approach would work. The most important thing for us is to build their capacities, and local NGOs' capacities, and to create that by sharing learning, which is the place for developing a community movement that supports children's universal rights.

Challenges and barriers

Age, power, resources, and social and cultural norms are the challenges. We are not calling our partners CBOs, but community organizations; they could be local NGOs, women's groups, or adolescent groups. If anyone in the community is organized and ready to organize themselves, we are happy to support them. We are trying to address it by understanding the situation in that community, not coming top-down. Community organizations are closer to the community and most of the staff are from the community. One or three years could not change that situation. That is why we have a long partner-building process. It could be six to nine years in the same community, with the same partners building their capacities and supporting them throughout that process.

Key barriers in supporting the process include adults' understanding of giving space for children and adolescent girls, and the power relations between men and women, adults and children, teachers and students. All are there, but we are starting the work. This is a long-term process. Currently, donors are committed to supporting us. We continue working at that level. I don't think that anyone who is part of the regional level has this kind of cluster placement approach at the community level. We have been working in their communities in a long-term strategy.

Other key barriers include poverty of course, and government sometimes doesn't understand what we are planning to do. They want the money for themselves. They encourage us to give them the money and we say no. There are a lot of challenges.

Policy frameworks

Most of our work is linked to government policies, in the CRC and adolescent girls' policy, the gender policy. Each country will review that. We are saying that we are addressing government policies by working with community organizations. We look at the Sustainable Development Goals as well. We look at violence prevention policies. We use all the available resources.

We are going to follow with qualitative and quantitative research, on whether bringing three, four, or five organizations together to work in one geographic area rather than working in isolation makes a difference or not in creating safer environments for children and adolescent girls. We are looking from a research perspective at the cluster's approach, partners, strategies, how they engage communities, and how they are supporting networking not only in their communities but also in local government structures to create safe environments.

Key funding priorities for the future

We are revising our strategic plan. Previously we started the violence prevention programme and then got funded for the adolescent girls' programme. But with our new strategy, we are merging the two together; we are going to have a theory of change and a learning agenda. Our support, our community organizations, and local NGOs are critical. I think most of our resources will be directed at building and encouraging adolescent girls to establish their own initiatives at the community level and support them. Even going to the extent of training adolescent girls' leaders and young girls to take leadership training, so that they can take over and work in their own organizations and build their own institutions at a community level. We believe in establishing community movements that support children and adolescents safely and with dignity. We want our community partners to lead this advocacy work and campaign as most of them are the residents of the same communities, rather than us implementing it with them.

Beyond financial support

I am a practitioner. I am not a researcher. I am more interested in engagement. Doing and implementing research, not only evaluation research, is very important for us. Understanding what works well and not well is critical in identifying the factors to understand how to scale up our programmes or even duplicate our programmes. So, implementing research and supporting that kind of research, not only evaluation research.

Sharing best practices and experiences is one of the critical areas. We are going to organize learning and experience-sharing forums every year. Once we identified our learning agenda, we are going to follow up on whether we are moving in the right direction or not. We want to bring our partners along. This may not be all the partners as we are planning 73, 74 participants for the adolescent girls' power programme. We might limit to a national or sometimes regional level: national level every year, and some kind of strategies to accommodate our financial limitations as well.

For the September [2019] forum, we will have an initial four-day meeting. The first two days will be sharing learning experiences with our partners. The two last days will be to look at the future direction and understanding, maybe identifying national and regional learning agendas for us. That is what we are planning to do. We discussed it with our consultants, and hopefully by the end of this month we will have a clear agenda.

CRVPF has developed its own manuals such as Parenting for Respectability, VSLA (Village Savings and Loans Association), and Good School, and plans to develop men's engagement manuals. The challenge of using other manuals is considering that most of the partners are community organizations and the need to tailor it to their levels of understanding.

I am very much interested in child participation and in safeguarding. We are developing a safeguarding policy for all our partners that have child participation. For us, participation is critical. Agency building and resilience building are critical for us. So, that is where our focus is.

Note

1. INSPIRE is a set of seven evidence-based strategies for countries and communities working to eliminate violence against children. It was launched alongside the Global Partnership to End Violence Against Children in 2016.

CHAPTER 11

Engaging with urban informal childhood: lessons from an informal settlement

Yaw Ofosu-Kusi and Phil Mizen: Ghana

Background

My engagement with children's studies goes back to 1998 when I enrolled at the University of Warwick as a PhD student in applied social studies. I chose to look at child labour referenced to children on the streets of Accra, Ghana. I had the opportunity to communicate with Professor Phil Mizen at the University; our initial engagement about research.

Street children

In 2000 I went into the field, and did interviews with street children and some adults in the street situation. It was a great eye-opener for me. I had certain ideas and hypotheses about certain issues; some tended to be as I expected, others were different from my expectations.

There is this idea in Ghana that I subscribed to at that time, that these children on the street would not listen to their parents, take things in their own hands, do what they thought, for their personal interest, which in Ghana is quite different from what we expect of children. We live in a society where what adults want generally predominates, especially for children of the age you find on the streets of Accra. So, I bought into the idea that these children are there because they don't want to do what their parents were asking them to do.

But interviewing and looking at their circumstances, especially the challenges that some were facing and why they have come there, went beyond disobeying their parents. With some background I had in economics, it made me become much more interested in poverty from the global perspective, global as something that does not just concern parents, but lots of people in the country, and creates a sense of insecurity or inadequacy for parents, and the inability to properly look after their children. As part of what came out, children are much more adventurous than, at least in my society, we usually allow them to be. Some learned from others in the cities and chose to replicate the same things.

At that time, I interviewed 45 children over three or four months, but went back to reassess some things. In Ghana, you cannot engage children in a research environment without necessarily engaging adults. You have people choosing to volunteer to take part in what you were doing. As a PhD student, fresh from the lecture room and having learned about methodological process and how you have to seek consent and deal with gatekeepers and so on, I felt quite obligated; the children were there, but I wanted to go by what the book says.

When Phil and I started working, we involved children and adults, but in the initial stage I only engaged children in the research. I had to engage adults because I needed consent from them to operate in an environment where the children were. It is a huge slum. You go there, and see a structure where children and people were informally organized into ethnic groups and communities based on where they have come from. For instance, most children don't have their parents with them, but there was some sense of control and regulation. Just walking to that area and conducting research was a way of inviting trouble for yourself. I learned this in all kinds of ways, because sometimes in the middle of an interview they would ask you, what authority do you have to do that?

Researcher obligations

When you conduct research in a more organized environment like somebody's house or going to school to interview children, the protocol is clear: the steps to follow, the people to seek consent from. In the streets, I like to say that is not organized but Phil argues it is organized but not in the conventional way. In the streets, sometimes the fact the child talks to you as a researcher could put the child in trouble. I remember interviewing a girl aged about 15 years who just had a baby. While we were chatting, some guy passed, and she was telling me about how some children have easy access to drugs. Somebody passed by and told me, do you see that person going? He sells drugs. Obviously, that act could potentially endanger her; that is why we anonymize some of our interviewees. But if this person knows that this girl has pointed out that he works as a drug dealer, that obviously would expose him or put him in danger.

The mere act of talking is why sometimes the adults feel reluctant to have children participating in what they are doing. Some are perpetrators of the violence and insecurity children experience. Even when children are not talking about that, some may assume they are talking about things that have gone on between them. For that reason, you feel a responsibility as a researcher to clear what you are going to do with people that are authorities in those areas.

If there were no protocols or institutional requirements for conducting research, a responsible researcher must feel an obligation towards the security of the person, of the child especially. You can assume a certain sense of adult personal capacity for themselves, but with children, at least in my culture, every adult has some degree of responsibility for the child, regardless of relationship. If you are in a street situation where undoubtedly there is some amount of violence, or some children show visible signs of illness, you have to consider all these things. There is a personal moral obligation on a researcher to not bring any harm to children. At the level of institutional requirements, we feel a certain obligation, even if we are not going strictly by any particular protocol. We feel that my work will be out there, people might look at my methodology to find to what extent I have dealt with the ethical issues.

A great emphasis should be on the sense of obligation the researcher himself or herself has. I can sign the university requirement about conducting research with children; it could be talk to parents or significant adults and let them give you permission; or do it in an environment that is inclusive and gives some protection to children. Sometimes these things are not available. Street children by definition are people who don't have parents with them, even when you deal with the other ways of defining street children, which they call children in street situations. Still their parents are not available. You cannot have a situation where you say, go home and tell your parents that tomorrow you will have an interview with somebody, or I am going to go to your house and seek permission from your parents.

You cannot have the luxury of conducting research in an organized environment like a classroom. Also these children, some have very short attention spans. You are talking to them about bottles, but they are interested in the next vehicle, which is overloaded. It all adds up to you knowing the limits to what you can do with a street child when you are conducting an interview.

When I got into teaching we would discuss challenges that made it impossible for children to be in school. I began to have an interest in children not in school, where they are supposed to be. There was a sense of national awareness about street children in Ghana, there has always been talk about children who sell things, instead of being in classrooms.

Participation and rights

In Ghana, because we don't have a very well-developed social welfare system, people don't put the blame on governments. Mostly, they say that your parents are responsible, that is why you are here. My first time going to Accra, people selling on the streets became visible. When the idea of doing a PhD came, I thought this is something that is visible, society talks about, for me it was also a concern that children, who should be in school are not in school. You can only do all right in our society if you have an education. If some children were not having an education, they are not necessarily going to do well.

When we had the Convention on the Rights of the Child in 1989 everything blew to the surface because Ghana was among the first countries to sign, because we had a president called Rawlings who was quite revolutionary. Very radical. He appeared to be fighting for some degree of equality because he was very much against people who were supposedly of the economy and who were sources of inequality. He was passionate about things like that. So, quickly he signed this. They set up the Ghana National Commission on Children. Then they came to have a Children's Act, called Act 594, that talks about most of the things in the Convention. Clearly, it was developed out of the Convention.

When I was in secondary school, many years ago, the school didn't have student representative councils. Now, every secondary school in Ghana has a student representative council. That gives a good level of participation and decision-making, regarding some of the important issues in the schools. I don't know what happens in the primary, at the very low level, but in secondary schools that is one good step.

There are two ways to talk about that. One thing is having children talking, giving them a scope to participate. It is another thing to talk about what they have done. That is probably the strategy of adults not just with children, but politicians and people do that. I will give you the opportunity to talk, but after you are gone, I will put everything you said aside, and I will do whatever I want to do. Participation must not necessarily be equated with achievement. They can participate in decision-making, but because they do not command resources, they do not have the capacity to actually implement. Maybe the example I gave about student representative councils is just window dressing. So, children, some of them know about the Convention. They know about their right to participate; they know that they have to be consulted. We will do that for them, but what about the challenges they have raised, rather than going to the roots of the issues? ... But it is better than nothing at all.

If you ask me what we can do, then I will probably say the primary thing is awareness, creation, and education. If we got to a point, I am talking about Ghana, where most adults in a decision-making situation are aware of the Convention, aware of the Children's Act, know what the Act expects them to do, know that children need this, and that you have to ask them about this before they make decisions; that is one big step.

Currently, one challenge for us is that in spite of the fact that the Convention is 30 years old, there are adults who are not aware of it. There are adults who are stuck in the belief that children do not have the capacity to participate in certain things.

Awareness creation is important. Education is important. Maybe through education, getting adults and parents to factor what they do with the fact that children, regardless of age, as long as they can talk, if they are given permission, could make important contributions. These come out when you interview street children. That is why I said that my expectations were proved wrong when I went there. You assume somebody that dropped out after three years of school, what does he know? That is a prejudiced situation. If you go with a clean slate and you talk to them, you will see that they have many smart answers to certain things. That is why we have written books and articles. It is about the sort of insight; you cannot assume that they are incapable of forming ideas about things. They are very capable, but participation and education are about making as many adults aware of children's capacity as possible. So that we don't assume from the beginning that they are incapable of doing these things. Beyond that, maybe organizing children, engaging children. It could be a two-part way of solving it. While we deal with adults and parents, we deal with their children also.

Child-friendly cities

Child-friendly cities: I don't know how that would work in a developing country like Ghana. It is worth trying but I would say that the government seems to be more concerned about bread and butter things. Secondly, in the normal scheme of affairs, getting the city to organize in ways that allow certain things that are more formal to happen appears to be unachievable. That is why we have informal situations. Obviously, I am sure that the government would not want children to be in the streets, but this is because of the inability to regulate fiscal planning, etc. This is why the children are there. It is an innovative idea, but it is contingent on how the public is. It might work; I am not sure in the Ghanaian situation for now.

The question is: do you want to do something? If the answer is, yes, we want to do something, next is what do we have to do? But you go to what we have to do by looking at what we have been already doing, and trying to figure out why it has not worked and look for ways to make it workable or try to find completely new ideas, innovative ones. Phil and I have, on a couple of occasions, gone to a drop-in centre operated by an NGO, Catholic Action for Street Children (CAS). We found that to be a very convenient place to talk to children, but when we talked earlier about the inability to find people to seek consent from, we found that environment is different because they have social workers there. They have an improvised classroom where they teach basic numeracy and literacy.

If you think about child-friendly cities, if we had a couple of such places, then, at some point, you can take out children from the streets. Even if they go out to the streets some of their needs must be met. In a number of interviews we ask children, what do you do when you are ill or when you have an accident? Some would say self-medicate, some that my friends will bring me. But a good number who have been to the NGO before will say that I will go to that place, they will look after me and if it is something that needs attention of a proper doctor, they will give them a sheet [letter of referral] and go to the nearby [services]. That probably is the only NGO that has a very organized structure like that. There are others doing this, but not at the scale of CAS.

So, the idea of a friendly city, if we have a couple of those in places where we have high numbers of street children, it could provide them with medical help. Having said that, I might add that not everybody in Ghana is happy about that. The history of CAS is that, when they started, the government was adamant they did not want them to do it. The argument was that the moment you do that, you encourage more children to come to the street. I don't know if there is any research that shows that the number of street children has actually increased because of the presence of CAS. But in the absence of anything, that seems like a responsible way to deal with some of the challenges the children are faced with on the streets.

A good place for starting any kind of project can be in schools, with teachers, because our experience with talking with children is that almost all have been to school. Most were in schools and for some reason dropped out. Perhaps in schools there is engagement with children to continuously remind them of the challenges of being on the street and for that reason, they don't see the street as a simple solution to the challenges they have at home. Maybe, it won't solve the problem, but it would definitely get some to reassess their situation. It could be mobile teams that go to schools, and show videos about street situations to children, give them the opportunity to talk and ask questions about what has happened, to visualize what actually happens in the city to children who are potential migrants to the city. It is something that works for adult migrants. There is always the belief that if I get there every problem is going to be solved. But it is never the case, some people get there, they find themselves in deeper trouble. Our research tells us that most of the children you talk to say, I eventually plan to go back after I have enough money or I am able to pay for school expenses and so on. So, perhaps a mobile team could go around schools and communities, not just to children, but parents and other people, to see real-life experiences of children on the streets and take a lesson out of that. That could be useful.

Phil Mizen

The CAS run outreach, not quite what you are suggesting. They used to set up mini-refuges established in different points of the city centre and would do what sounded like traditional forms of outreach work. What are your rights, how you deal with the law, maybe health and education, sexual health, those sorts of things. Those were too controversial, they had to be stopped, the city authorities did not want them.

Participation and agency

One of the things we often discuss is what at the very minimum we try to do, in terms of ideas of children's participation. It is just allowing children to join the conversation in a very basic way, without the debate of what voice means. Talk just about children joining the conversation. That is one element of it, really fundamental, children are routinely included in the conversations that we have about their lives. That relates to the problem that once they begin to participate in the conversation, what substantive difference will that make? That is the really difficult thing.

My own view is that children's interest is fundamentally linked to their families and communities. That is always a popular thing to say, and I always say that because there is a tendency in a lot of research around children to fetishize children as individuals rather than recognize that they are even children embedded in sets of connections and relationships, which still involve their families, but are centred on communities, and where they find themselves in communities. Allowing children to have some say in the conversations that we have in their lives means recognizing the similarities and interdependence they have with their families and communities.

We spend a lot of the time talking about children's agency at the moment; children are rarely passive. We have some fundamental sense about that and can point to lots of examples in the ways in which children are active. Our problem is not so much that; our problem is looking at their capacity to realize that agency. What we are finding and what we are doing with quite a lot of detail is to actually point to the fact that children's attempts to make their ways through their lives are often confounded, limited, denied. When you see it in those terms, it brings back the fundamental recognition that children's lives are embedded in all sorts of social relations.

The issues and problems that children confront are often the same ones that their families and communities confront. They might choose to solve them in different ways, but that is something else that we have come to the same conclusion about. I don't want to be rude about anybody, but personally, I have become a bit fed up with research projects that say, all we need to do is to listen to children and everything will be all right.

Terminology: child-centred, child-focused, child-sensitive

Yaw Ofosu-Kusi

Child focus? Child-centred? Child-related? Certainly there is a lot in a name. Some names get people to stand still and reflect. I would say that child-centred has been around a long time and probably is already familiar and you won't have to spend time and energy explaining this term to people so that they relate to what they are doing. Even if we were thinking about doing things for adults, we could not think of them as independent entities.

It all comes back to communities and in the case of children, even if we gave them legal legs to stand on, it is still going to be, they belong to the family, they belong to the community. Even me, as a Ghanaian, I cannot walk to a village and say that all children should come and then start talking to them. It won't work.

You go back to the interdependency, they belong to families, you need to negotiate with families to have access to them. For instance, if they can read, you can give them an abbreviation of the Children's Act. They take it home and the father takes it away from them and throws it away if he does not believe in what you are doing. So, you would think that you have a solution, but you will get to every child's house and see what happens.

In our societies, like African societies, if you would have something as child-led, it would be the doom of it. Adults have always been taught that they have the wisdom to raise their children. You are telling them, you sit back and follow what your children are doing. That is probably the literal interpretation people will give towards the end.

Phil Mizen

What would be interesting is you say child-centred and start explaining something about children's rights, it will stop them in their tracks. But if you say, how do children participate in this community? I think you can have a much more fruitful conversation. We have not just researched street children, we research this huge slum. We interviewed children living with their families, their mothers, in the slum, and find these children are actively integrated with their communities, not just work. So, they might form the basis of conversations where child rights begins to be recognized.

Another thing that myself and Yaw keep talking about is we have this idea about informal urban childhood; the idea that greater proportions of children in major urban areas are growing up in contexts of childhoods that are weakly regulated by formal state mechanisms around education and work. All child work is by definition informal because most is illegal. The legislation, that passes in terms of children's rights, presents a huge problem. If we are right, more and more children are growing up outside or in spite of these existing regulatory frameworks, which in theory could give children some rights.

Education is a great example. Where we work, because there are squatters, the metropolitan authority wants to get rid of them and would [not] give them any local government provision for schooling. So, we assumed there are no schools there and then found several but all informal schools. Although they follow the national curriculum and guidelines, they exist outside of the framework that governs the education system.

Yaw Ofosu-Kusi

I was going to make the point about IDs. In some West African countries, francophone countries, they always have IDs since probably the colonial times, but in anglophone countries, maybe as in Britain, we don't have a national ID, but sometimes you go to the bank and they say, you should have an ID. I could use my driver's licence, my passport or the voter's ID card. All these are things that children can't have. You cannot have a driver's licence, because you cannot drive; you cannot have a voter's ID, because you don't vote. The government authority for national identification is speaking now about the process for ensuring Africans get an ID, but this has not been formalized yet. Only a few people have national IDs. I am not sure whether children are allowed to. I think that is for people at a certain age.

By law, any child in Ghana must have a certificate and anyone who dies must have a death certificate. Birth certificates are very valuable documents. Even if they have one, their parents will keep them; parents will have got them their passport. They won't be in a position to carry it with them, wherever they go, use it as a form of identification. That probably won't be a workable way of identifying children. This is the national health insurance card, even children are entitled to that.

Community

I don't know what the official English definition of a community is. But if you ask me, I will say that it is the aggregation of people at any place with some common interest. If you think of it in that sense, community should not necessarily be where someone is coming from when children talk about community or when government or people talk about community development. They are thinking in big terms, spatially and numerically.

For example, a group of about 20 young and inexperienced people congregate every night. For them, in those particular moments, a small number of people, it is a shifting situation, but momentarily a community of people who have a common interest. They have no place to sleep. They need some sense of security at night. They have a certain level of sociability. For that moment, they bond together, linking to each other. You would do that for someone met for the first time, when you don't know anything about them. There are very small levels of consistency in terms of what they do every night. You trust that other person. You are going to allow them to put their leg on you while you go to sleep.

Particularly in urban areas and in rural areas as well, things are in flux. Old communities are being subject to pressures. They are changing as a consequence. Children and their parents are finding themselves in new situations where they are trying to build communities. That is a tough thing. The girls that live in those shacks, and the girls who prostitute themselves. How can they build communities? That is really difficult. They are doing things. They are not passive. They find themselves in certain social relationships where it is very difficult to build, let's call it communities. If you are living in a private shack, which is half the size of that table and there are five of you who live there, and you rent.

You see a sense of oppression. There are times that some, at best, provide a place to sleep for the night. Share resources. They have a very organized system. You come for the first time and they will find a place for you to stay. When somebody has a baby, they will have one or two people that will look after your baby for you. In the end, it is about the community, a group of people. The basis of community. It is not a mature community, but it is the beginning, it is quite a fluid thing. It is not stable like a village in Accra, where people come, and everybody knows what the other person is doing. Here, there is a group of people who are united maybe by insecurity; so, the poorest stay together, but there is a very good sense of looking after each other in certain situations. We made an explicit point in an article about not glamourizing the street, but the reality also is those street children, many of them have a good heart, could be altruistic; this is the sense that we belong together. We share some of the things that we have together.

In Fadama, a big slum in Accra, the first time I went in 2000, I spent almost a month trying to get there. I could easily have gone, but my thinking was, go through these people. They had a youth leader who says I have to talk to this person and get permission from the chief. These are things you don't know on the surface but underneath what you see there is organization, hierarchical systems and people respond to the wishes and demands of others. And I suspect they probably even make some money from the people to keep the structure intact.

CHAPTER 12
Changing concepts: mobilizing peace, accountability, and education

Shubhendra Man Shrestha: Nepal

Background

I have worked in the area of child rights and education, and with young people in national and international organizations. My career started with research with children in conflict with the law, with juvenile delinquents – it is a widely used term in Nepal. I worked with them for more than two months when I was studying, and after this one organization called me as a researcher to work with juvenile delinquents in the reform [unit]. I have also worked with children in the street situation and done research, but many people were involved in finalizing that research paper (see Sharma et al., 2007).

Children as Zones of Peace

After this I went to work for the National Coalition for Children as Zones of Peace in Nepal. It was started in the time of conflict, when children were recruited as soldiers by both the Nepal Army and the then Maoists. The school became shelter homes. I was a national coordinator; it was a loose coalition. It was a movement; now this coalition has been registered under the Associations Registration Act of Nepal.

During that time I went to different parts of Nepal to monitor the rights situation, and we started to talk about facilitating young people's actions. I was very much involved in child protection issues; basically, child protection and child participation. How do they raise their voices? How do they enhance their participation in order to protect their own rights? So, I facilitated those child clubs, the members, the training, collected information from them, and monitored the situation. We used to collect that information at a national level and disseminate it at national and international level.

When I was national coordinator, I had to carry everything because I was the only paid staff. Because it was a loose coalition, I had to mobilize all

35 organizations involved, coordinate everything and provide the input at the local level. I was very young, and I enjoyed it a lot, I learned a lot, and during that time I realized what exactly the child's right is at the local level and what is their condition. I got an opportunity to work with young people at the local level in different parts of the country, because when you see the children and you talk to children in Kathmandu it is totally different, and has been highly influenced by the social-economic situation.

After the peace process we lobbied at the national level and we used to meet with both parties. How we can support the rights of children through different kinds of mechanisms, for example, in the comprehensive peace agreements, in the elections, in the manifesto. Everything we demanded we reflected in those documents and later on got the constitution also to recognize that we should not recruit children in those kinds of armed activities. Later on, what happened is that there are still shelters in schools and the children were used for political purposes. We educated groups of children about being vulnerable politically, we produced short briefings as advocacy, based on our experiences.

Then the government declared the schools as zones of peace: schools should not be used for any armed purposes; children should not be used by political parties or political interests; and children need to be protected from all kinds of violence, all kinds of abuse. I was invited by the Minister of Education to make that draft and then we consulted on it at different levels. And then, the government came up with those 'schools as zones of peace' guidelines. We had that guideline and that became a great instrument for all the organizations. I am proud because I had to work a lot and all the organizations that were involved in that supported this kind of campaign.

Then, I joined ActionAid where I learned some important things about participatory approaches, tools, methods, the education on rights. When I went into the field the approach helped me to know how these participatory methods can be used at the local level. Basically, my work was to facilitate different networks and organizational work. Providing training, programmes, capacity building activities, and lobbying at the national level, engaging with policy-makers, and at the same time linking our local work with the national and international level.

Then, I had the opportunity to work with a team from Ethiopia and with colleagues from Nepal in YOUR World Research (Johnson and West et al., 2022), where I got incredible experiences to work with the young people who are the most marginalized, living in different situations.

When I was with ActionAid in Nepal I supported Youth Alliance, facilitated their movement and advocacy work. They are working in different districts, all interrelated, and there are young people, from different organizations but in one alliance, and I am closely working with that as an adviser, sometimes as a facilitator, sometimes as a presenter. They have got experience advocating and campaigning with and for youth.

Gaps: beneficiaries and the most marginalized

In my experience, first of all, the whole development work framework is driven from the level of funding and their own strategies. The one thing missing which I can see is that they did not consult at the local level. They did not consult with the main beneficiaries. They consult with the bureaucrats, they consult with the local government, but they do not consult with the main beneficiaries, and the most marginalized are always excluded from those kinds of issues. They call it rights-based but sometimes they have very populist programmes. That is the gap, that is why they have not had good reports, but the most marginalized, the main beneficiaries are not actually benefited by those kinds of interventions. So, there is a gap.

The most excluded, the most marginalized, and most target groups must be able to benefit from those kinds of programmes. At the same time, it is also important that all the policies and the government stakeholders need to be accountable. There is another gap, the gap between the most excluded and the duty bearers. These gaps are maintained by the local organizations themselves because they have made it a kind of a business; they always create, they always maintain that gap so they can work forever and ever. So, that is why I am telling this to you.

Accountability

In my experience, there are people who want to work with young people and now are also interested in [working with] children. The context has been changed, but we need to facilitate their agencies, their actions. We need to make consensus among those adults as well, after the restructuring of our administrative system. The local [administration] have to show responsibility to protect and promote child rights. They have a huge responsibility in the area of child development issues as well. It is now our opportunity to support local government and at the same time, to make them responsible.

How can we reach the children? How we can develop that kind of mechanism where children and young people can be listened to, can be heard, and their voices reflected in local governing planning and policy-making processes. Sometimes, local and national government can be targeted as can the children who are living in marginalized areas. At the same time, not all adults are the barriers, because they are also our supporters. However, some allies performing in the name of social organizations can be transformed through our positive actions.

We need some people, social organizations and children's clubs, young people's groups whether they are a loose forum or a registered one, to make sure children and young people's representatives are there, as the champions of youth rights. Rather than thinking about what they don't know, we have to make sure that we are listening to the young people's voices.

When you talk about the Nepalese context, the typical NGO programme would not help those kinds of initiatives. We need to carry out this kind of programme in a different way. For example, we have more than 24,000 government schools here and the teachers are highly paid compared to private school teachers; more than 80 per cent of the children go to public schools. But when you compare the results of public schools with private schools, the results are very good in private schools, even though the teachers are paid less in private schools. But that is why we are advocating for the strengthening of public education.

The problem is the accountability of the duty, the accountability of the stakeholders on the one side. On the other side, there is the problem of our social context. It is not a problem, but it is ignorance of the social context, because who is coming to public schools and who is coming to private schools? These two things are different. So, the most disadvantaged and most underprivileged children are going to public schools, those parents have not time to give even one hour to their children for their education. That is why one organization, *Teach for Nepal*, is promoting volunteering and providing training and mobilizing them in different schools just to facilitate one or two subjects in one school. The result is not only to facilitate the subject but also to facilitate the whole community, just to increase the quality of public education. This is transforming that education.

The lesson is we have to work in campaigning, promoting volunteering, preparing that critical mass who have that kind of passion and capacity to deliver at a local level, to listen to the children, raising the voices of young people at a local level and the wider context. We need to make this happen, we need to make a plan, strategically, on how to promote it.

Frameworks

Living rights definitely, the UNCRC, but we need to connect this to the national context and globally to the SDGs [Sustainable Development Goals]. Everybody is talking about the SDGs. Most people use UNCRC. We need to deepen the discussion about the UNCRC and how we can influence international policies. At least, we need one framework. Right now, at a national context, we cannot say that the UNCRC is not relevant, and we will not use UNCRC, we will use living rights. We need to organize that kind of dialogue. We need to have more evidence so that we can influence people and we can have a critical mass. We can influence those kinds of things at the international level.

Participation

Agency is [more useful] than participation, the word participatory or participation has become jargon and people are used to using it. Most of the NGOs are using it just for the word, to make their programme more flowery, attractive, but agency has some power in the word itself.

The term development still carries several concepts. Still, we can use community development because everybody is talking about development, but it depends on how we interpret, or we define it. Because the word development still carries several concepts, so define it very clearly.

References

Johnson, V., West, A., Tuladhar, S., Shrestha, S.M. and Neupane, S. (2019) 'Marginalized youth navigating uncertainty', in C. Walker, A. Zoli, and S. Zlotowitz (eds), *New Ideas for New Times*, pp. 425–445, Basingstoke: Palgrave.

Johnson, V. and West, A., with Church, A., Getu, M., Tuladhar, S., Getachew, M., Shrestha, S.M., Ahmed, A., Neupane, S. and Gosmann, S. (2022) *Youth and Positive Uncertainty: Negotiating life in post-conflict and fragile environments*. Rugby: Practical Action Publishing.

Sharma, H., Ghimire, R., Shrestha, T.P., Shrestha, S.M. and Dahal, K.P. (2007) *Rehabilitation Reintegration Denied? A critical analysis of the juvenile justice system in Nepal*. Kathmandu, Nepal: PPR Nepal.

CHAPTER 13
Involving children: pathways of participation and terminology

Harriot Beazley: Indonesia

Background

I conducted my PhD research with street-connected children in Indonesia during the mid-1990s, at the end of the Suharto regime. I was in the Department of Human Geography at the Australian National University and geographical literature informed my research design and analysis. I was looking for appropriate child-focused methodologies to design my research with street children in the city of Yogyakarta. At the time I was doing some work with a community development organization in Vietnam, and they introduced me to the IIED [International Institute for Environment and Development] *Participatory Learning and Action (PLA) Notes*.

My PhD research design was subsequently guided by Vicky Johnson's work and PLA Notes 25 (Johnson, 1996), along with Hugh Matthews' (1980, 1986, 1992) work on mental maps with children in the UK. I found these resources very useful to help me develop my research protocol, because I had not conducted research with children before. My thesis was an examination of street-connected children's geographies in the city of Yogyakarta. I used a lot of techniques described in the PLA notes: including mapping, drawings, spider diagrams, and focus group discussions. I also took photos and asked the children take photos of places that they liked to go in the city for different reasons. They borrowed my camera and I would then develop the films and discuss the images with them. I found those activities so incredibly useful in terms of understanding their lives from their own perspective, and that was the focus of my thesis: the geographies and identities of street children in Yogyakarta, through an analysis of these methods. I later found *Stepping Forward* (Johnson et al., 1998) and that was very useful for me too when I was writing up the thesis.

I was just really lucky at that time. In June 1998, I went from Australia to the Urban Childhood conference in Norway. I was a PhD student and had been in the field for two years. I was a bit in awe of all those people whose work I had been reading while I was in Indonesia and Australia (Hugh Matthews, Ben White, Vicky Johnson, Roger Hart, Judith Ennew, Brian Milne, Rachel

Baker). I met so many different people and I got so much out of that. It was really amazing and inspirational to listen to Judith's paper on 'Children In Place/Out of Place', for example. There were so few people writing about participatory approaches in research with children at that time. The conference galvanized me to go back and finish my fieldwork and my thesis.

Then, I was very fortunate again when Stuart Aitken, at the beginning of the internet, advertised scholarships for PhD students to go to San Diego, for a children's and young people's geography workshop, in late 1998. It was amazing because it was so well organized and enabled me to meet other children's geographers conducting child-focused research (for example, Gill Valentine, Sarah Holloway, Elsbeth Robson, Sarah Radcliffe, Tom Herman). At that time children's geographers were interrogating the same issues, but mostly from a first-world perspective. That time in San Diego was quite defining for me, theoretically.

Community development, research, and children

Once I completed my PhD in 1999 (Beazley 1999) I got a job with DFAT (Australian Government Department of Foreign Affairs and Trade), for AusAID (Australian Aid), as the Community Participation Advisor to the Indonesian Provincial Government in Eastern Indonesia, based in Lombok. The project was a women's health and family welfare project focused on reducing infant mortality and maternal mortality in Eastern Indonesia. It was a huge project across two provinces and 16 districts, with three main components focused on health, training, and community participation.

The project wanted me to inform them on how best to engage the community to improve their health-seeking behaviour, especially in relation to neonatal and postnatal practices. People at that time in the development sector (at the multilateral and donor level), were not really using participatory methods in their projects. The whole notion of participation was like an add on, an afterthought. It was a buzz word but no one really knew how to do it. For the particular project I was working on they had not factored in any community engagement; it was only training of midwives. Then, they added another component, which was community participation, but no one knew what it really meant. My understanding of community development was very much community-driven, but there was this idea among the project team that I could somehow train the community to use services provided by the Indonesian health department!

My Indonesian colleagues and I led participatory fieldwork in several villages, with pilot projects. At the time I felt that I was in a vacuum: while the rest of the team were all training midwives and nutritionists, and doing household surveys, I was trying to conduct community participatory rural appraisals, to understand what the community issues were, and why they were not using government health services for birthing and for infant and children's health. We went to a number of villages and conducted participatory research with the community to try to understand the antecedents and causes for the high infant and maternal mortality rates in Eastern Indonesia. But in that project, nobody was talking to the children. Trying to understand and develop the best ways to include children in community development, especially in Indonesia, is really important to me, as children are often left behind in the planning stages of development initiatives, particularly when they are implemented by external donors and government agencies. Because I had conducted my research with street-connected children, I used the same methods to understand their health-seeking behaviour and their nutritional needs and obvious stuff, really. I got great data and we presented it to DFAT and AusAID. They were like, 'we have never seen data like this before, it is so detailed and informative!'

But even when I had the data I found that it was absolutely impossible to feed that information back into the project because of the project design. It was awful because I felt that I was raising hopes in the communities where I was working and there was no way that I could actually make something happen or implement the changes they needed and asked for.

One of the main problems with that project was that it was designed in five weeks by a team of experts who went around Indonesia seeking information. They visited high-level organizations (no one at the community level) and came back and wrote the design. But then, when we were in the field and actually living it, we were saying 'no, the design cannot be like this', but they replied that we could not change the design. Any design, whatever you call it, has to be from the community perspective. Or a design must have something built into it so that you can implement necessary changes at a later date. Flexibility is key in any project design. For example, saying that 'this is going to be a maternal and health project and it is going to be doing x, y, and then z. We are going to train the midwives and we are going to send a trainer and then, all will happen as we planned'. That is not the way to do it. You need to be much more fluid and flexible, which donors hate. It is essential to have some flexibility in any project design in order to be able to adapt and create a project that is right for the community. In the end we were able to support an initiative to develop traditional herbal medicines from the surrounding forest, which was an income generating project for the women, and also a way of supporting the health of the community.

I went back to the same village recently, 15 years later, as I had formed a really good relationship with the village head. I went back for another project funded by the SSHRC (Social Sciences and Humanities Research Council), in Canada. We were looking at the issues of statelessness and birth registration among children of transnational migrants in Lombok. Many parents migrate to Malaysia and Saudi Arabia to work, and their children are left behind. We went to these villages because we knew them very well and I had a good relationship with the gatekeepers and the parents. Some of the parents I have known since they were children, but it was still really hard to access their children, especially as in Indonesia children's perspectives are not seen as important, or something to be taken seriously.

I remember being sat on the ground; I had managed to gather a group of 13-and 14-year-old girls together, who were children of transnational migrants, including migrant mothers, and who had been identified and selected by the village head to participate in our research. That in itself was problematic, due to the power dynamics. The village head stood over us where we were gathered, and he listened to their answers and corrected them when he saw fit. All the dynamics were wrong. You have to actively embody the research process, and it was at that point that I realized that is what I do. So, I asked the village head 'could you go and get me something' (to make them feel useful and important), but really just to get him out of the way. When you are operating on your own you can find ways to short-circuit those kinds of power dynamics. Perhaps it is that I don't want to meet here in this particular place, surrounded by all of these people (which often happens in Indonesia). So I ask 'can we go into that room over there and with the permission of the children? I think it is best if we don't have so many people around'. Or 'let's sit under that tree over there'; just finding a polite way that reduces the power dynamics, and gets rid of onlookers, that is what I normally try to do. It also helps to speak the local language.

Intergenerational

The IOM (International Organization for Migration) recently asked me to write a paper on intergenerational cycles of migration to work for women and girls in Southeast Asia and the Pacific. Writing the article made me question the whole notion of intergenerational because I had not really focused on the issue before. I have used it but not in any deep context, and I now find it quite problematic. Everybody seems to use it differently. You don't automatically understand what the term is describing. While I like the term on the surface, it does worry me that people will use it in different ways and that it will cause confusion.

Participation and terminology

'Participation' is another buzz word that everyone used to pay lip service to. Now 'children's voices', are the buzz words. But as Vicky Johnson and Andy West (Johnson and West 2018) say, our attention and understanding has to move beyond children's voices. It is everywhere now; you keep hearing it. Even 'lived experiences' has become a catchphrase, everyone is talking about the lived experiences of children and young people, to the extent I want to stop using that phrase because it has become overused currency in development speak.

I personally use the word agency all the time, implying something needs to happen, rather than saying what is happening. I do find it helpful. Sometimes I have to explain what I mean by agency. I don't think it is a problematic concept for practitioners; that children are able to express themselves, and do things in their lives which they make the decision to do, rather than us trying to interpret and decide what is best for them. It is the opposite of passive. But in the end we must not overstretch this notion of agency. This is something Karen Wells has pointed out; that sometimes children are vulnerable, and they do need protection and they don't have agency because of their complete lack of power.

In my research I have used the term child-led, I have used child-focused, and child-centred, I think was the term. After the AusAID project I got to know Judith Ennew much better (as she was living in Bangkok and I sometimes went to visit her there). Judith invited me to join her in training local researchers in participatory research approaches with children, with UNICEF (Indonesia) and Save the Children, in a number of different countries in Southeast Asia. One time we were doing work with UNICEF, with child sex workers in Central Java. Judith and I had such interesting conversations, interrogating the terminology in currency at the time (early 2000s). Especially from the analytical side of things. UNICEF called the children 'victims' whatever their circumstance. Later, when I was writing [about the vulnerability and agency] of adolescents working in the sex industry in Indonesia some people said that I was overemphasizing their agency. I get that. I get the criticism and I think that it is important to move back a bit and give some space to the theoretical discussions and drilling down on these concepts. It is like participation. Everybody gets excited about participation but you cannot always be partici-patory in your research approaches. You also can't be 'child-led' the whole way through either, especially when the children are extremely vulnerable.

Child researchers

The best child-led research project I have ever worked on was with the Save the Children child protection unit in Aceh (northern Sumatra), exploring the experiences of children living in orphanages after the Tsunami in 2004. Save the Children had a child-focused research project with trained child researchers who lived in the three orphanages where the research was conducted. I liked that terminology and I liked their approach very much because they really let the children run the research project. I felt that was the most successful child-led project I had worked on, even though it was based in an institution (orphanage).

References

Beazley, H. (1999) 'A little but enough': Street children's subcultures in Yogyakarta, Indonesia, unpublished PhD thesis, Australian National University, Canberra. https://doi.org/10.25911/5d78db149c5f7

Connolly, M. and Ennew, J. (1996) 'Introduction: Children out of place', Childhood, 3(2). https://doi.org/10.1177/0907568296003002001

IIED (n.d.) *Participatory Learning and Action.* https://www.iied.org/collection/participatory-learning-action

Johnson, V. and West, A. (2018) *Children's Participation in Global Contexts: Going beyond voice,* Routledge, New York.

Johnson, V. (ed.) (1996) *Special Issue on Children's Participation. PLA Notes 25.* International Institute for Environment and Development, University of Sussex.

Johnson, V., Ivan-Smith, E., Gordon, G., Pridmore, P., and Scott, P. (eds) (1998) *Stepping Forward: Children and young people's participation in the development process,* London: IT Publications.

Matthews, H. (1980) 'The mental maps of children: Images of Coventry's city centre', *Geography* 65(3): 169–179.

Matthews, H. (1986) 'Children as map makers', *Geographical Magazine* 58(3): 124-126.

Matthews, H. (1992) *Making Sense of Place: Children's understanding of large-scale environments,* Hemel Hempstead/Lanham: Harvester Wheatsheaf/Barnes & Noble.

CHAPTER 14

Reflections from an engaged researcher in Brazil

Irene Rizzini: Brazil

> *Since we did this interview in 2019, some 'future' events have now happened, such as the author's trip to Brazil.*

Background

I have been teaching for 40 years. I started as a young person, as a professor in Brazil but I had been working directly with children voluntarily since my teenage years. That had a very important impact on my trajectory because since I had experiences talking to them and working with them in different contexts, I brought to my work as a researcher always talking to them, and understanding their environments as being something very important. At the moment, I am a professor at PUC-Rio, the Catholic University of Rio, a major private university in Brazil. I am very happy that they brought me in 2002 from another university and I was able also to bring my centre, CIESPI, the International Center for Research and Policy on Childhood, with me.

It is a very small centre, with a lot of brave people who have been working with me. It depends on grant and contract funding. When there are resources, we have more projects and more people as part of our staff. In synthesis, it is a small centre with 10 regular people working together for a long time to develop research areas where we think we can make a contribution. I am settled in Rio, but working with partners all over Brazil, and several partners in Latin America remaining from Childwatch International, which I directed for about seven years (I was involved in the network for about 15 years). It is a network of over 40 university-based research centres in over 40 countries. The Latin American representatives survived as a group. We continue to interact; in fact, next week [in 2019] I am returning to Brazil after participating in our 13th conference which took place in Mexico. We keep updating and supporting each other in the region.

Terminology

I think we need to recognize the complexity of understanding the meaning of concepts, particularly in different contexts. Simple translations of words and terms often are misleading. In different contexts, cultures, and languages, concepts have different meanings. Take for example, when you say 'children'; are you defining them based on the Convention on the Rights of the Child? Are you thinking about the age range 0 to 18? In my part of the world, we never say 'children', for example, to refer to adolescents or youth and we distinguish between those two categories. There are other complexities and it is important to go beyond legal definitions. Looking at how Latin American researchers and scholars have been thinking about young people's participation, I think that there are nuances; the term participation is used and misused.

The term agency tends to sound a bit strange to us, particularly in Brazil. We have been using it because it comes from childhood studies, but it does not sound very good in Portuguese and Spanish. The terminology of *protagonismo* is really what resonates in our part of the world, referring to children and young people's place and roles in society as active citizens (see Cussiánovich, 2013; Rizzini, 2021; Collins et al., 2021).

Another interesting question is about community development. In South America I think we reject a lot that comes from North America, because it is basically focused on the US. But I had the opportunity to study at the University of Chicago, and got some understanding about community development as a broad and a very strong field in the US. When you say communities, you are thinking about neighbourhoods, people associated in a neighbourhood. But in Brazil, when the word 'community' is used, it tends to refer to *favelas*, or low-income neighbourhoods that need development. The notion is they are underdeveloped or not developed enough.

When I think about community development, I think about engaging young people who live in low-income communities or *favelas*. I am using this example to explain this idea of working with them and supporting them as young citizens, with autonomy to develop their own work as young people trying to improve their own communities. In our team, we tend to emphasize the idea of the context where children are growing up, as well as their relationship with their families and their communities; we don't see them as vulnerable young people; they live in challenging contexts and that makes them vulnerable.

Social justice is a completely different thing than community development. If you are thinking about community development, if you define community as anywhere where children find themselves in relationships, that is OK. Social justice is another thing. It comes from another theoretical background. Maybe we should bring back that concept more often. It became a little bit lost over time. It is out of fashion. It is a different thing. I love the idea of 'rejuvenating' in some ways; it is really good. English is not my first language, but it seems to me that if you say rejuvenating communities, it could also mean that young people are very important actors in those communities.

Child participation

A process involving different generations is how I understand participation, social, political or 'citizen participation'; a kind of integration; the young people should be integrated with adults all the time, finding their own voices and strategies to be heard. This is not to say it is an easy process; there are multiple barriers due to adult-centric attitudes, as we heard so many times from young people (Rizzini et al., 2005; CIESPI/PUC-Rio, 2022; Taft, 2015; McMellon and Tisdall, 2020).

In terms of child participation, I have an interesting story. As President of Childwatch, the whole idea was to stimulate the academic world internationally, to produce information related to children's rights, after the Convention on the Rights of the Child was ratified. University of Oslo researchers found me and we started to work together. We started by attracting other researchers or research centres. We ended up working with over 40 countries. Child participation became a very important theme. I resisted for years to enter deeply into the debate. I believe that there still is a lot of rhetoric rather than action to change the fact that young people often continue to be left out. A lot of, 'oh, this beautiful work' is in fashion. I have done all my work in research and action because that is how I understand my work. Policy is part of it. We want to help change things; we want to support and strengthen other actors that are out there trying to improve children's lives. Translate research into action, to inform social change. I believe that children are part of everything, they are participating in different ways. But we keep telling them that we have to give them a voice.

There is still a lot to be understood and changed. From where I stand, as a researcher with the soul of an activist, I kept working and writing. I have had the opportunity to do this with partners in many countries and different cultures, but my priority is to focus on my part of the world – with 300 million people in Brazil. There are 26 countries in Latin America, one cannot do everything.

My perspective has been to look at what children already are, the ways in which they are part of society, and then there is this other side of it, which is them developing their own ways of engaging with adults, always there supporting, interacting with them with respect. Especially the very young ones, they depend on adults, not only to take them to places and allow them to participate. Adults have also to be open to what comes as a consequence of children becoming empowered. So, adults have to be, like children, part of this debate. They have to be a part of this everyday practice of opening spaces where traditionally children have been excluded and devalued as people who have not lived enough, who have no experience, and therefore should not be included.

There are areas where I see my work developing in relation to this broader view of participation; one that is more connected to community development in a way, I think, that is engaging young people to participate in developing an agenda where children become priority. You see, children are not usually part of those political agendas. There are so many priorities and urgencies in our low-income communities that even if, for example, sanitation is priority number one, which it often is because there are many diseases in those slums, children won't be a part of the debate, despite the fact that they are probably the main victims of lack of sanitation.

I am talking about low-income communities, not that I see that it should be this way, the divide between classes. But in our region the economic division is huge. I think this is also true in all the countries. The segregation is there. In some communities, in countries like mine, it's appalling. For example, at my university, we are on the side of high-income residents. We are basically separated from the *favela* by a street that they call 'the asphalt'. Children being born on one side or the other side of the street will have completely different trajectories in their lives. That is social injustice, let's put it this way.

One way of understanding the work we do in terms of participation is by engaging all kinds of people, but we have a particular interest in engaging young people in our projects. We have always done that as a principle, not so much to stimulate participation, because we see them as part of everything, but it is also to give them an opportunity to be supported by a university where they very often see they cannot even come inside. They could be one of our students in the future, but the divide is such that they cannot even imagine that possibility. It is a form of exchange as well. As we involve them in research, as we work with them, we can also help them strengthen their own resources as they strengthen ours. We are always learning with them. So, we see it more as a way of exchange, and their participation is crucial.

We usually engage young people from the communities we work with in advisory committees to work with us in research projects – and adults as well. The idea is also to support young people that are starting to appear as possible community leaders. People who connect younger and older generations. That has been fascinating work.

Another way is doing research, not with them directly involved, but doing research where we can better understand the way young people participate: their roles in political spheres and in public spaces where policies about children are deliberated (CIESPI/PUC-Rio, 2022).

We have been researching the use of the term political participation as applied to young people in the Latin American academic literature and developing some theoretical approaches related to political participation and activism – their *'protagonismo'* – where young people find their own spaces and strategies to be part of processes of decision-making about children's rights. It is the role of young people as advocates for children in general. Here, I hope that we will be able to engage with middle- and upper-class youth as well, and be able to have kids from different socioeconomic groups together to talk about their views and concerns. I am pretty sure we will be able to do that eventually.

Contrasts project

The Contrasts project started in partnership with Norway. It started when we had the opportunity to work with a young professor from Østfold University College. He has come many times to Brazil and is fluent in Portuguese. Once I told him that our university was full of Norwegians, mostly engineers discussing petroleum and gas with no interest in social issues. Back to the notion of social justice – they basically served economic interests linked to corporations – not giving anything to this country. We thought we could do something about that.

We found a way to call their attention to children's diverse realities in our city by creating a simple exhibition of photographs focusing on children in different contexts, contrasting different childhoods in Rio. We called this project 'Children in Rio: Contrasts'. Young photographers produced the photos and it was really beautiful. We exhibited in various parts of Rio and in Norway too.

Then my team came with the idea we called: 'Children in the City – methodologies for listening to children'. As we brought these pictures to schools and other places, children immediately took an interest in them and had a lot to say about their own childhoods. They were really excited as they started creating stories and making comments about what they saw in the pictures, mostly about what children were doing, describing their surroundings and so on. A professor from the department of design, part of the CIESPI team, came up with the idea to create silhouettes of the positions that children had in those pictures taking away much of the background. These images were presented to children of various ages ranging from early childhood to 10 and they had some time to draw on the silhouettes and tell stories about what they produced. We slowly improved the methodology and took it to various settings – schools and even an early childhood education centre.

The other fascinating thing was that the methodology was also applied in a school in Norway where there are people speaking many different languages. We are still discussing the experience in both countries and starting to write about the learnings. Over the years, we have been experiencing different kinds of methodology and more recently some particularly designed to listen to young children in their early years. It has been fantastic.

Political participation

Decision-making about children basically excludes children's perspectives – they are simply not considered. There are young people who have not been given training or even exposure to political participation; quite the contrary. They are kept apart, even older kids. To engage them is important. They will replace us one day, like it or not, and we should have people that are more prepared to occupy public spaces or public policy arenas. They are not prepared for that. But when given the opportunity, which only happens in a more democratic political atmosphere, what happens is impressive. This is for me the foundation of democratic societies (CIESPI/PUC-Rio, 2022; Pérez et al., 2008).

Children everywhere are massively influenced by the internet, but they are rarely exposed to civic and political participation. It doesn't seem to be an option. They have been included in the category of citizens, they are entitled to rights, but they have very little opportunity to be part of collective actions, social movements, and so forth. That is even more true when our countries are under right-wing governments, which has happened several times in our part of the world as well. And when that happens there is even less space for political participation. So, we need young people that will stand for themselves and will say no, we won't vote for those people anymore. It's my hope and my wish.

References

CIESPI/PUC-Rio (2022) *Youth entry into work and social participation in Brazil: Young activists conduct research on problems and solutions.* Rio de Janeiro: CIESPI Research and Public Policy Bulletin # 11.

Collins, T.M., Rizzini, I. and Mayhew, A. (2021) 'Fostering global dialogue: Conceptualizations of children's rights to participation and protection', *Children & Society* 35(2): 295–310.

Cussiánovich, A. (2013) 'Protagonismo, participación y ciudadanía como componente de la educación y ejercicio de los derechos de la infancia', in A. Cussiánovich (ed.), *Historia del pensamiento social sobre la infancia.* Lima: Universidad Mayor de San Marcos.

McMellon, C. and Tisdall, E.K.M. (2020) 'Children and young people's participation rights: Looking backwards and moving forwards', *The International Journal of Children's Rights* 28(1): 157–182.

Pérez, B.C., Pérez, C., Póvoa, J., Monteiro, R. and de Castro, L.R. (2008) 'Cidadania e participação social: umestudocomcrianças no Rio de Janeiro', *Psicologia & Sociedade* 20(2): 181–191.

Rizzini, I., Pereira, L., & Thapliyal, N. (2007) *Percepções de crianças e adolescentes sobre cidadania e participaçãocidadã. (International research project: Children's perspectives on citizenship and nation-building. Childwatch International, Oslo).* Rio de Janeiro: CIESPI/PUC-Rio.

Rizzini, I. (2021) 'Jovens na luta em defesa dos direitos das crianças', paper presented at the *ALAS XXXII Congreso Internacional ALAS Perú 2019.* Dossier Sociología de la Juventud, Grupo de Trabajo 20B. Asociación Latinoamericana de Sociología, Lima, 757–768.

Stoecklin, D., Rizzini, I., Mizen, P., Johnson, V. & Geneva, U. (2023) 'Children in street situations and their rights', in: *The Palgrave Handbook of Social Problems.* Baikady, R., SM, S., Prezeperski, J., Nadesan, V., Islam, M. R. & Jiangio, G. (eds.). Palgrave Macmillan

Taft, J. (2015) '"Adults talk too much": Intergenerational dialogue and power in the Peruvian movement of working children'. *Childhood* 22(4): 460–473.

CHAPTER 15

We already have the answers

Jessica Nowlan and Tenaya Jones: United States

Background – Young Women's Freedom Center

Jessica Nowlan

Some history about the Young Women's Freedom Center (YWFC): I came to the Center in 1996, as a young person from incarceration, and in that same year, the organization was left to us by the founding executive director (ED). I came at 17, and the new ED was my supervisor. She was 19.

We became a youth-run organization and the whole idea behind our work is that girls who have grown on the street, experienced incarceration, are really powerful and resilient and that we have everything that we need. That we are, and young folks are, the ones who can radically reimagine something different and transform lives and communities. I say that is really important, because in this work, what does it mean to be an organization that is led by 19-year-old ED? I became the deputy director at 17, as a young person who has lived in the street since 13, has dropped out in the 7th grade. There were no adults in the background telling us what to do. So, we were really stepping into our power in a real way. We also had to do our own fundraising, from grant writing to cultivating donor relationships.

The work that we were doing in the 1990s and 2000s was really revolutionary and forward thinking and now we are 26 years old. We are not youth-run anymore, but we are still youth-centred and still led by folks who have experienced incarceration and life in the street. The things that we were saying back then are actually the things that society is talking about right now in the United States. Mass incarceration, gender-based violence, poverty, and these were things that as young people we already knew.

We already had radical ideas for transformation, but because of adultism both in the political landscape and in society, also with funding, our ideas were not looked at as solutions. They were looked at as not powerful. As an organization centred on the voices, experiences, and ideas of young people, it continues to be a struggle for us to really prove that young folks do have the answers. This shows from positioning; funders requesting young speakers to speak and only tell a story and not be valued as experts. We actually launched our own research department, because we decided, 'Fine, let's use the tools that are accepted, vital for capitalism, white supremacy, and patriarchy.

We actually already have the answers, but we need to use the tools that are accepted because we have to challenge adultism in a real way'.

That is a little bit about who we are. Other ways that [adultism] shows up is that I am not a young person anymore and as ED I am often asked to be the one to speak, represent, articulate what we do. So, even in my own role there is constant repositioning of who the experts are in my team because my role is to facilitate space for young folks to actually be in power and have a platform to share the solutions.

Tenaya Jones

I got into the young women's centre after I had been incarcerated. I got introduced to them when they were doing groups there. When I got out, I started participating in the groups that would help me in my leadership, help me with probation, and the system that is trying to keep me there. As I was in the YWFC as a participant, I noticed that my work in this would be good and focused, because I am a youth.

I am still in the system and my voice should be involved in this. But once I got introduced to them, they see that my leadership has gained over the time that I have participated with them and they actually hired me as a community organizer. Once I started there, I was one of the girls to do outreach to the youth LGBTQI folks that are on the streets. I was one of the first people they see. I let them know about the resources they can have to work and programmes that could support them.

I let them know what we can do for them and tell them about the SD (self-determination) plan. It is a self-determination plan that helps set goals for yourself, and your coordinator will help you achieve them, and once you achieve them, you will leave with a stipend. I also joined the research team. Right now, we are analysing and coding surveys we gave to 100 girls that have been incarcerated, LGBTQI folks, and I asked them questions about their experiences inside. Also, the resources they would want inside or any alternatives that may help them throughout the time they are there or out.

Adultism

Tenaya Jones

How I define adultism is by them not listening to youth [and] the things they need. Then, assuming why we did something, why we are going through this, and the outcome of things. It seems they won't let the youth or child express themselves to what is going on with them and how things should be handled in their way, because adults mostly think they know what is best for us because they think that when they were young, at our age, they were going through the same things. So, they know how to fix it. But the times are different now. It is 2019 and things are happening now in our society, our world. Youth can only express what their experiences are, no one else can have that advantage of knowing what they have been through or how they feel about it.

Jessica Nowlan

I think adultism is the prejudice that adults carry towards young people and the idea that I know better. In our world we cannot talk about adultism without also looking at gender and race and class. The YWFC is in California, which I believe is the fifth largest economy in the world, and so when we are talking about young, poor, women and girls, and non-binary people of colour, we are looking at huge inequity.

San Francisco is in a crisis when we look specifically at poor, black, young women, for example: 3 per cent of the population, black people overall; 58 per cent of girls on detention are black. They are from the exact three neighbourhoods where young people are going into the welfare system. These three neighbourhoods have the highest level of incarceration of parents, have housing [issues]. People are being displaced. When young people are being targeted, being incarcerated, we know and we have been saying for 26 years, that poverty is driving this, that inequity is driving this. When you talk to young people who are being incarcerated, they consistently say: I need a job. I need economic opportunities. It is literally not that hard.

Because of adultism, and because of the values that folks in power who are adults bring that are also influenced by race, class, and education, those values are projected on these young people who have completely different experiences, and that experience should be the centre and driver for solutions.

How does this relate to local government and structures? Through the overall narratives that are happening, the culture and also funding. One good example, and Tenaya has been the leader, we have just passed legislation in terms of closing our youth detention centre. This is something we have been working on, led by young people, for years, but funders have been very slow to respond. We are saying that this is what needs to happen. But now that we have been able to build traction, pass legislation, folks are coming to the table. Again, I think that this is rooted in the ideas that we know best: and if we are able to support young folks from the margins, and with the deep belief that they actually know, and that there is something, a lot, to learn from them, and if they lead the way and they are supported with resources, time, development, opportunities, then we actually could go with our own way and imagine a different society. I think that those are things that show in our work, including from funders.

Challenging adultism

Jessica Nowlan

When I think about ways in which we can challenge adultism in the work, I think about what I can do personally. As a young person, I mentioned, coming to an organization, I have been incarcerated many times, I have been on the streets for years, but coming to the young women's centre, it was the first place where I was told that I was powerful, I was brilliant, I had everything I needed, I was not broken, I did not need to be fixed. So, I felt my power and I had economic opportunities that allow me to go out of the streets. That changed the trajectory of my life.

So, being able to do this work is for me, now [aged] 40, how I can continually challenge my own beliefs as an adult to make sure that I am creating a space for young folks' leadership within the organization. One thing in the non-profit sector that happens is pedestal leadership. 'Oh, that is the leader. Let's only focus on them'. So, for me, it is continually creating space for other leaders in the organization and using my privilege now with funders, with politicians, with whoever I am with, to make sure that I am not somewhere without a young person and that we are giving space for young people inside the organization to know what they know.

Just because I don't understand the definition of adultism yet, does not mean that I don't know it viscerally and though my political, economic, and historical experience of my own and my community. What does it look like to create space for young folks and all directly impacted people to go deeper, to be able to put language to what we know? I think again that it goes back to how you show up as a leader.

I think that that is my call of action for other leaders. Whether you are in philanthropy or government, we have to recognize that because of structural racism, class bias, gender inequity, that the values we all have, have been shaped by white supremacy and capitalism and that those values value a certain belief system. We have to challenge that within ourselves and we have to transcend the way in which we approach solutions, which includes really creating intentional space for other folks, specifically young folks at the margins.

Tenaya Jones

Personally, making sure that we as young folks have a voice, but also collaborate with adults. They have been through similar things that we have been through, although it is different timing. It is good to understand both sides and points of view, not just my side. It is good to have an adult actually looking down to see what they see, and also letting you know what you are going through and how their ways actually help you, instead of tearing you down and letting you feel that they already know what you are going to do. They think they know how you feel, so they think they have a solution. Just basically making sure that the adults listen. Also, let us make a decision and let them know that this is what I need, this is what works for me. I feel that you (as an adult) should support me and if in the future my decision doesn't work for me, you can help me and give some of the reasons that you have when you were my age.

CHAPTER 16

Reflections from community work practices promoting children's well-being

Gabriela Trevisan: Portugal

Background

I started as a sociologist fresh out of university to work in a community centre in a deprived area of Porto; a poor area with a lot of social issues. I started working with young people because I did my final degree thesis about teenage mums. We tried to give them different perspectives on what they could do and finding training opportunities. We found with that community, they were very poor in every sense, even on structures where you can have young people having their say on whatever they would like to do. Basically, they were school dropouts also. We wanted to create a place where they could feel they have their own interests. That's where it started to hit me, this idea that if you ask people, they will let you know what they want to do.

After three years, I went to do a Master's degree because I felt I needed to learn a little bit more about childhood and children. I had all that experience, but I didn't feel that it was organized. I needed the theoretical background and that's where I started to learn about children's rights, which was a surprise because I didn't know about them when I was a child.

The Master's was at the University of Minho, in Sociology of Childhood, where you have this construction of theoretical background on childhood, on children's rights approaches. I was trying to combine it with basic principles of community work, which really is about the need to start working from the communities, from within and not from the outside. We tried to combine both of them regarding work on children's rights.

Intergenerational

For the PhD, I moved to the political parts of children's rights and political participation. Participation was a huge deal in community development processes. For a long time, I had this idea that participation would be about listening, but then you would be the experts coming from outside. When I started to do this from a children's rights perspective, I kind of started to think that we don't do this with adults, we don't really listen to them, and as an adult even I don't feel I participate that much. I'm hyperactive as compared with a lot of people; so, one of the big learnings I got and I think it was universal to children and adults, is that participation is the key if you start from within, and if you also go into a joint perspective.

When you work with children about the city, for instance, it was a big surprise for me listening to their views on the city. It's a very intergenerational view. It's not like a selfish thing saying I want a new park, or I want this. They have very specific concerns with other generations, like older people, people who live in the streets. They have concerns with poverty and with the most structural issues in the communities. Not just about their own places to be or to hang around, as you might think. These perspectives are valuable. Valuing of these intertwined views is something that I took from childhood studies to community work.

Theoretical and practical

For the theoretical part we[1] drew on the community perspective, from Paulo Freire to all the emancipatory theories, and also inspired by authors such as Nicky Nelson (Nelson and Wright, 1995). We worked a lot with the inside-outside perspectives, with perspectives of strangers and not strangers. A lot with emancipatory theory; those would be Paulo Freire's liberation theories (Freire, 1983). This idea that you need to gain your own consciousness on your own power in your own community before you start to do anything else is a very powerful tool for us.

On the practical side, we usually do these kinds of community projects that are European-based, funded like the first one. Now, we are working with one municipality, which is called Guimarães. They were very active in doing a community process of listening to children and young people, but adults were also involved in this listening process, which is very cool. It was locally funded; it was the city council that decided to bring some money into that.

Now, we got funding for a collaborative laboratory to work on children's poverty and social exclusion in Guimarães. It is called the ProChild CoLAB project.[2,3] We already had different projects in place over the past years and the idea is that we developed them in different territories in the country, so you could find which kinds of actions starting from the communities could actually work, in a comprehensive perspective. They involve families, they involve institutions, they involve children. It is like trying to bring everyone together from different disciplines. It's a big challenge.

Key indicators and criteria of success: what makes it work?

Money of course, but we are starting to get more conscious about the need for having people from different field areas. We work from a sociological point, then, you realize that when you are working in such a complex phenomenon as community development issues you need to bring everyone on board. You need anthropologists, economists, people from history, that will give you the background on the specific community. We bring people from different areas, and we need people that could stay in the field intensively. That's a big issue for me because you cannot really talk about involving communities if you are not there on, I would say, basically, a daily basis or on a very permanent basis. You will have to have people that go that deep in the community and not just go there like once a week.

I would believe in an interesting team made by community leaders. Let's say, one person from practitioners would be the link between communities and the services that are provided to that community. Also, researchers would bring a team of three or four people from different areas that will discuss a comprehensive view of the community. Someone from the community will be my priority other than academics. Someone from the inside would be really important.

Youth-led and child-led

In most issues, I would not say youth-led from the beginning because in these projects we are working on, the theme was not chosen by children themselves. But I do believe that you can, as an adult, discuss with children and young people some of the main issues of the community. Partly these issues were discussed in the previous project that I mentioned, that was of citizenship. So, they already identified parts of these issues that are now also in this project.

But I don't think it's a bad thing, even as an adult, to propose something, as long as it's significant to children and to young people. As long as from there you involve them every step of the way. You can start doing it with basic regular meetings or you could ask them which interest they have and they would organize themselves into different responsibilities inside the community or to solve a specific issue, but I do believe they need support from adults. I just don't think they need paternalistic support. They need someone to be their ally in a sense. To help them get the resources they need and to help them organize their own ideas because other than that they can do it themselves, I think. So, that would be the main purpose.

Useful initiatives

One of the first initiatives could be to train community leaders, to give them a chance to have the tools and resources to be more active, because all communities already have their informal leaders. They know who they are, but what I feel is that sometimes they don't really have the power or the connections to go to the right places. So, if you could pick a number of people that could be your specific connection to a community. Adults and young people of course because we also have leaders among the younger people.

Then, from there, I think you would need to create, I don't know if it's a centre, or just an informal place where people could gather around and draw their own actions from what they want to do. Then, take it from there, I guess. So, you would need the money to start with those two things and those would be key.

Most of the experience I've had on working even just with children and young people is that I find the territories are very important when you are talking about community development. It's not the same thing to do something now, let's say, in the north of Portugal as to do something in the south. Even though we can take the same principles, I am sure we would have to have a lot of different adaptations regarding culture, regarding history. That is why this kind of multi-discipline thing would be very important to address those issues.

Networks and communication academics and practitioners

I think it is useful, and could also be very interesting to take some of the main principles of what you can do in the network and see how they can be translated into the specificities of each country of the network. You could have a base where we all agree on basic principles or basic actions we want to take within communities. Then, they will necessarily change because communities will give you different feedback on that. So, it could be very interesting to take like a macro approach and then to see how it happens in the specific realities.

Definitely you should try to avoid, for example, one of the issues when these projects emerge, that people get a lot of interest, the press, and the media. Be very careful about who you choose because, for instance, we had wonderful reporters doing work on childhood but then we have others who did not know anything about it. So, they just get, you know, very frenzied with things that are nonsense.

Also, to avoid those who have a political advantage from this because one of the real difficult things when you work in specific communities is that you have political leaders. They will take advantage of the nice things you do. They will try to put a mark, a political mark on the things you do, when actually that's not what people want or are interested in. For me there could be a big strategy of trying to avoid that, especially if you run into elections, they could be a big thing for communities.

Facilitative states

For instance, if you talk about this municipality, about Guimarães, it is quite open, because they have been doing work on child rights for a long time. They actually believe in it. It is not that hard. I think one of the main reasons why it works well in southern Europe could be because of personal connections. The personal connection that you have could be helpful because people are more informal in certain ways and that could help to get through the people that you need to get through to get clearances. It has a downside, if you think about ethics committees in some countries for instance. For us that's not really a big deal and it should be, because some universities have ethics committees. You have it in the Ministry of Education and in health sectors but that's it. But opening informal ways of getting to people I think it is one of the things that facilitates more participation of children in decision-making, when you can get there.

Notes

1. The work on the community centre was coordinated by Irene Cortesão, who brought different readings to sustain the work proposals with young people to the team.
2. ProChild CoLab: https://prochildcolab.pt/en/4014-2/
3. The work developed by ProChild CoLAB was supported by: (i) FCT (Fundação para a Ciência e Tecnologia, I.P.) and NORTE-06-3559-FSE-000044, integrated in the invitation NORTE-59-2018- 41, aiming to hire Highly Qualified Human Resources, co-financed by the Regional Operational Programme of the North 2020, thematic area of Competitiveness and Employment, through the European Social Fund; and (ii) Mission Interface Program from the Resilience and Recuperation Plan, notice nº 01/ C05-i02/2022, approved by ANI (Agência Nacional de Inovação, S.A.).

References

Freire, P. (1983) *Educação como Prática de Liberdade*. Rio de Janeiro: Paz e Terra.
Nelson, N. and Wright, S. (1995) *Power and Participatory Development, Theory and Practice*. Rugby: Intermediate Technology Publications.
Quintas, S.F. and Castaño, M.A.S. (1994) *Planificación e intervención socioeducativa*. Salamanca: Aramú Ediciones.

PART THREE

Youth activism into thinking

CHAPTER 17
Youth activism into thinking: an introduction

Many people who work with and for children and young people do so from a commitment to change; for example working towards rights, participation, social justice, to address circumstances of gender, ethnicity, (dis)ability, sexuality, marginalization, discrimination, and problems of poverty, exclusion, inequality, violence, abuse, justice, and other issues. In many, if not all such cases, aspects of this commitment might be externally viewed as activism: the notion and role of professional practice has a part to play, but the commitment to change, the pursuit of change, may override this. For example, many active practitioners feel frustrated by bureaucracies, measurements required, and other aspects of project frameworks that can stifle initiatives responding to the moment of opportunity or crisis. This contrasts with practitioners who see their work as a 'job'; or organizations that prefer a fixed transferable skill set, also perceived applicable in commerce and business, to a personal commitment and the empathy and abilities to engage with children and young people.

In this framework contributors to this book might all be seen as committed and dedicated to what they do, and might see themselves or be seen by others as 'activists'. Allocation of some contributions to Part Three of the book does not mean that those in other parts of the book have not been involved as activists: clearly some became engaged with child and youth issues when they were young themselves. As throughout the book, the chapters are based on personal experience, and open with a brief personal account providing an overview of how they came to be engaged and involved in working with children and young people. The issues, dilemmas, methods, and other points emerge from their practical experience. Contributors to this part became engaged on children's and young people's issues when they were children or youth themselves – as did other contributors in this book.

As always, circumstances and organizations change over time, which is a main feature of the chapters in Part Three. Since the interviews were conducted in 2019, the degrees of social change make us attend to the importance of process and recognition of time and place as significant components of child and youth participation, along with child and youth rights.

Eric Braxton (Chapter 18) helped to found a student union organizing with young people around educational justice when he was just out of high school. He discusses the work of the Funders' Collaborative on Youth Organizing. This national collaboration of funders and youth organizers supports young people in social justice work in the USA. This is focused on groups led by working class youth, young people of colour, and gender-oppressed youth.

Lakshitha Saji Prelis (Chapter 19) became active growing up during the conflict in Sri Lanka, and after experience with responses in Sri Lanka and Indonesia to the 2004 tsunami, became engaged in working with a coalition towards creating a global policy framework around youth. This culminated in the UN Security Council Resolution 2250 (2015) on Youth, Peace and Security. He also leads work in the peacebuilding organization *Search for Common Ground* and describes approaches to involving children and young people, particularly in Africa.

Chernor Bah (Chapter 20) talks about how he became involved in children's participation in Sierra Leone in his early teenage years just after the war, having grown up during the conflict. He describes the growth and spread of children's clubs based in schools. He goes on to discuss the development and work of *Purposeful* (*Productions*), focused on girls and developing girl-led processes, looking at issues affecting them, including violence.

Blair Glencorse's work is about issues of accountability in government, local and national (Chapter 21). He points out how these are often seen as negative, and the organization *Accountability Lab* aims to be youth-focused, creative, and positive, and working from the grassroots up. They use role models and creative people, including musicians and artists, to engage children and young people in different ways, moving away from older approaches, to activities such as seeking honesty in government and enabling the most honest to become a national celebrity.

Karl Hanson (Chapter 22) worked voluntarily as a practitioner youth worker while he was a student. He worked with immigrant and other groups of children and young people, some focused on clubs in a European city, while studying the law with the intention to take up social justice work. He found he was able to combine a legal and practitioner side to some extent through children's rights work based in universities. His work has included not only the development of concepts of living rights but also raising some of the contradictions and dilemmas in children's and young people's participation that crucially need ongoing study if there is to be any coherent movement.

Perhaps the key focus is the need for continual reflection and debate in order to recognize, identify, approach, and respond to emerging issues. At the same time there is a need to address the contradictions and dilemmas arising from social perceptions of what childhood and youth should be like, what it is like, and how such idealistic conceptions and the reality of childhood behaviour and relationships can be reconciled. Activism brings all this to the fore.

Activism as with any and all forms of work with children and young people depends on context (cultural, social, political, economic, environmental, emergency) and groups involved: not only age, class, caste, ethnicity, gender, disability, sexuality, and other given or claimed identities, but also processes and places such as custody, detention, and alternative care, as well as forms of violence.

Many contributions in this book discuss children's and young people's participation sometimes in ways that might be considered as facilitating activism, for example in promoting and facilitating child and youth decision-making and action to resolve issues and problems. Children and youth may become involved in various activities that fall under the rubric of participation, including children's clubs, research, community groups, campaigning. Some continued in related activities as they grew older, while others, as an example given by one contributor pointed out, got married and life changed.

Many of us who become engaged early as a child or youth on child rights issues (before or after the inception of the CRC) may continue working in the field, or return to it off and on, but this is in a different capacity. One of the main issues of child and youth-led organizations, as participants point out, is moving on: ensuring those who become the lead and the face of a movement and who are seen by outsiders as the key representative, pass over the reins. Change is obviously a main component in being a child when childhood is defined on the basis of age: children grow older. Many social structures find that difficult, in terms of regular change within the organization. But change is a main focus of activities discussed throughout Part Three.

CHAPTER 18

Supporting youth organizing

Eric Braxton

Background

I've been on staff at the Funders' Collaborative on Youth Organizing (FCYO) for about eight years, but I was on the board for 10 or 11 years before that as one of the youth organizer representatives. When I was just out of high school I helped found the Philadelphia Students Union that does organizing with young people around educational justice, and did that for around 10 or 12 years.

The Funders' Collaborative on Youth Organizing

The FCYO is a national collaborative of funders and youth organizers that support young people on the forefront of social justice work in the US. Our primary work is supporting groups that are organizing young people age 13–18, but some 18–25 as well. Our focus is on groups led by working class young people, young people of colour, and gender-oppressed young people. Our work is a mixture: some grant-making, some convening, and capacity building of youth organizing groups. We do a lot of funder advocacy and education, supporting learning for funders about the multiple benefits of youth organizing. We do research and communications and try to build and share knowledge about the ways young people are engaging in social change efforts. In some ways we're the primary institution that tracks the development of the youth organizing field in the US.

The multiple benefits of youth organizing

Part of the value of youth organizing is that it's like a three for one investment. Some particular funders often feel they have to choose between programmes that are about the individual transformation of young people on the one hand, or systemic, structural change on the other hand. Part of what we think is valuable about youth organizing is that it does both and more.

We often talk about three categories of outcomes. The first being the benefits to individual young people for participating. Our research indicates that engaging young people to solve problems in their communities is one of the best ways to support the holistic development of young people. If you look at social and emotional learning capacities – that is, the 21st century capacities – of all of the things that researchers now think are the best predictors of future success, engaging young people in organizing in their communities is one of the best. For young people who are the most marginalized, this is particularly relevant. Whether it's leadership skills, goal setting, handling difficult emotions, academic aspiration, all these kinds of things, engaging in organizing is one of the best ways to meet them. The research far outstrips where the funding is for that work these days. Engaging in organizing is highly effective for individual young people and for their development. There are starting to be more longitudinal studies that even show that engaging in organizing really supports young people academically, career wise, and other things.

The second level is community outcomes; young people are organizing campaigns that create real structural change in their communities. In this country, if you look at particularly the last couple of years, the ending the school-to-prison pipeline, the fundamental change in the way that we understand school discipline, immigration policy, in these areas the leadership of young people has resulted in policy changes that benefit not just the individual young people that are in youth organizing groups, but whole communities.

The third level of outcomes is long-term civic engagement; we are building the capacity of young leaders to be both present and future leaders that are really needed to build a robust and inclusive democracy. There's more and more research that shows that there's no better way to build future leaders than to have young people engaged as leaders right now. The research indicates that engaging young people in organizing is much more effective than student government, and other similar kinds of youth participation. We did a research briefing document, about two years ago that laid out a lot of the latest research on all of this (see Shah et al., 2018).

The youth engagement continuum

This is the tool the FCYO and partners developed about 20 years ago. It talks about a continuum of different ways to engage young people. At one end you have strategies that are directly about meeting the individual needs of young people: services.

The next step: you have youth development that says, hey not only do young people have needs that have to be met, actually young people have assets that should be developed, and we should create safe spaces for them, that kind of thing.

Then the next step says, hey, not only do young people have assets that should be developed, but young people have voices, and we should listen to young people and they should have a voice in the programmes serving them. That to me is where participation comes in, youth voice, and participation.

The next level is youth civic engagement: not only should young people have a voice in decision-making but in fact they have valuable contributions to make, and can make recommendations about how to solve problems in communities.

Finally, at the other end of the continuum, you have: youth organizing. The idea is youth organizing builds on all those other approaches. So young people in youth organizing are being met with their basic needs, are helping to develop skills, are being given the opportunity to have a voice and solve problems, but they're all organizing and building a base of constituents to whom they are accountable who are ensuring that policy changes are actually implemented. We think that a healthy ecosystem for young people requires all of those elements, and young people need different things. All those elements need to exist, but we also do think what is powerful about organizing is that it includes all of those things, when it's done well.

The continuum was developed by FCYO and some partners. In the US, in the mid-1990s, there was a real explosion of youth organizing. We always start by saying that youth organizing is not new. It did not start in the 1990s, young people had always been in the forefront of social movements. There was, at least in the US, for better or for worse, a field of youth organizing, a field of practice. Then, an expansion of new organizations that started in the 1990s.

The 1980s saw the creation of youth development and the idea, 'hey, young people don't need services, we develop assets'; and instead of youth workers they said, 'that is not enough, young people are not only assets, but they could have power'. How do we build the power of young people, instead of youth workers, who could have gone beyond the youth development paradigm?

The 1990s also saw in the US some public policy attacks on young people of colour, the notion of the super predator. Young people responded and began organizing as young people against those public policy attacks. You saw a form of organizing, where young people have always organized for social justice. They were actually organizing as young people against attacks that were geared at young people in that time period.

Those are some of the main factors that led to the development of that youth organizing field. FCYO came from a set of partners who recognized that and wanted to support and said, how do we build philanthropic support for this work? How do we develop some theoretical frameworks to help funders and others understand the importance of this work?

Where youth organizing has been successful and why

On this, speaking at a national level: the school discipline work. Ten years ago, the trend in school discipline was about zero tolerance policies and that translated internationally. We tend to export some of our worse ideas. I think that youth organizing groups were pretty instrumental in shifting the common sense around school discipline. Over the last 10 years we had dozens and dozens of districts that have passed new policies around implementing restorative justice, away from zero tolerance, recognizing that we needed to address the school-to-prison pipeline. There have been significant policy changes and a change in the fundamental common sense around school discipline. That is at a large scale.

To talk about a favourite trajectory of an individual organization, I think of InnerCity Struggle in Los Angeles, which is a group that started in the mid-1990s. In many ways, their leaders came out of the fight against Proposition 21 in California, which was criminalizing young people of colour, and then developed this organization, InnerCity Struggle, that begun organizing around education. In 2005, working with a number of partners, not alone, they got the District to pass a policy that ensured college preparatory education for all students in Los Angeles. Now, in 2019, they can report dramatically increased graduation and college attendance rates for young people in the east of Los Angeles based on that policy. You can really follow the 25-year trajectory of this organization in transforming education in East LA.

That organization had leaders that were tied to the Chicano Movement in the Southwest. They had deep roots. InnerCity Struggle did not come from nowhere, they were really tied to the history of the Chicano Movement in southern California. Those ties allowed them to build a strong institution. I think that is one key.

Another key is they were really good at both organizing young people to create policy change and supporting the holistic development of young people at the same time. They have a really strong academic support and college support programme. Not only were they organizing the schools to make sure that the schools were preparing young people for college, but they were doing that work themselves. Part of that is what allowed them to bring all these people back; they have all these people who are now staff members, who were young people, went away to college, got some other experiences, and were able to come back as staff people. The work they did around college support and combining that with organizing was pretty unique and powerful.

What not to do

People try things and they don't work all the time. What not to do? We make so many mistakes all the time, all of us, and hopefully we learn from them and move on.

There are a lot of attempts at youth voice and youth engagement that are not authentic. A lot of them are too tied to the institution. A lot of things get done in the name of student governments that are not focused on young people really developing critical consciousness and understanding the root causes of the problems they are trying to address. It is like, let's create a voice for young people, give young people a voice; but it does not actually support and develop them to be able to play those roles and to really develop critical consciousness, and that is a very important component to what youth organizing groups do effectively. Also, the structures doing it are so tied to the power structures that exist that they are not really going to allow young people to develop and build power. I think this work is about power.

If I think about things not to do, there are two mistakes at the opposite ends of the spectrum. One is putting young people in leadership roles without actually developing them to be in those roles. Great, you are in charge of everything right now. We have not supported you in any way to play that role. It is sort of an extreme focus on youth leadership: young people are in charge of everything and adults have no role.

We really believe in the leadership of young people, but we believe in multigenerational alliances as well. We believe that youth–adult partnership is really important, and that there is a role for adults in helping to support and develop young people to be able to play leadership roles. So, there is a set of mistakes that are made about putting young people in charge of things without actually developing them to play those roles.

On the other hand, there is another set of mistakes like never allowing young people to build real meaningful power. The strategies for youth participation are so limited in scope and scale that it does not actually allow young people to really change and address power.

Key barriers

We certainly have seen an increase in the support for youth organizing. But when FCYO started 20 years ago, our idea was, could you get 1 per cent of all the money that goes to youth and development go to youth organizing? And we certainly have not achieved that. It is really hard to get data on what the real numbers are. We are not cracking the larger thing.

We had these communication researchers look at who is not funding on youth organizing that could? What messages could reach them? One of their findings was that funders have a flawed mental template of organizing. I really like that term, a flawed mental template. What they meant is that what they think of all the time is protest and uprising. And they don't understand the rigorous cycles of learning, preparation, action, reflection, which is another key component of what makes youth organizing effective. That cycle, of learning, action, reflection, a lot of people don't understand that and they think that it is just rebel uprising. Another reason is ageism, and not believing in young people and their potential. Another reason is people that have the most resources are invested in the status quo and young people tend to challenge the status quo. Those are probably the main reasons.

Advocacy and frameworks

We don't do advocacy or organizing ourselves as FCYO. We support groups that do that work. The most common issues that we see groups working on are education, health, immigrant rights, and criminal justice. The single most common one is education, within that there is a big focus on the school-to-prison pipeline. That is the most common thing that we see groups working on. Health, and health means a lot of things, that is a very broad category, but there is a lot of different ways, from reproductive justice to food issues, to social and emotional mental health. Those issues, then immigration rights in the US is a big issue. Organizing among youth immigrant people is a big deal here. And then all this stuff about mass incarceration. Those are the four largest issues that we see groups addressing.

For the most part, many of our groups are organizing around local issues. One of the things that we keep in our website is a searchable map of the database of youth organizing groups in the US. There are about 300 groups with active profiles here. You can search it by issue, geography, constituency, and all that. The vast majority of these groups are organizing around local issues.

They are state-wide groups and there are national groups that are organizing around federal policy, but mostly it is local. I don't think most people are intentionally grounding that in Sustainable Development Goals. I don't think most people are really aware of that. I think, my sense is within the US context, we don't have a lot of faith that our leaders are bought into the UN or that the UN is going to push local policy change.

There are groups that do have a human rights framework that I think has influenced their work. There are groups who really believe in international solidarity. It is not dominant. Within the immigrants' rights world, 'immigrant rights are human rights' is a common slogan. The immigrant rights world has embraced the human rights framework. Then, in the school discipline world, one of the big networks around the school discipline world is the Dignity in Schools Campaign, which is a network of 300 grassroots organizations across the country and they very much ground their work in a human rights approach.

There are definitely places that are grounded in the human rights approach, but I would not say that it is the dominant frame. There are probably places where that [UNCRC] is happening, more than others, but mostly no. We are uneducated in the international frameworks around this stuff for the most part.

International work

There are groups really interested in that; there was a lot of interest last year. We did a little bit of sharing about equal education in South Africa. Folks were really interested in learning more. At one point we were talking about organizing an exchange with them. That did not end up happening for various reasons but there was a lot of interest in that.

There is an intergenerational network called Grassroots Global Justice in the US. It is not just for youth, it is not even mainly youth, but it includes youth and they do a lot of international solidarity work. They were really active in the social forum process when that was a thing. Some of the folks on the movements in Black lives, a bunch of them came back from an exchange in Palestine. I am talking to some young people, there has been a bunch of work around solidarity between Black-led organizing groups in the US and in Palestine. Definitely some things like that exist, and I think there is interest in more but it is limited.

Key funding priorities and criteria

We are a funder, but a lot of what we do is advise funders (Equal Education in South Africa 2018). We do more of that than actual grant-making ourselves. What do we think are the key priorities for funders within the US? We have been encouraging funders who support youth work, but don't support organizing, to develop an understanding of how engaging young people in organizing can get the outcomes that they care about. For funders who don't support this work, we have been saying: you care about youth development, about policy change, about any number of these things. We have been trying to encourage them to lean in to understand how supporting youth organizing can get at the things that they care about effectively. Pushing funders who care about young people, but who do not yet support organizing, to support organizing is always kind of our biggest priority.

Within the funders that are already supporting our work: what does it mean to support it strategically and to really support the best of this work?

In most cases, what we want to do is follow the leadership of young people. It does happen to us sometimes that somebody is working in some issues and they are like: can you get young people involved? I was talking to some funder about ocean conservation; they were, we love this idea of young people organizing. How do we get young people organizing around ocean conservation? I was like: you know, this is not really how it works. I think it works best when we follow the leadership of young people, what they themselves have identified.

When we think about how this work would look at its best we are looking at groups where young people were able to organize significant numbers of young people and build a base, and build power that way, and therefore, achieve.

So, criteria would be looking at how many young people they were able to organize and mobilize and build the leadership of. We look at what are the actual policy changes they are able to achieve. We are looking at the impact that they are having among young people themselves. All those levels of outcome I talked about [earlier]. All of those different things help us to indicate where this is being done really well.

We have some criteria that we use for our grant-making programmes and we encourage our member foundations to utilize and tweak those for their own purposes. Criteria we look for include: authentic leadership with young people within the organization itself; formal structures for developing the leadership of young people; formal structures for membership; and kind of an internal ladder of engagement; the ability to articulate a track record for leading campaigns and articulating clear campaign demands. Those kinds of things.

We are supposed to have an understanding of how do we support the development of anchor institutions that really know how to do these things well. InnerCity Struggle is a finely tuned machine. We need those anchor institutions that have the practices down and we need to support emerging groups that are learning how to do this.

But we don't want to throw money around at anybody and say, 'It is emerging. It is ok. They don't know how to do it.' I think one of the most challenging things to do as a funder is to identify where there are nascent and emergent efforts that really have potential. And how do you recognize when one is really going to have that potential? I think that this is a really important thing as funders: how do we both support the anchor institutions and support the emerging groups?

References

Equal Education in South Africa: website: https://equaleducation.org.za/
Funders' Collaborative on Youth Organizing (FCYO) website: https://fcyo.org/
Funders' Collaborative on Youth Organizing (2018) 'New research on the impacts of youth organizing' [Webinar], 2 March 2018. Panel: Veronica Terriquez, Associate Professor of Sociology, UC Santa Cruz; Roderick Watts, Professor of Psychology, CUNY; Ben Kirshner, Professor of Learning Sciences and Human Development and Faculty Director, University of Colorado Boulder; Rossmery Zayas, Youth Organizer, Communities for a Better Environment. https://fcyo.org/resources/new-research-on-the-impacts-of-youth-organizing [accessed 13 June 2023].
Kirshner, B. (2015) *Youth Activism in an Era of Education Inequality*. New York: New York University Press.
Shah, S., Buford, W. and Braxton, E. (2018) *Transforming Young People and Communities: New findings on the impacts of youth organizing*. Funders' Collaborative on Youth Organizing. https://fcyo.org/uploads/resources/webinar-new-research-on-the-impacts-of-youth-organizing_resource_5aa1 95dc4ab462417b3d7ea7.pdf [accessed 13 June 2023].

CHAPTER 19

Youth as a political force for peace

Lakshitha Saji Prelis

Background

The fields of children and armed conflict and women, peace, and security are well established, yet the concept of youth has been falling through the cracks; no longer children, not yet adults, there was little attention to youth (defined as ages 19–29) within peace and security discourse. To make sure there is a global focus on youth as it relates to peace and security, a collaborative effort was started, led by civil society and youth in partnership with UN agencies and intergovernmental bodies. I helped convene civil society, youth groups, and the UN to collectively shape what we call the youth, peace, and security agenda. The collective work has led to a set of political norms, institutional commitments to act on these norms, and now, increasingly national governments are exploring how their commitment to youth can be strengthened while youth leadership is better financed. I am co-leading this work as the co-chair of the Global Coalition on Youth, Peace and Security and represent Search for Common Ground (Search), the world's largest and oldest peacebuilding organization, where I focus on providing technical support to our country teams.

Global coalition

I grew up in war, seeing the ugly and good side of human nature, realizing that violence is committed by a few individuals and the vast majority either stay silent or act in constructive ways. One person can make a difference but we need the silent majority to wake up and to get active. I saw that from a young age and was part of groups able to do things constructively.

After the 2004 tsunami, I ended up by default creating and co-chairing the largest coalition of humanitarian, peace, development, business, and security organizations and President Clinton and his staff (as he was appointed the UN Secretary-General's Envoy for the Tsunami Response) to collaborate in responding to the 2004 Asian Tsunami that took the lives of over 300,000 people from Sri Lanka to Indonesia. To me, collaborating across various groups toward a collective level impact is something I truly believe in.

In 2009 we started to look at ways to shape the discourse on youth through a set of global policy frameworks. Frameworks that would shift a policy panic-based response that saw young people as troublemakers toward seeing young people as partners in peace. At the beginning, institutional leaders dismissed our efforts saying youth issues are not the domain of the UN Security Council. The dismissal was a wake-up call for us. The task was daunting and we realized that our work requires people coming together who speak different languages; the UN, civil society, youth groups speak very different languages. How do we enable these communities to understand each other?

By setting up a global coalition, we were able to bring people across agencies to collectively accomplish this. The first document was the guiding principles that unified what we knew and need to know around how adults and ageing Western European institutions can adapt to engage young people in conflict-affected countries that at the time were not Western. The guiding principles created that common language to advocate for what we all wanted. That requires a collective effort; participation and trust-building were at the heart of these efforts. Because of this work, we collectively recognized that the youth, peace, and security agenda is a human agenda. Currently the Coalition is co-chaired by the United Network of Young Peacebuilders, the United Nations Population Fund, and Search for Common Ground, and includes over 110 organizations including UN agencies, intergovernmental bodies, INGOs, youth-led organizations, and scholars.

UN Security Council Resolution 2250 (2015) on Youth, Peace and Security

The coalition led the advocacy efforts that resulted in the historic UN Security Council Resolution 2250 on Youth, Peace and Security.[1] This is the first resolution that recognized young people as partners in peace and by doing so introduced the normative framework for supporting young people as partners. The relationships built over three years helped members of the coalition to successfully convince the member states of the Security Council to unanimously adopt this resolution. (See Berents and Prelis (2020) documenting the journey of this resolution.)

At the time people realized young men with guns were a threat and young women were victims, and we wanted to transform that mentality.

Our guiding question was not, why are young people susceptible to armed violence or drawn to violent extremist groups, but why are more young people peaceful? We hardly ever ask that question. Evidence shows that even though young people are surrounded by exclusion and violence, most young people are not violent. Why are we neglecting the vast majority who are not violent? Resolution 2250 and two subsequent resolutions make a powerful case for how and why young people are a powerful force for peace.

Listening and learning youth research

A lot of work pushing for guiding principles came from the field. For many organizations children under 18 were seen as beneficiaries of aid, a group that needed protection and were too young to advocate themselves. The reality, especially in conflict-affected situations, is that a child who is nine can be a mother and also a breadwinner. A young girl or a boy is playing multiple roles. That required us to see their agency differently, as not just rights holders but also as resilient actors for peace.

Violence is a societal issue. So, at Search we grappled with the question of how to get society to understand how to deal with grievances and differences constructively. Radio is a powerful way to do that in sub-Saharan Africa, where the median age on the continent is 19. Having young people design and broadcast their interactive radio dramas and talk shows enables their peers to know they are not alone, while also building the confidence of adults to learn about issues young people are experiencing. The shows have a broad societal reach and act as a powerful tool for listeners to learn how to understand their grievances and act on the commonalities people have; or, said differently, to separate the problem from the people, so that people can attack the common problem as opposed to each other.

The question was: How do we engage young people? Engaging them requires us to reimagine our relationship with young people, away from seeing them as those needing our assistance, or as troublemakers to genuinely seeing them as co-leaders and partners. For Search, it was very difficult in some countries to get staff to see them that way, but in other countries it was quicker and we were able to pilot different approaches. For example in Liberia, Guinea, and Sierra Leone in West Africa, before and during the Ebola crisis, we were managing an EU-funded project focused on the worst forms of violence against children. And instead of accepting conventional wisdom on the topic, we designed an approach led by children and youth, so that they can define what the worst forms of violence are to them and the ways they could address it.

We developed an approach called 'listening and learning' as opposed to traditional focus group discussion or survey methodology. We got children and youth to do something they do every day, which is to use an everyday conversational approach among their peers as a form of rigorous inquiry. One of the key findings was that hunger, according to the young people, was one of the worst forms of violence they experience and can lead to other forms of violence such as child labour and early child marriage.

This project and other similar efforts helped us discover a mistake we were making. The mistake was, we were not taking into account issues of vicarious trauma. It was a real shock to us, because we were thinking if young people are seen and engaged as partners with agency, they are able; we didn't think about trauma in this situation. The evaluation discovered some researchers were re-living events, vicarious trauma among three individuals who were part of a

23-person team. That was an embarrassment and stark shock to us. As a result, we refined our methodology, learning from our mistake, and included a trauma-informed approach of children and youth-led inquiry. This included practical ways to account for it in our programming budgets too. Next time in Tanzania, in mining communities where we were engaging young people in research, we were able to implement our improved approach and ensure we had a budget to support them and took steps to minimize vicarious trauma. The biggest mistake was not taking into consideration mental health issues of young people going through this work.

Children in mining

In mining and extractive industries we learned how some children were doing this to make a living for their family, and there were no alternatives. The issue continued to come up, not only in Tanzania. A common thing we heard was, 'Look, the benefit of education I won't see for five to seven years at least, if not ten. And that is still not guaranteed. What am I going to do to survive today? I may not be alive in two years. Education is not going to be guaranteeing my safety or my stomach. I need to do things today, to face the consequences of today.'

Some of our efforts enabled us to convince some children to go back to school. These were kids who dropped out of school; they went during the morning and left school halfway through to go to the mines. Was it perfect? Absolutely not, but showed evidence that when people are made aware of how to manage immediate versus long-term needs, there is a spark that helps them see there is a possibility to manage immediate basic needs alongside thinking of their future and the role education can play in both.

Need for protection

Young people's peacebuilding work is deeply political. From Kyrgyzstan, Pakistan, and Kashmir to Central African Republic, Nigeria, and Colombia, young people are leading non-violent efforts and are mobilizing their peers calling for a more just, more equal society. Often these efforts are being misunderstood as going against the government's work. This is increasingly leading to governments feeling threatened and many youth groups experience threats, harassment, intimidation, and even imprisonment. How do we protect young peacebuilders and human rights defenders whose work is perceived (often incorrectly) as a threat to governments? Under the leadership of the Global Coalition, we have made progress in calling attention to the importance of protection of young peacebuilders and young human rights defenders. UN Security Council Resolution 2250 has a whole pillar focused on protection. The recently adopted UN Security Council Resolution 2535 for the first time recognized the shrinking civic space young people occupy and called on governments to protect and safeguard civic spaces for youth.

Conditions for successful participation

A starting point was to see adolescents and youth as mentors and role models for children. We learned they are more likely to trust a peer than adults because they fear or have lost respect for adults. Due to cultural norms, they may listen, but they don't trust them.

Conflict situations are one of the only times adults' power can change. In normal circumstances the adult will say something and the child or youth will have to listen, but in violent circumstances a young person with a gun can get an adult on their knees to do what they want.

We try to engage our cohorts to see young people as potential partners, and what they are advocating is not that different from what adults also want. Trust is first built across youth groups and then using media to socialize young people's ideas and actions that are contributing positively to society, so that adults can learn without feeling they are being lectured at. Their solutions are similar to what adults want. But the resonance of our programmes has to have a different tone speaking to adults as opposed to speaking to children and youth.

Programming requires trust and time. It is equally important to understand how; enabling young people to be part of a process, without feeling a sense of exclusion from it. Our research highlighted that young people are excluded from situations and decision-making. This sense of exclusion is structural and psychological and hence the first global study on youth, peace, and security (YPS) couched it as violence of exclusion. If we are trying to transform violence, we need to address the violence of exclusion from policy and programming perspectives.

That requires us to see young people as partners not only that need to be consulted, but consulted in a way that they feel engaged and trusted. We civil society actors are not so good at this, violent groups and gangs are much better at seeing young people as partners. We can learn from that. This is important; we learn from troublemakers also. That is humbling; our exceptionalism, sense of arrogance, our ego that we are doing good needs to be broken up so we see that we can learn from people who are much better at this.

Supporting locally led, locally resourced efforts is really important. This is not new. But often international actors like us get in the way because of financial mechanisms.

We have been piloting, for example in Sri Lanka and Nigeria, how local civil society can work in partnership with young people to address violence-related issues. We wanted to be completely led locally; our role as enabler of initial facilitators. We learned valuable lessons on how international actors can do that. It has taken so long to break away from this idea that people come with projects and tell local communities how to do things. Transforming that mindset takes a while, working with the state, private sector, and communities together. It needs this trifecta of groupings to work together to address what people feel as a sense of exclusion from society, the violence of exclusion.

It requires a new operational mindset we are calling a collective impact approach; we bring different actors to collaborate, to address interconnected issues.

The steps: engaging children and youth to ensure more trust; making sure their partnerships are there; addressing the violence of exclusion; developing a collective impact mindset; and steps for acting on this collective approach. This requires bringing people together across dividing lines. Traditional funding can often disrupt these well-intentioned efforts; therefore, donor education and ensuring risk-taking to try new approaches is critical so that donors can also better support local ownership of peace and security processes. Ensuring funding provides support for young people to safely participate is also essential.

The last thing would be to not neglect mental health issues; this is a peril to programme quality. Mental health issues need to be thought through. Sometimes they are seen as a developing country problem, not necessarily a developed country problem. But even in the US or Europe, mental health issues are a leading cause of child and youth adolescent suicide rates. The pandemic has exacerbated it and showed the world that mental health and well-being is universal for young people and adults alike.

Child/youth-led and child/youth-focused approaches

Child- and youth-focused work and children-led work are not mutually exclusive, but mutually inclusive. You cannot have one without the other; both are necessary, especially in situations of conflict. For the issue of protection, for example, child- and youth-focused work gives the impression there is international attention to young people; which enables them to be protected in some way as well. When I say international, us Western internationals need to leave a lighter footprint behind: How can we be responsible actors who are accountable to young populations, but also enable them to lead the efforts?

Mental health and education as rights issues

This is where children and youth become mentors and mentees to one another. They can lead in partnership with adult counterparts, and address dividing lines that are keeping people apart. In Niger or Mali, the median population age is around 15 years; in Nigeria, 18; in Congo, 19. In the continent, especially sub-Saharan Africa, you are looking at a very young population. If 60–80 per cent of the population are below the age of 30, it requires us to think about engaging children and youth very differently, enabling them to engage each other in a youth-friendly way, supporting them in their efforts. Supporting their leadership helps strengthen state–society relationships, which can lead to healthier societies.

We create processes to measure how effective young people are. I think that does harm because the way young people articulate impact is very different from our institutionalized way of measuring impact. We need to adjust as international organizations, as outsiders, how we measure impact; not bureaucratized, also not NGOized, because a lot of movements are not NGOs and far more effective in creating change. As outsiders supporting child and youth efforts, we want to enable them to be successful without becoming NGOs like us. Measuring impact is another way of making sure we are supportive; we need to do better in understanding impact from children and youth perspectives.

We as international actors need to recognize young people are organized and affecting change locally in different ways, sometimes using different governance, organizing principles, and networks we are not aware of or understand. We don't understand it, because they speak a different language, are organized differently, and their leadership model tends to be more horizontal when compared to ours, which is vertical and hierarchical in nature. We need to embrace that, understand how they are organizing, the language they are using, how they are connecting and empowering one another. This is why the concept of listening and learning was at the core of how we at Search started this work; to listen, and understand, as adults, to collectively address their needs. This listening and learning approach has become a standard practice at Search.

Acting and rooting work locally

We often see conflict as an opportunity, to do better, correct wrongs, and build back better relationships that could endure. In doing that, we see violence and peace issues are supremely local. What we ignored in peacebuilding for many years, and now the violence and extremism field realizes, is the key driving factors are local as well. From one neighbourhood to another, it might be different. While the roots of violence are local, other roots are regional and international in nature. So responding to prevent violence requires us to understand the contours or the geographies of a conflict as opposed to narrowly looking at conflict from simply a nation-state perspective. Conflicts often are not bound by a national boundary, just like a pandemic.

A young person growing up in a village or city might be connected through smartphones and internet to a whole other world that sees issues differently and they see a world where adults are holding them back. When we respond, while it is important to make sure issues are locally grounded, locally owned, there is a need to ensure outside actors do better in making sure problems are addressed locally. We cannot neglect the intergenerational distrust that should be addressed within our various interventions. As international actors, our role is critical to ensure our efforts are locally owned and grounded and yet support intergenerational trust and collective action.

In Search 93 per cent of staff are local; in many countries where we work, all staff are local and also represent the diversity of the country including religion, ethnicity, tribe, sex, and age. This has often given us a unique advantage to understand complex contours of a conflict and the various grievances that are common across society. Even though Search is an international brand, our staffing and local governance makes us locally rooted. In West Africa, for example, we are better known as Talking Drum Studio than Search for Common Ground because our local brand is locally rooted in the powerful traditional role drums play within the culture and its significance to peace.

Barriers to participation

Power is often a barrier. Who actually has power? Often people do not see themselves as part of the solution because they see government as the solution-maker. When governments fail to live up to expectations then people get agitated, try to take the streets or do something about it. Then they try to change power dynamics.

A second barrier is the apathy of elected government officials to live up to expectations. Another barrier is that people do not realize the power within themselves to make change happen. Sometimes, the silent majority stays silent until it is too late. The fourth barrier is policies, systems, and institutions that are too outdated to deal with problems of today and those to come. They need to be reformed and transformed.

The fifth barrier is instruments we use to advocate for change: funding, policy, and institutional instruments. There is no sense of urgency. The most powerful example I can cite is Greta Thunberg, the 16-year-old who revolutionized climate change conversations and introduced a sense of urgency, saying, 'we need to act as if our house is on fire'. This came from a young person, not scientists with 50 years of experience and 300 publications.

A sense of urgency is needed and we don't see this. We don't see violence, climate as urgent matters. Climate and violence are two of the greatest risks to humanity's existence and are interrelated. We focus on Band-Aid solutions, projects that are short-sighted, not transformative.

The sixth barrier: we don't see efforts for collective action and impact, because we see our superiority and exceptionalism as the way to make change and it's absolutely foolish to think that.

For young people, we mapped out globally a set of barriers they experience globally, based on their own prioritization. The key barriers they have identified (see Izsák-Ndiaye, 2021) in order of importance for them are socio-cultural; political; financial; legal; digital; physical; and impact of the pandemic. The most common barrier is socio-cultural, which means the barriers exist in their families and their communities. So, we have to ask ourselves how our programme interventions are trying to address these barriers. These barriers are a form of violence, and together form the basic structure for the violence of exclusion young people face daily.

Specific policy processes

Building on the global YPS agenda, one of the key priorities is to strengthen institutional commitments to act on the political norms set by the UN Security Council Resolutions on Youth, Peace, and Security. Working with institutions to strengthen their commitment to the agenda is critical. The African Union (AU) has really stepped up and has made a robust effort in institutionalizing the YPS agenda in the continent of Africa. The AU is also working to get the other regional economic communities and regional mechanisms to adopt youth-inclusive strategies. Similarly, we are working with other institutions to adopt policies and strategies that commit them to the agenda that sees youth as partners.

The rubber meets the road at the country level. This means national governments need to rethink their relationship with their youthful populations. We are encouraging governments to design and implement youth-inclusive national action plans, policies, programmes, and services with young people as partners, not just beneficiaries. The YPS agenda is a universal agenda, not an agenda only relevant to young people predominantly in the Global South or countries with significant populations that are black or brown. Youth-inclusive policies have the ability to create enduring change. Policies or legislation can do that. The US is the first country to introduce legislation to develop a whole of government and whole of civil society approach to supporting and strengthening youth leadership in peace and security efforts. Other countries that are considering a legislative agenda are Cameroon and Kenya, which see young people as partners in peace and security issues at the policy and operational level.

All our efforts will not be successful if we do not strengthen our collective commitment to improving how youth leadership is financed. To support this, the Global Coalition is leading multiple efforts that are improving traditional systems of support while also looking at disruptive models that support youth leadership at scale.

Global frameworks used regularly

The UN Security Council Resolution 2250, the guiding principles, the Sustainable Development Goals (SDGs). I was in the policy planning committee that helped influence what the SDGs could be. The SDGs have become an instrument to talk and feel good about, but not actually act on. It is sad, because globally governments agreed to the ambitious goals on behalf of their people. But we are seeing how far behind we are in meeting our progress towards the SDGs. My fear is that with such an ambitious global agenda with all countries committing to meet, and yet we struggle to maintain our commitments to, how can any new global agenda secure better commitments?

With the YPS agenda we are focused on strengthening state–society relationships and ensuring that people, in this case the vast majority being young, have better alternatives than violence, and they inherit a world more just and peaceful where they are co-partners and co-leaders in creating that world. This is why focusing our efforts at the country level is critical. While global agendas are important, if there is no ground support, global agendas remain good on paper but not in the lived realities of everyday people. This is why we are focused on national-level commitments, trust, and collaborative action between state and youth to prevent violence and sustain peace.

Key funding priorities

First, the YPS agenda is still in its infancy compared to, for example, the children and armed conflict agenda or the women, peace, and security agenda. Our research has shown that 64 per cent of youth-led organizations/groups/NGOs operate with a US$10,000 budget. We need to think differently about young people's leadership and find ways to finance their leadership across multiple sectors. We know that young people don't typically identify as peacebuilders or human rights defenders. They would say they focus on climate change, on peace, on human rights, and a host of other things because they all collectively lead to a more peaceful and just future for them. So, we have to ask ourselves how we support that multisectoral approach to youth leadership. What role do donors play? What role does political leadership play? Resources are not just about money; political capital is critical for ensuring youth leadership has the necessary civic and digital space to flourish, not shrink.

Second, we need to think of supporting youth, beyond a short-term project that feels good. For example, some gangs and violent groups engage young people as partners and make them believe they are part of something greater than themselves. Our value proposition as civil society is a project-based approach and often this is short-lived. Our value proposition to youth has to be more powerful than what gangs and violent groups provide. What do they do? They provide mentorship, guidance, tactical training, and skill building. We need a holistic approach to strengthening young people's capacity and agency to be effective and not make them become NGOs to do so. A holistic approach that is cost-effective and innovative needs to be supported.

At Search, in partnership with the United Network of Young Peacebuilders, we have tested a model called Youth 360 that adopts a holistic approach to youth leadership. Youth 360 is based on four principles, transforming traditional relationships between youth and the international peacebuilding community:

- First, placing power in the hands of youth, including power to define key problems, determine metrics of success, and direct resource allocation.
- Second, working with the excluded majority of youth often overlooked by the international community, including young people organized through small and informal youth groups.

- Third, rethinking what sustainability means, emphasizing sustainable impact rather than focusing on sustaining NGOs.
- Fourth, enhancing young people's collective impact on conflict systems, by supporting young people's collaborative leadership across divides.

It's critical for donors to support more holistic approaches such as the Youth 360 approach as a way to decolonize their funding instruments. One way to prioritize support and limited resources is to invest in collective impact initiatives not just individual impact. Donors need to help facilitate that together with implementers.

What would help support practitioners and researchers in the field?

First, actively support youth-led research: support young people in the Global South to create content and get their work published. As a community, we have to do better at ensuring there is Southern knowledge that is more publicly available. This requires enabling Southern scholars, practitioners, and young people to make their work more public. For example, there could be regional research collaboratives for young people to create thought pieces on a regular basis, case studies, white papers, policy papers or regular blogs, about how young people are influencing and impacting their societies and communities. This is essential and can cover different topics or themes. The point is to enable young people to create knowledge and content that people can actually use in a way our academic research is not. Our position will be to help cross-analyse multi-country, multi-thematic issues; there is space to play collaborative roles, as opposed to taking over the role in knowledge creation versus knowledge curation.

Second, recognize that young people in universities from the West and developing countries can become allies. The idea of insider and outsider needs to be nuanced and understood. Creating clusters of young professionals, students, exploring the research, policy, and practice triangle and creating content around it can make a big impact for the field. Doing so well will require a strong understanding and acceptance of diversity, strengthening inclusivity, equality, and equitable access to opportunities and resources, managing power and a nuanced understanding of decolonizing learning and practice.

Criteria for supporting groups

These are things I would look for in a group to support, not necessarily an NGO; we need new ways to support groups and movements that are not NGOs. The NGO model is ageing quickly, especially because of legal, financial, administrative, and human resource requirements, that continue to exclude not include real youth leadership. A mapping is critical to understand who is doing what.

For example, I would look for those making a difference in the fringes, promising practices, organizations, and individuals, because in the middle there is a crowded field that is part of the system; a lot of donors working in the middle space. Often those on the fringes are the most innovative and trying to shake the system.

Second, groups and individuals within them trying to transform, not get into the system, are people to invest in, because they are not trying to accommodate, to fit into a failing and broken system. I would look to understand how they are doing things and why and what are their practices.

Third, there are organizations still collaborating within the system, and transforming it from within, not trying to completely rip it apart, but are thoughtful, trying to do it in a systematic and collaborative way.

Also look at those trying to change the system at a policy and at a practice level. Both are required to create that seismic shift. Climate groups are a good example. They have worked to educate governments about their responsibility to commit to 1.5 degrees of warming, yet they are finding that path difficult. Some are now evolving their tactics as they are critically looking at systems change on behalf of humanity, not their own bottom line profits.

I would look at investing in those types of groups on a five to eight year commitment, not just a one-year project cycle. Have some broad benchmarks, but not indicators saying you did not do that so you need to give us money back; if you don't deviate from that, change is impossible.

Sharing best practice

Search set up a system called Design, Monitoring and Evaluation for peace. We were struggling to get other organizations to collaborate. How do we publicize our evaluations? That was an eye-opener: a lot of organizations did not want to put their evaluations out there. But eventually people adapt to change. Now, we have a large coalition of organizations sharing information, learning and trying to improve practice. There are webinars, there is a blog post around it.

Lessons are not going to change practice unless communicated in a way that empowers people's change. That requires branding and communication to go hand in hand.

If we are able to say, for example, if women are not involved, in five years or less the peace process will fall apart. In education, $10 has a $90 return on our investment. We need to be able to articulate the return on investment and impact on the children and youth field much better when it comes to violence, conflict, and peace. Then communicate in a way average citizens, policy-makers, and young people understand so they can use the messages as tools for advocacy in their work.

We don't have good examples yet. We need to be better at measuring, not measuring how many people took training, but how people feel about it afterwards. That is not good enough when it comes to changing practice.

Measuring outputs like numbers is not going to make a difference; it is useful, but needs to be correlated and triangulated with more sophisticated outputs. That is where we need as a field to be more accountable, because if we are spending millions of dollars, then you need to have responses that are also at that level.

Note

1. The UN Security Council adopted Resolution 2250 Youth, Peace and Security (UNSCR 2250 (2015)) on 9 December 2015. *'Young people play an important and positive role in the maintenance and promotion of international peace and security.'* There are five key pillars for action: participation, protection, prevention, partnerships, and disengagement and reintegration. https://youth4peace.info/UNSCR2250/Introduction

References

Berents, H. and Prelis, S., with Tibe, I. (2020) *More than a Milestone: The road to UN Security Council Resolution 2250.* Search for Common Ground. https://youth4peace.info/topic/more-milestone-road-unscr-2250-yps
Izsák-Ndiaye, R. (2021) *If I Disappear: Global report on protecting young people in civic space.* United Nations Office of the Secretary-General's Envoy on Youth. https://www.un.org/youthenvoy/wp-content/uploads/2021/06/Global-Report-on-Protecting.-Young-People-in-Civic-Space.pdf

CHAPTER 20
Go work your magic

Chernor Bah

Background

I joke I was the poster child for children's participation because I started in Sierra Leone after the war. I was about 13 or 14 years old and I liked asking questions, being in and out of the war and seeing what had happened to us children. My experience of war was the beginning, when we came back having been refugees.

We went to one of those school-organized conferences, a debate competition, between a number of schools. I was one of those kids always going to those things and I said to my friends: we should (at the time my idea) organize a children's parliament. I'd read one of those UNICEF leaflets in one of the debates, which mentioned a children's parliament. I was fascinated and I wanted to set one up in Sierra Leone. I started talking to a few of my friends. I said: we should do it. Let's organize ourselves to meet. Let's basically demand children's rights. Let's have like in parliament, we could be here all day, talking, being part of the conversation.

The other desire I had was to be part of, have a voice in, the peace process after the war. I had a lot of friends and family lost in the war. I knew what we had gone through and I felt we needed to be part of those process talks going on and obviously children were not part of it at all. We had an epidemic of child soldiers in Sierra Leone; they just set up a Ministry of Children's Affairs receiving less than 1 per cent of government budget allocation. This Ministry was not doing much, but the lady who was head of the Ministry at the time was very approachable. We thought let's reach out to this Ministry. We were this bunch of 14-year-olds saying we have this idea to set up a children's parliament. I remember them saying, 'Parliament is not for children. No, we cannot have a children's parliament,' and that basically we could set up children's forums for schools, and organize ourselves. We did that.

In a few months we'd set up about 40 children's clubs in schools. I went into schools with a bunch of friends. We had a letter asking school principals to allow us to speak in the assembly. We spoke about children's rights and our right to be heard, and if anyone was interested meet us at lunch time, and we will take names and set up a club in the school. We didn't have any tools to help the clubs on what to do. It was about the setup; there is a club.

Then, Plan International heard about what we were doing. They called me and said, you can organize the first meeting of all these clubs, send representatives, and the Ministry agreed to host workshops, train us in basic children's rights. We organized that. We decided we should have an election at that meeting so that we could have national representation. That's how they elected me as the president.

So, I became president for the children's forum of Sierra Leone. We continued to go into schools, to speak up. There were so many issues about children's rights. Luckily there was a mission at the time, they had a child protection unit that heard about what we were doing, and offered to help us go across the country. We started having partnerships with people involved in the peace infrastructure, the truth commission, special courts, the disarmament process. We would be invited to talk to children that were disarmed or being demobilized. We spent time with them.

So, my own beginning came from one leaflet, a debate in schools, talking with my friends and acting on it. Doing that over the years, I continue to see the value of substantive children's participation. I have a lot of regrets, about how some of that was managed, how we were used or not used, some were inevitable, but some we could have done differently.

A focus on girls

Our work now focuses exclusively on girls. My experience over the years exposed me more to the exclusion and marginalization of children from power. I realized that girls were having it much worse overall. Just recognizing their agency and their humanity is reason why we set up Purposeful. There is a really strong institutional and structural focus on girl's rights, power, voice, and agency. The decisions we make, making sure they involve girls.

I'm not necessarily a big fan of posturing representation. I understand that representation is not just about what we extract; at Purposeful we really try to focus what we give, understanding and recognizing the agency, power, and expertise of girls who come here. My opinion is that something is missing in child participation and structure; it is the way of saying that it is just decorative; there is a lot of that.

I worked with Plan, part of the team that set up child advisory panels they have now in most countries. I have set up UN advisory panels and advised organizations who want to set up children's panels or groups. I come to them with a lot of scepticism because I think that a lot are so very extractive, not tailored for what young people themselves want and need. The other thing is that they are very elite. It's kind of selective, it is for outstanding young people.

It is not just about that. We try to think about agency, and about social capital, because we believe that helps bring systemic change. I think participation can be a tool that is institutionalized and lead to systemic change.

What happens now is that participation is about reward of the individual, and gives individual opportunities but without thinking about, how does she understand that? Not just because she is outstanding, but we are taking her connectedness with other people of her communities. And how do we make sure that the rewards, the relationship we are having, translates not just to that one girl? It's about how she can use that power, experiences, benefits, and rewards for the people in her community because that is how change happens. It is not about taking that girl in the village who can speak and dance or sing and do well out of the village. It is about making sure that there are many more girls in that village that can transition from primary school to secondary school and stay there. That is how we are trying to focus our programmes.

Successful participation

Over 17 years ago we started the Children's Forum. It still continues. In fact, a number of people who came into this new government were members of the Children's Forum at schools at national level. We have been able to build an enduring platform for young people to have agency, to have voice in certain ways. There are many things I would transform about it, but it's an example.

Successful participation is about process. Who is participating? Who is in the room? Who do you represent? People should not only represent themselves. When I say who do you represent, it is making sure they have that connection to the people they represent.

The other thing, especially for children, there has to be tangible products throughout the participation. In Sierra Leone, we were very focused on the peace process and the aftermath. We wanted to be in negotiations, to make sure children's issues were there. We wanted to make sure we testify in the truth commission, so we could mobilize children and share their stories. That was very important, collecting those stories, children going to the commission. It gave us momentum, we could be part of something. Out of that, one recommendation we have was to make sure every truth commission included child-friendly environments. It was followed up by UNICEF. That was really important.

In my experience, outside Sierra Leone, and the ways in which I have seen children's participation work, I really like the idea of solidarity and the movement, not just coming to sit on a panel for an organization. I have worked with Malala [Yousafzai] in the education space. This was powered by children across the world and youth who heard and wanted to be part of the movement; who wanted to share their voices and take them to the highest level. Malala came and spoke, and it is really demonstrating to the world the power of children's voices. It is important to mention that Malala was not only given that voice because she was shot, she had been advocating for her voice before she got shot. In fact, she was attacked because of that voice. I think that gets missed sometimes when you talk about that, she got shot because of that.

The organization and the structure after she got shot, we worked on that. We encouraged people around the world. The sense of a movement had very tangible goals, advancing education. Now it has been recognized by the Nobel committee, and that gives it power. This is an example of how children's participation works at a global level.

At the local level, I have seen in rural areas like in Liberia, girls come together and say they want to be part of decision-making in their community. Having support, I have seen girls set up a collective, work together, sell goods and the money they make they use to support individual activities and organize events in their communities. That support gives them the possibility and now they have a voice they can use to ask specific things of the community and to ask for action.

There is a lot of thinking that somehow all participation is organic, but there should be infrastructure and resources to have organic organizations funded, supported, in ways that are relevant. In Purposeful we provide support to girl-led groups that are not registered. We are going to pilot a cash grant incentive. Support is a critical component of how you get genuine participation.

Children's participation not working

Not every children's advisory group has worked in my experience. Some try to remove the power and magic of children's voice and children's participation and combine them into the status quo of adult platforms. When that happens, it is about making the organization better, not about making children's lives better, because then they can say they have done children's participation. This doesn't support the individual transformation of children and children like them within the societies they come from. I have been part of setting this up. I think that they are examples of children's participation. Actually, they are quite tokenistic. These are super complex things that these organizations themselves cannot solve or cannot do. So, we are going to bring a bunch of kids to solve these problems for us, in our own language. Not their language. So, it becomes incredibly cosmetic, even in cases when you get substance.

Child/youth-focused and child/youth-led work

Girl-led, for us in Purposeful, is projects that are initiated and led fully just by girls. Child and youth-focused work is what we do now, which is we focus entirely on girls; the implementation certainly is not led by girls.

This is why we talk about allies. You cannot have a radical transformation of the systemic barriers that hold children and young people behind, and limit their access to power by essentially saying that people without the power now are going to be able to talk about their problems. At the same time, you cannot do it by just saying that the people with power, the allies are going to do it.

If you think about it as a movement of people that are victims, or people without power, in this case, children and youth, their voices should lead this movement, but you certainly need allies as well, and this is where youth focus comes in. But it needs to be better integrated, coordinated, to understand that the focus work should be guided by the children's led work. It should support it, it be integrated with it, be existing for that work. Especially in the youth sector of course, it is very different in the child sector. The idea of centring the voice and agency of children and youth is often an afterthought and that is why sometimes you have children's advisory panels, because it is the perfect cosmetic solution. There is not sufficient critical thinking on structurally and systemically integrating and being led by the voices of children.

Barriers

Power does not give away power voluntarily. There is a power discourse there. Adults grew up not having power when they were children. They were taught it is their time now to have these decisions. It is very difficult to unlearn; people don't know how to.

People say that groups are difficult because they are difficult to reach. Everybody says it is impossible to get females in the workplace: 'we had an open call application and we only got two women'. But we run an organization, Purposeful, and 97 per cent of our staff are female. That is the same thing when it comes to children's **participation**.

People go quickly for the low-hanging fruits, the things you can do to seem like you are doing participation but not being transformational enough. In general, we are not people who are used to upsetting the status quo. Think about these big organizations; to really look for children's participation and voices, they have to knock down structures they have, and people are afraid to do that. People think that's the way things have been done and that's the way it should be. They don't question the structures.

There are different levels to why it is so difficult for institutions. The biggest one, that is relatively easy to solve, is that people don't know what to do, how to do it, and they don't feel they have the power and the freedom to make the radical transformation that will build meaningful participation. Everybody is, 'If I do this, it's fine, I would have shown that I care about children, children's voices, the voices of the marginalized groups'. It requires an investment; there has not been a commitment for an investment, including from donors that claim they want children's participation. We see the same thing with girls, the same thing with girls' disabilities. Donors want to count how much per girl when you do a project, and the project becomes expensive. But the reason why these groups have never met is exactly because they are going to be expensive. If you are aiming for people with disabilities, they are going to be expensive. You need a commitment that understands that; you need that investment when you need it.

A man directing the organization

I am one of the two co-founders of the organization. I am very aware of the privileges that I have, especially being a male. I have talked about being a feminist fighting for abortion rights, for girls' right to go to schools; a shock value of that. I think that's power. Obviously, I hope that I am using that for the right reasons. What we do at Purposeful is about creating opportunities for females and for girls specifically. Now we are hiring and everybody is calling me, there is a job problem, and everybody is like, you have to at least hire some men now. We try to show the community what we do, and the credibility of doing this for the long term. I think for women's groups and organizations my leadership still raises questions. I try to be sensitive about it. It is in my interest to fight for girls' rights, because everybody would be better in society when females are emancipated.

Policy processes

We are involved in policy processes all the time. In Sierra Leone, the president declared a state of emergency on rape and sexual violence, and Purposeful was invited to advise government on the policy landscape and response. I spend a lot of time in the state house, trying to help them think about what to do, how to develop the right set of policies. Last week we were invited to parliament about a new law. I have been asked to advise on international youth policy.

We think about Purposeful as a movement, we want to think about trying to keep girls and their allies, their voice and agency within their communities. We try to provide support to do that, but we also want to be part of policy discussions, to bring the voices of girls within the space. At the United Nations we are involved in that. I was on the international task force at UNICEF on the workplace, gender discrimination, harassment, and abuse of power. We made massive recommendations of what needs to happen and change at UNICEF. There was a lot of policy work involved in that. We work at various levels and we try to focus on how we can affect girls.

Purposeful

In 2014 we started to focus initially on getting girls the right set of information to help them survive and thrive. We did a lot of media work, and launched a couple of brands that will engage girls. We used brands like the face of power. In the middle of that we switched to the things we do now and think about it more holistically rather than being media-heavy and media-led. We had the name: Purposeful Productions. Our tagline at the time was going to be around how to use the power of the media and girls' voices and movements. We dropped 'Productions'; officially, we are now just Purposeful (https://wearepurposeful.org/).

Frameworks

We do not necessarily align or ground our work in UNCRC or CEDAW [United Nations Convention on the Elimination of All Forms of Discrimination Against Women], or any of those. We call on those as and when is convenient. Mostly, the underpinning of our work is around this idea of feminist transformation of the world and thinking about girls' agency. We refer a lot to the SDGs, but you cannot achieve any of the SDGs if you are not intentionally focusing on girls or females in general. So, we use those, not as the underpinning of our work, but depending who the audience is. We try to demonstrate how girls can achieve. Our discourse is not entirely like a rights-based discourse, because we understand the limitations of that. It depends on the audience and the occasion.

Limits of rights-based discourse

In a society like Sierra Leone, on human rights people say 'these westerners come and tell us all the time'. Human rights get paraded. Some people would tell you that it is a human right, but we don't have the resources to enable everybody to realize their rights. We pushed back on those arguments. We engage with policy-makers because, for example, on education policies, they understand a human rights perspective. They say that education is free, but the discussion is not going to be about girls, not about rights, it is going to focus on economic implications, the correct economic focus on girls, even in reaching our goals.

To educate all in Sierra Leone, we need to free our discourse of the cost and the dividend of that investment. Rights are too generic from this perspective. Everyone has rights and they should have them. It is not a debate about rights, but about what the viable options are. And how you can get that done. We want to be a part of that conversation as well. So, I just can recognize this right; you have to demonstrate how you get to it.

It is a useful framework, but we are aware it has its limitations. Especially in this context, people resort to their culture, to tradition. It is an unproductive conversation because, then you are creating a false binary where they are holding on traditions and you are holding on to rights. You want to say, 'In your, in our, tradition what do we want? But this is the way we are going to get to that stage. If you don't do this to boys and girls you are not going to get to that. We are trying to use the rights framework. We go back to your history, your culture, even before the advent of rights, what was it like for females?' I teach gender at the university and I push my students on that. Before colonialism; what was the situation of girls before colonialism, before slavery? We can find a lot of anecdotes that become arguments, more than the rights discourse.

Funding priorities for the future

Donors need to offer flexible, long-time funding; to change the form of funding. When we started Purposeful donors said we never qualify for anything. Why? They said, elimination by complexity. Because for donors we were not qualified at all, and that was a problem for the infrastructure. Amazing grassroots organizations and groups do not necessarily have the technical expertise to write complex proposals or don't have the time, because they are busy doing the work. Very needy donors, they needed a report every month, every two months.

Donors should look for opportunities, including people not coming to them for funds. I will give you an example. At Purposeful, we obviously care about sexual violence. Recently, we got a national emergency declaration. A media personality here had received too many calls about rape. So, she organized one day that she called Black Tuesday. It was going to be one event. We were invited to be in the panel she organized. She invited students from different cities. After the event, I called her and said, you have a very big platform, you have a voice. Let's do it multiple times, in multiple places; we would find flexible funding. We will run a couple of consultancies to organize it. Let's make sure people no longer deny this subject. You have media, we can put in the structure. She has a foundation in her name. We never qualified for any funding, because there was nobody, just her. We went to several parts of the country, hosted TV, town halls, radio. The president referred to the work we were doing when he declared the state of emergency. If we had started with a plan: where can I find the funds? It would never happen. The power of just being receptive and looking for opportunities like that, you can help accelerate something that is important.

In Purposeful we try to do that kind of funding. We are moving away from this idea of grants. In fact, we are having discussions, we don't just want to be a grant organization. We want to be an organization for people we believe in. We want to see possible change-makers in society and provide support to them and say, 'We believe in you. Go work your magic and figure ways to do that.' Particularly for children and young people that level of faith in them can be really transformational. It can give them the freedom to do amazing things.

I know that is a difficult part for all our donors. But in general, invest in people. There are people here who have demonstrated potential. Some of us have been around for a while, we now have opportunities, resources. But a lot of people, if you demonstrate any capacities, they want to buy you over or suppress you, because there is no sufficient investment in the alternative, the progressive side of things. Whereas the conservative or negative side invest in the system, education, and structures that link people with each other, the good side has too many barriers for that kind of investment in informal structures. Just to have registered NGOs in Sierra Leone disqualifies so many good initiatives. That is why in Purposeful, we support groups that are not registered.

If you really want social change, to build that social movement, especially for these groups we are talking about, for children and young people, you have to be willing to say, 'I am going to take a risk with you'. It is risky, but you want it. Despite all this incredibly rigorous processes and structures, the amount of corruption in the aid industry is just amazing. I would rather take a chance with these groups, who are credible, who are connected with society, who are there, sometimes informal. We are looking for opportunities; be flexible, moving resources fast like we did with Black Tuesday and initiatives like that, is where the magic is.

What would help to achieve this is money, flexible money, faith in us, in our approach, supporting exchanges. In Purposeful we fund, we support different coalitions, we encourage them, and it sometimes feels that is frivolous money. But there is a lot of power in bringing like-minded people together and supporting them with the right set of tools.

I was invited with some kids to meet one donor. They are going to set up a platform and I said, 'Who do you think credibly is going to be in your platform with the internet situation? Dump all these tools. That is a waste of money. It does not make sense at all. You have to bring people together. You have to invest in people, it is costly.'

Bring people together, give space and time to talk, engage with each other, share experience, and support an exchange programme. Act on social change, social communities, supporting them to invest in organizing their own community. You have to invest and build that infrastructure, that foundation. Flexible and long-time funding; community support.

There are other things that I want to be able to do to take on issues. We have this situation of FGM [female genital mutilation] in this country and everybody is afraid to tackle it. I cannot take it on with Purposeful resources, because this is the infrastructure; you have to fight back at different levels, fight smart, but we need money. There are so many allies out there, but they are not even recognizable, because people don't give them money. These are women who were subjected, who are terrified, whose voices have not ever been heard. A politician has to support it so their voices could be heard. It is hard to write a project on that, because it is going to require flexible thinking. It is based on talking about the rights of people; girls want to share their stories and figure out ways to fight this. Use the power of media to share their stories and help them to organize at community level, come together and start to create the alternatives required. Saying: we are not against our culture, but we are against bloody culture. And finding the right message in it.

Whether to invest in a group

It is challenging, but success [is] what is happening in the conversation in country about rape and sexual violence. Silence is broken, and I think it was connected with the work we wanted to do. Success is looking at how we can shift the conversation.

I was asked to advise the president about policies; if I had not seen that opportunity of investment, I would not have had that. Be sensitive to the opportunities because the way that social change happens, there are moments. To take advantage of moments you have to have an infrastructure that you have built for that. I don't think it is sporadic. You need to have a base of organizing an ally, and credibility and trust. So, when it happens you can take advantage of those moments. You can go chase one after the other, but you have to be sensitive and have the flexibility to respond in real time when those moments show up.

To share good practice we are going to have to use social media, media in general, the power of technology. I think we will move on from physical interaction and connection. We should not underestimate the power of media and the power of telling the right story. In this field there is not a real investment in media; we have left that exclusively to the private sector and the market.

There is a real power in how the media shapes social norms. We need to think about how you create things and make them part of the culture. Also finding the right set of allies, people who are doing things in their communities and finding ways to reach people where they are. Take risks. I think that that is a dirty word for the donor community. The whole premise is, how can we give this money without this risk? That is bullshit; the ideas are very, very risky; therefore, you have to take risk, on people, on informal structures, institutions, finding ways to meet some of the risk with the right way of adjustment.

Website

Purposeful: https://wearepurposeful.org/ [accessed 17 July 2023].

CHAPTER 21
Making governance work

Blair Glencorse

> *Since we did this interview in 2019, the government of Afghanistan has changed.*

Background

I'm from the UK but came to the US for graduate school and then worked at the World Bank on post-conflict and fragile states. While I was there I met the [former] President of Afghanistan Ashraf Ghani. I worked for him for five years writing his speeches and thinking about strategy.

About 10 years ago, having done all that, I came to the conclusion that accountability is what it's all about. Unless we can get this relationship between people in power and citizens right, it's going to be very hard to deal with everything else.

The second realization, which is more relevant here, is that it has to be about young people. It has to be a generational change because it's going to take a long time, it's not linear, and it needs a movement of young people who are going to push for a different way of doing things, and for more inclusive and fair and accountable societies.

The third realization is, if that's the case, we have to engage young people where they are rather than where we want them to be, and that means creative approaches, ongoing support, and finding ways to shift norms.

I realized that there is an emphasis within the governance community on institutions, rules, compliance, and enforcement. This is important, but we decided, with young people in particular, it just wasn't filling them with much energy (and didn't give them a sense of a different future that they could help to build). In many cases there was mistrust in government.

Accountability Lab

We do things a bit differently from most other organizations in the field. We've tried to flip that narrative and make it positive; to make it solutions-oriented, to hold up people doing the right things; role models with positive energy. These issues of accountability can often be very negative so we're youth-focused, creative, and positive. Our work tends to be very bottom-up, grassroots stuff. That's the broad overview.

When it comes to meeting people where they are, that means building what we call 'unlikely networks'. In development we often default to 'the usual suspects', in all sorts of ways, and we haven't really seen impact from that in the way I think that young people would like. So we're trying to build different, unlikely networks. We work a lot with musicians, rappers, filmmakers, creatives, and interactive muralists for example; all kinds of people who are inherently thinking accountability but aren't invited to the sorts of conferences that focus on these things. We try to make the connections between them and support them to push together in the same direction to try to overcome the usual piecemeal, supply-driven approach the aid industry tends to take. Young people everywhere have great ideas, but it's very difficult for them generally to connect to each other and to access the kinds of resources and support that they need to create the change that they want to see.

That's how the Lab started and that led informally to work with some young people initially in Nepal and then in Liberia. We support good ideas: for example, a filmmaker in Liberia who wanted to set up a film school around accountability; or a young woman in Nepal who wanted to create a crowd-sourced 'wiki' type website for government services to help young people navigate government effectively. That support grew into what is now our 'accountability incubator'; a year-long training and support programme, a bit like a business incubator with support from entrepreneurs but for civic activists we call 'accountapreneurs'. That's in 10 countries now and all sorts of interesting ideas have come out of it and grown significantly.

The other campaign in which we adopt this positive approach is called 'Integrity Icon'. This is an effort to rethink the way we understand people in government, find the most honest of them and turn them into national celebrities. In the same way we celebrate sports stars and musicians, why don't we celebrate people who are truly serving the public good? The campaign started in Nepal six years ago, now it's in seven countries. It creates a positive conversation about what the word integrity means, what kind of people are wanted in government, and then celebrates them very publicly to shift the narrative around these issues.

The people who become Icons are not necessarily young people, but the campaign itself is very focused on the younger generation. All the volunteers and the outreach tend to focus on young people. The point is to encourage them to rethink how they understand their aspirations and possibilities. We've seen some amazing feedback where young people, who'd said previously, 'I'm a person with integrity and I thought I'd never work for government because it wasn't possible', and are now saying 'actually I realize this is possible and I want to go into government and serve my country'. This is exactly what we want; good people going into government trying to do the right thing.

Now we're supporting them to grow and to build coalitions for integrity and shift the way decisions are made. For example, one of the Icons in Mali was previously a middling level justice official but after he won his campaign last year the trust and credibility it gave him led to his promotion to Minister of Justice. We are now finding this is really helping get people into positions where they can implement decision-making from the top down.

The Civic Action Teams [CivActs] began in Nepal after the earthquakes eight years ago [in 2011]. We had large networks of young people in the worst affected areas, but we're not a relief organization so we mobilized them to begin to collect information on the response to the earthquake, support people to solve problems, plug gaps, then feed this information up to decision-makers; and then communicate decisions being made back down to communities. We created feedback loops in this way that became a central piece of the earthquake response because no one was really integrating citizen-generated data into the relief process.

That's still going in Nepal. We've collected hundreds of thousands of pieces of data, solved hundreds of different challenges, and built trust between communities and government. It's evolved to focus on other issues including migration and public service delivery.

In Liberia we've adapted it, working with gold mining communities to understand their rights and responsibilities vis à vis gold mining companies and local government. In Mali we're doing this around justice and security issues in the north of the country; and in Zimbabwe Accountability Lab is using CivActs to focus on local level issues including climate.

It's become a methodology we're beginning to test in new places and is again very youth-focused. The data collectors are young people. The data we generate is put out in easy to understand infographics given to local radio DJs who use it as the basis for Q&A shows with young people about what they want and what the future should look like.

Finally we have begun to try to create physical and intellectual spaces for young people to come together and build these unlikely networks. We are part of a co-working space here in DC called The Open Gov Hub which is about 90 organizations working on open governments and accountability. Accountability Lab has set up Open Gov Hubs in five countries, Mali, Pakistan, Nepal, Mexico, and Liberia.

These are physical spaces where young people can come together; and we host events and trainings. There's co-working space. In Liberia we have an audio-visual studio which has state of the art equipment so rappers, citizen journalists, and media-makers can create content and meet each other and feel part of a community which is generating lots of ideas. Lessons show this work is beginning to get better at feeding into policy processes. For example, the Open Government Partnership, the international effort to make governments more open, had a conference in Ottawa. We brought 20 young people from around the world to that conference for a two-day open government bootcamp, then worked with them to systemically integrate youth into everything that the open government community is thinking about.

That's one angle, getting young people's voices heard at those levels, working with them at country level on different policies and procedures related to youth in accountability. In particular, trying to connect the dots between initiatives like SDG 16 globally and young people in specific countries.[1] Trying to make sure their voices are part of the conversation and they are seen as equal stakeholders in decision-making and not a group that somehow needs to be separately consulted on the side.

Funding and advocacy

We are registered in the US as a '501(c)(3)' [tax-exempt], but also registered as a local organization in all the countries we work. We operate as what we call a 'translocal network': we share values and approaches but are a community of independent, proximate organizations. We are funded by a mixture of foundations, governments, and multilateral organizations, such as the Open Society Foundations, Ford Foundation, MacArthur Foundation, Luminate, and multilaterals like UNDP [United Nations Development Programme] and the UN Peacebuilding Fund. We're about to start some work with the World Bank, and with bilateral organizations in the US, Germany, Sweden, and the Netherlands. We do a bit of crowdfunding and there are a few individuals that support us too.

Strategically, we want to become the hub within the accountability space that supercharges the future of the field. We have made great progress building the organization we want to be and want to work for. Now we want to ensure we are building the accountability field. We are in a position in which our programmes generate learning for others around how to change systems; our networks can become the spaces in which young people learn about these issues; and our ways of working set new standards for other organizations.

Example of youth participation

One of the best recently is a music contest we run in Nigeria called Voice2Rep [also V2R below: Voice to Represent]. It was a competition for first-time musicians to sing songs about participation and engagement in democracy and accountability around the Nigerian elections. We partnered with a large music company called Chocolate City that manages many of the most famous rappers in Nigeria. Of course, if we're talking about shifting norms, then music is a fantastic way to do it. There's actually an approach to this that was outlined in the World Bank World Development Report a few years ago on governance which talks about 'norm entrepreneurs', and musicians are definitely norm entrepreneurs. They talk about issues that young people care about, they have voices that they listen to.

The traditional approach has been inauthentic, with donors perhaps saying, 'hey, sing us a song about this thing that we care about'. We would argue work with music needs to be organic, and about things the musicians themselves care about, and then they are challenged in the right sort of ways. I think through V2R we managed to do that to the point where we had just tons of engagement, tons of people applying, some amazing music being made.

The success point was not with the musicians in the competition but with much more senior rappers in the music industry who acted as mentors for the young people coming through. Many of these guys are also young of course and have followers of millions, and they came out publicly. There was one newspaper article that quoted some of these musicians saying, 'Previously we used to be co-opted by the political parties and we would sell ourselves to the party that would pay us the most to sing for their campaign, but this time we're not going to do that. We've realized through this process that it's all about integrity, accountability, and candidates that actually have policies, not about who is going to pay us the most to talk about their campaign.' They encouraged young people to vote for the candidates that will do the right thing. When you've got very famous people that lots of young people respect and follow saying that kind of thing, it's a really interesting example of how you can begin to shift messages and understanding of what kinds of behaviours are acceptable.

Learning from failure

We would argue that failure isn't failure if you learn from it. A lot of what we do is try new things and see what works and what doesn't. We recently in Liberia created a network of women filmmakers all over the country to make films on accountability on gender issues. We've done it but I think it was a bit of a missed opportunity. I think we failed to understand how difficult this was going to be. The idea was to create films and then build an advocacy network around them, and get more into pushing at different levels for policy change.

That advocacy piece has been very difficult for a number of reasons. The logistics were incredibly difficult because there were delays. It was rainy season and it's really hard to get to big chunks of the country. Policy-makers have been consumed by other issues because the political process is very difficult, inflation is extremely high, and the government is not listening. So we put a lot of time and effort into building this network and telling stories in ways we thought everyone, including lots of young people would get behind, and it hasn't quite happened. Lots of lessons in there, not just about project planning but also about how you do advocacy, how to tell stories within specific contexts, and how you manage this kind of thing.

A bigger failure, and relating it back to music, was in Liberia during the Ebola crisis. The international community were trying to explain why it was dangerous, and it was so haphazard and inappropriate in the way they tried to communicate with young people in particular. For example it was a lot of posters in English saying things like 'don't touch each other there's Ebola here' without any understanding that many people don't speak English, many people can't read; so these posters didn't really tell anyone anything.

We were working with some of the most famous musicians to think through how to authentically message music around Ebola. There are examples not just from us, but many others in the region who did this really well. Again use an audio method which is understood by everybody to communicate in a slightly different way what this meant.

We also did a lot with film at that point; young people made films about why this mattered in local languages around local community issues related to Ebola. Then we activated local mobile cinemas in many communities showing films with young people talking to their contemporaries about this. It was difficult to measure success, but a very different approach at the time.

Primary conditions for engagement or participation

It begins with trust and this we've learned repeatedly. To be legitimate in any community there needs to be trust and that comes through repeated interactions and highly contextualized knowledge of a place, often through people who have lived the challenges in those communities. We have local teams who are doing all of this, but of course there are many marginalized communities who don't necessarily trust an organization like ours, as hard as we try to build trust. There can be issues and that takes a long time, years in some places, and we didn't necessarily account for that.

Trust is the starting point, then delivering on your commitments and promises. That is part of what creates that sense of co-dependency and of trust.

Third is living by your values. We take this extremely seriously because we are about accountability, often in difficult places. If we have new team members who haven't been as imbued with our values as others, sometimes that can be challenging.

Fourth is having the right stakeholders engaged and involved from the outset. We had difficulty sometimes getting those people on the same page, and for them to understand why this was important. For example at political levels, there were elections and many newly elected officials had other priorities and other things going on, so it was difficult to get people to engage and focus on accountability.

In most cases money is the least valuable resource. There is a lot of power inherent in all of this. Liberia, as an example, creates massive amounts of dependency. Because of some bad behaviours of people in the past, it means it's very hard to get things done. I'll give you a good example; in Liberia, I talked about the Civic Action Teams and how we collect information from people and feed that up to decision-makers. Now, asking questions in Liberia, even in the most remote communities, they will ask to be paid because there's been so much of this aid-driven information collection. They know people have money and that's part of the way they see this interaction going.

That is partly because it's been a highly extractive process; collecting information, collecting data, doing something for these communities, and then leaving and never coming back, never showing them what happened, never showing how this led to any bigger change, or how this information was used to advocate for their interests. Never communicating back to them is highly inefficient, highly frustrating, and creates suspicion. It undermines the trust which is needed to build relationships to create the kind of change that we might collectively want to see, which is why we spend massive amounts of time in these communities and work on the feedback loop.

Also, for example, with our incubator, we began by giving what we call the 'accountapreneurs' some seed grants, but we've stopped doing that, at least at the outset, for some of the same reasons. Once we mention that there's money involved, often it's very small amounts with us, $5k [US$5,000] over two years, it distorts the conversation and becomes, from their perspective, very much about what they need to do to get that money, not about what they need to do to create the change that they actually want to see, or that might be needed.

We do help them when we can financially – and we don't deny the critical importance of finance, of course – but we don't make that explicit from the outset and put the focus much more on the ideas, the networks, the communities that can be built, the communication that we can support around these goals and so on. The real resources are the ideas and the human capital in many ways. There are always solutions to challenges in communities, it's a question of supporting them where they need it, drawing them out, connecting them, and giving them the space to physically go on to do this.

If funders understand there are organizations in communities doing good work, it's so incredibly valuable to give them the money to get on with that work and to trust them, rather than place constraints and parameters around it based on their own understandings of what might be needed, when they don't necessarily know the context as well. Long-term, core, flexible support is the way to go, and the opposite can actually make things extremely difficult.

Assessment criteria for donors

It would come down to the legitimacy, creativity, and positive energy side of things, and integrity rather than systems and processes and so on. It's perhaps more subjective and it takes being in these places to really understand what's needed, or at least having very good networks that can help you assess these things a bit more effectively.

There are constraints for donors when they are generally in the Global North, don't always have offices in the Global South, and are not embedded in communities in quite the right ways. It's tricky, but I think there are ways to do this. There are a lot of shortcuts that donors tend to take that are unfortunate and undermine their own impact.

There was a very large scandal in Liberia recently with a girls school run by an American woman that was funded by all the big donors and became a kind of rock star in the development world. We knew for years and years there were very bad things happening in the school, told everyone, no one wanted to listen, because she has an amazing [social media] account and told all these stories about young girls. We pushed and pushed and eventually managed to get two incredible journalists to write a story on it, which blew the whole thing open, and it closed down the school.

What was pretty shocking about the whole thing was the reaction of the donors, many of whom refused to acknowledge that they had funded this organization and had perhaps not done the due diligence needed.

Donors can perhaps find ways of better contextualizing what they do in some places, and develop good networks on the ground that can inform them of who's doing the right sorts of work. Then work in organizations that are legitimate locally, that are pushing in the right direction, and which may not have all of the systems and compliance processes in place, but support them to do that in different ways.

To give an idea of an organization that does this well: GlobalGiving is a crowdfunding website which funds many grassroots organizations around the world. They send field assessors to all of these countries. They are generally volunteers, or young people who are travelling around but go and do interviews about what's going on, talk to people about who's doing the work and what perceptions are of their platform. For example, when it comes to this organization in Liberia, GlobalGiving, they were on their site, they were fundraising through it. We were telling people what was going on; GlobalGiving were the only people who sent someone out, did a review, and then retracted the money and took them off the platform because they actually did their due diligence. Other organizations that do this quite well are the Fund for Global Human Rights and the American Jewish World Service. Again grassroots funding, really know the contexts in which they're working, take time to listen, and identify organizations that are legitimate. Then provide them with the support they need, and often that is not just financial, it's capacity building, supporting them to improve their communications and so on.

Sharing learning

We have what we call quarterly learning calls, a bit like quarterly learning schools for companies, where it's an open call but anyone can share publicly what we're working on, and challenges, failures, and successes. We have monthly open-board calls, which are open calls with our staff globally and all our board members that anyone can join, about different thematic issues or challenges. We have functional working groups in the organization. For example all the communications people from every team have a group, all of the finance people across the world have a group, and they have at least monthly calls to talk about challenges and share ideas. We have WhatsApp groups for all of these team members which are very active every day.

We share our learning through blogs, podcasts; we are getting a lot better at connecting learning with the communications, so now there are videos on some of these things. We try wherever we can to get external evaluation of what we're doing; we managed to occasionally build partnerships with universities and find ways to get them done. There's a page on our website all about impact and learning. It has all of our resources, and there we talk a lot about what we're learning and try to say what's going poorly and well, and on how to improve.

Note

1. SDG 16 is about promoting peaceful and inclusive societies, providing access to justice for all and building effective, accountable, and inclusive institutions at all levels.

Website

https://accountabilitylab.org/

CHAPTER 22

Think twice: travelling between academia and practice in children's rights

Karl Hanson

Background

I studied law out of a motivation for social justice, with a rather vague, naïve idea. My ideal was that I could use the law to fight injustice, to save widows and orphans. Of course, when you study law, things quickly move to the needy-greedy things of positive law, like in contract law or business law, and you get something else compared to grandiloquent fights against injustices.

When I was a student, I did volunteer work as a scout leader in my hometown and worked as a volunteer for the national scouts' movement. I took up a similar volunteering job in the city where I was studying for an organization that worked with immigrant children. I really liked working as a child and youth worker, which also made me aware of the importance of carefully thinking about how to work with children. This became even more obvious when I later got involved as a trainer in these movements to train young people who wanted to become involved as a volunteer in child and youth clubs.

At one point, I was offered the opportunity to combine my technical legal degree with reflecting on the social status of children and young people; that was at the Centre for Children's Rights at Ghent University in Belgium, which is the university where I later did my PhD. I felt it was a great chance to start working there, and once I was in, I did not want to leave.

I started to work at the Centre for Children's Rights Studies in 1992. The Centre, which had been created by Eugeen Verhellen, was attached to the Faculty of Psychology and Educational Sciences and offered a genuinely interdisciplinary setting. Having a law degree, I was hired to do editorial work for a publication that combined law and social science approaches to children's rights. I felt that my work was in line with my initial quest for justice that had now taken shape through the cause for children's rights. After a few years working there, I discovered how much I enjoyed working on social movements from an academic point of view, and I decided that I wanted to stay. But then I also understood that if you want to stay in academia, you need a PhD. So, I resolved to go for a PhD, and wrote my doctoral thesis on juvenile justice and criminal responsibility.

Participation conundrums: justice and labour

At the beginning of the 1990s, the field's main themes had to do with child protection and youth justice, and of course with children's rights more generally, with the UNCRC being adopted in 1989. Within the broader children's rights field, the right to participation was put on the table very early on.

In my PhD research I explored the idea of minimum age of criminal responsibility, but with a particular question in mind: do children have a right to participate in juvenile justice? Can we take their agency seriously also when they do wrong? What is so against the idea of considering children and young people responsible for what they have done by looking at them as responsible beings also in the criminal sphere? That question goes against a dominant view held by many children's rights actors, who want to protect children against the criminal law system. Contrary to the cause in favour of participation rights in most other children's rights domains, such as education or local politics, in juvenile justice children are deemed not to be competent enough and hence don't have the right to be held criminally responsible. I found, and still find, these contrasting viewpoints on children's participation extremely interesting (Hanson, 2016).

Already by the end of the 1970s and during the 1980s, scholars had been working on such ideas, including my thesis supervisor Eugeen Verhellen and his predecessor Gerda de Bock, who both worked at Ghent University in Belgium. They argued, not from a law and order approach but from an emancipatory view on young people, that if you want children to become responsible, you must hold them responsible when they commit offences. In my PhD on juvenile justice, I have investigated further these ideas and studied more in depth the origins and evolution of children's criminal responsibility. What if children are taken seriously even if they do things we don't like, such as committing an offence?

In parallel with working on juvenile justice for my PhD research, I had also developed an interest in the child labour debate. In 1996, at the beginning of the internet, I received an email about a Declaration of Working Children that had been adopted during a meeting in Kundapur in India. Contrary to earlier discussions about child labour, this declaration was different in the sense that it had been elaborated by working children's organizations that had explicitly mobilized the right to participation to argue that they have a right to work in dignity. I still find this extremely interesting: what to do when you believe that children have a right to participate, but then children use that space to say things with which you don't agree? That conundrum puts many children's rights persons, including myself, before a difficult challenge.

Too often, organizations that officially declare that children have the right to participate very much remain at the surface of things. Take for instance UNICEF, which sees itself as one of the champions of the right to participation. But then these working children's organizations knock on the door and say that they want to participate. UNICEF funds their meetings and during these meetings, working children's organizations say things that go against UNICEF's position on the abolishment of child labour. What should they then do? As an academic, I sometimes feel very privileged, because I do not necessarily have to defend a particular stance but I can study the discussion.

It is extremely interesting to try to understand the politics of children's participation. When children say things we dislike, we immediately tend to assume that they have been manipulated. On the other hand, when children say things with which we agree, we think that this is great and that they should participate more. This happens in many contemporary discussions. When young people in industrialized countries take to the streets and say: we want governments to take action against climate change, we all think that is great and that we should listen more to children. But if young people in Europe gather to defend ideas that deal with national identity and argue that too many immigrants are coming to their country, we feel uneasy and rarely argue that we should listen more to children. I feel it is important to think these problems through and to work around what we mean by children's participation.

Children's rights, social movements

I now work at the Centre for Children's Rights Studies at the University of Geneva in Switzerland. Since I started to work in academia, more than 25 years ago, the broader field of children's rights has changed, an evolution I have witnessed from within and on which I have also written (see Hanson, 2014, 2019). I think that in the 1990s universities were much more involved in accompanying the social movement in favour of children's rights to put child participation in practice. Promoting children's rights and including child participation is still a strong trend within academia, even if I became myself more and more an academic compared to the child rights advocate that I was at the beginning. For me, this has created a critical distance from the social movement from which the study of children's rights at the universities emerged. It was indeed a social movement that has pushed academia to be interested in children's rights.

I think universities were interested in children's rights and childhood studies because it gave them the chance to engage with social movements, to step down from their ivory tower to be more directly socially relevant. But once children's rights were getting incorporated in the universities, the academic ecosystem in turn impacts the way that children's rights are being considered. Because it would say, OK, you can teach university classes on children's rights, but only if you have a PhD. These are the rules in academia. But then, to get a PhD, you must clarify what your theories and methods are. You cannot express ideas about children's rights simply because you believe in them; you need to build on more solid ground. Almost inevitably the academic ecosystem pushes you into a more reflexive, detached, and less passionate role. At least, that is what happened with me; instead of promoting children's rights through advocacy work, the main purpose of my job is to study children's rights from a relative outsider position.

Our centre in Geneva is called the Centre for Children's Rights Studies, whereas other similar centres are called 'centre for children's rights'. The fact that we added the word 'studies' summarizes through our name that we want to study, rather than advocate for, children's rights. In this sense our work is different from what child rights advocates do who want to improve children's rights. But this is where I now stand in the field. This position of course needs to be nuanced. I am not just a critical outsider, I am in general very sympathetic to the children's rights movement. But at the same time, I do try to take some critical distance, which I think is my role as an academic.

It is not just a game with words. Even if we share with them the ambition that children and young people's perspectives on the world deserve greater recognition, I believe that as academics in the field of children's rights we need to be emancipated from the social movement of children's rights. But emancipating and having our own agendas comes at a cost. Some people might criticize that we have climbed up the ivory tower again in which we are now stuck like so many others in academia, and that what we are doing is no longer relevant. I don't think such criticisms are correct. There is a lot of diversity within academia, you can find people that are very close to the field and who for instance collaborate intensively with youth-led organizations or working children's movements, whereas others take a more critical distance. I believe that the wide range of positions taken by academics, including on epistemic discussions about where one stands as a researcher in relation to social movements and how to analyse child participation, is now one of the field's major strengths.

Living rights, translation, and social justice

When Olga [Nieuwenhuys, see Chapter 27] and I developed our ideas on children's living rights, we were very much interested in children's agency and participation. We felt that many participation discourses remain at the surface, even if they build on children's rights and children's participation language. In a special issue of the journal *Childhood*, which focused on refractions of children's rights (Reynolds et al., 2006), we engaged with the need to both deconstruct and reconstruct the way we reflect on children's agency and participation, and from there we proposed living rights as a framework.

We have developed further this notion of living rights in a recent chapter in a handbook on children's rights (Hanson and Nieuwenhuys, 2020). The chapter starts with the story of Kailash Satyarthi and Malala Yousafzai, who were jointly awarded the Nobel Peace Prize in 2014. We felt it was very strange that such an extreme paternalist figure as Kailash Satyarthi, who constantly speaks 'in the name of' vulnerable children who are said to be voiceless and can't protect themselves, was hailed, in 2014, as the international champion of children's rights. Given all the fuss about children's participation, I had thought that we were done with these kinds of paternalist approaches. But apparently, we are not.

At the same time Malala Yousafzai also got the Nobel Peace Prize. She represents a completely different image of children's rights, being at the time a 17-year-old Muslim girl from the South who campaigns for the right to education for girls. The fact that Satyarthi and Yousafzai, an old man and a young woman who have such divergent views on children's rights, were awarded the Nobel Peace Prize together seems quite incoherent. What are children's rights then? And what place is there for children's participation? Satyarthi is relatively easy to set aside: he ticks all boxes of paternalism, with him we don't need to bother about participation and agency. But what can we make from Yousafzai?

From a living rights framework, we felt that also her position at times is disturbing and essentializing. She was presented as a girl who had suffered and therefore knows the truth. Her emphasis on largely uncontested rights claims, such as the right to education for girls, and her association with what I have recently labelled the children's rights aristocracy (Hanson, 2022) illustrates that in many instances child participation is not necessarily very new or challenging. We might in fact be turning in circles, and never touch on what is politically really important. I do not believe that things have changed a lot since 2014, and that this is where we more or less stand today.

We agree with the basic ideas about taking children and young people seriously and the importance of acknowledging their agency. But we felt that the language of child participation did not help us further, which is why we suggested the notion of living rights to change the language. If you provide space for children to participate and to have the right to give their opinion, that also includes recognizing their right to say things about children's rights. With that, we take the risk that children disagree with the way we ourselves see children's rights. There is the example of the claim of working children's organizations to recognize their right to work in dignity that I talked about earlier, but there are many other examples. What if children claim the right to marry even if they are under 18, the right to mobility and migration, or the right to participate in violent political struggles, including in warfare? How should we look at these kinds of questions?

We have supplemented the notion of living rights, which contains the words 'alive' and 'living', with the notions of translation and social justice. It is important to make space for people to express their opinions, but this does not automatically mean that what they are saying is now the new truth. To give space for children's viewpoints does not mean that we must sacralize children's voices. That would mean that once children have spoken, nothing else needs to be said; it would essentialize what children think.

This reminds me of when I was a youth worker. For one year, I was the editor-in-chief of Greenpeace's children's journal, which was made by a small group of adults and children. I was the one who suggested bringing children onto the editorial committee, with the argument that if we want to have a journal for children, children need to be part of the editorial committee. So, it was a participatory initiative where we had both children and adults on the editorial board. As final editor I made some changes in texts that were written by children, because I felt it was not at the level we had set for this journal. My adult colleague editors did not understand this, and asked, how can you? You wanted to have children as co-editors and as authors, but now you are the first one to censor things that they have written? They felt that I should have kept children's language without any changes, because what children wrote is authentic; this is what they say. For me, it was very important to have children on board as co-editors and to respect them as journalists, but at the same time we also have a readership of children for whom we write. I felt that out of respect for our readers the material we published must be of high quality, which implies that sometimes texts needed to be significantly edited.

We must multiply spaces where children can express their opinion, but we also need to reflect on how to go about it. Children's participation is not about simply accepting everything that children say, which would be very similar to populist right-wing discourses that pretend they are merely saying 'what the people think'. In addition, not all children have the same ideas about children's rights, so you need to assess their different perspectives. Yousafzai's message about the right to education of Pakistani girls fits well with what funders like to hear, so having her on stage during a Nobel Peace Prize ceremony is not that surprising. But for other kids who defend different claims, take for instance children who find that sleeping rough in the street is OK, it will be much more difficult to speak in front of the same audience.

That is what the notion of translation is about: some voices are heard more than others because we agree with what they are saying.

Filters in child participation operate everywhere, even among youth and in youth clubs where people are generally very much in favour of child participation. There are filters already from the very start, sorting out who is in the room and who is not, as well as among the suggestions and ideas expressed in the room, because certain claims are more difficult to sell than others, which is something youth workers know very well (Poretti, 2019). To analyse situations such as these, the notion of translation can be very useful.

Living rights, social justice, and translation can be tools to work around the limits of children's participation, as they tend to be more analytical. Olga and I have done quite some work on living rights and translations, and we want to continue working on the notion of social justice. What do we mean by it? How can social justice mediate discussions and conflicts around rights and so on? I was recently inspired by the work of Nancy Fraser (2009), who makes a distinction between different social justice claims around distribution, recognition, and representation.

I think that in children's rights we got stuck in the quest for recognition, in a similar way as what happened within feminism. In a sense, we want children to be recognized as persons, in their own right, and we greatly continue to invest in this idea. But in doing so, we tend to lose track of claims for just redistribution. Therefore, questions about social inequalities have been considerably left out of the gaze of child rights. Besides bringing those questions back in, we must also engage with Fraser's third claim for social justice that deals with children's representation. I contributed to a recently published edited volume that deals with children's representation as a site of contestation and power over who represents whom, what, when, and where (Sandin et al., 2023). Especially in transnational affairs, children as much as anybody else suffer from misrepresentation. In my chapter in that book, I argue that it is important to critically assess who is speaking on behalf of children and carefully consider where children's representation is being performed (Hanson, 2023). Questions about social justice are normative, they deal with what is right and what is wrong. In children's rights, it is impossible not to engage with such questions.

Children's themes

The Sustainable Development Goals (SDGs) are I feel rather problematic precisely because they are normative tools, or uncontested policy objectives that even many universities consider they should achieve. According to SDG 8.7, child labour must be abolished in a few years from now, an objective that is, given the actual social reality, quite ridiculous. By including the totally unrealistic goal to abolish the worst forms of child labour by 2025 – note that to end all forms of slavery the target date is 2030 – the SDGs illustrate how much a political organization, in this case the International Labour Organization [ILO], impacts how we think about children and their problems. According to the ILO's self-produced figures about the advancement of child labour abolition, we would need almost 150 years before child labour disappears. What then makes them think that suddenly, in a few years from now, child labour can be abolished? How come respected international organizations such as the ILO continue to set unrealistic goals? And why do people believe that? How have the SDGs become the new mantra? Now everybody thinks that they are great, and that we must not ask any further questions but only need to implement them. I am worried about the SDGs that pretend to fix certain things that in my view are extremely political, and hence need constant scrutiny and discussion.

An important question to ask students of childhood studies, as was suggested by former *Childhood* editor Dan Cook, is 'when is a child a child' (Smith and Greene, 2014)? The child is indeed not always a child, so you have to think about when a person is considered a child and when not? If a young person commits a serious offence, we tend to forget that he or she is a child and prefer thinking about an offender; even as a society, we consider child offenders mostly first as offenders, and only in a second instance we see them as children.

I find it fascinating to look at child or underage marriage, but from a critical perspective. Setting a minimum age of marriage at 18 undermines young people's agency and even undermines their right to marriage. A recent study of child marriage in Indonesia showed that many young people decided to marry because of love, a wish to belong to their community or to gain access to new opportunities, and tend to disagree with this paternalistic idea that you have to be 18 before you can marry (Horii, 2022).

From a socio-legal perspective that I have adopted in most of my own work, I also find child soldiering very interesting. In a chapter that I wrote together with Christelle Molima, we have tried to imagine new ways of looking at child soldiers by taking their agency as a starting point (Hanson and Molima, 2019). This is not an easy undertaking, as we always come back to this very vulnerable child image when we see children and warfare. We can criticize the essentializing image of the vulnerable child, but then what can we suggest as an alternative? How can we look at children at war and consider children as agents? The ambition of our piece was to try to understand what this could look like.

Another theme that I find inspiring is the role of 'the child's best interests' in sentencing decisions, which has been addressed in the work of Sophie de Saussure (2017). In the case where an offender is also a father, it is seldom in the child's best interests to have his or her parent locked up in prison for a long period. So, if the child's best interests would be at the centre of all things, a father who committed an offence would for instance be sentenced to a shorter period of deprivation of liberty compared to an offender who has no children. That would mean that when two persons get caught for robbing a bank together, the one who has children would receive half of the prison sentence compared to the other who has no children, to respect the child's best interests. Given today's discussions on criminal law, this seems very unlikely to happen, as it hurts most people's feelings of justice and equity.

Can you take a child-centred perspective in these matters, and take the child's best interests into account when deciding about prison sentences? If that is not possible, can you take into account the place where the sentence is going to be executed, or the practical implementation of the sentence? Can you for instance decide that in case the convicted person has children, the sentence should be executed close to the place where his children live, so his children have the possibility to preserve the ties with their father? What is fascinating here, is that at the end the discussion about the child's best interests is tied up with larger debates in criminal law about the detrimental effects of deprivation of liberty and the prison abolitionist movement. [See for instance the International Conference on Penal Abolition – ICOPA.]

Child rights: academia, practice, and policy

I strongly believe that NGOs and academia each have important autonomous missions, and that it is to the benefit of the children's rights field that both are strengthened. To put in practice the popular metaphor to bridge academia and practice and policy, each pillar of the bridge needs to be sufficiently strong in itself. Then you can establish connections between the pillars and ensure that results from academic research are shared with policy-makers and practitioners, and conversely that policy-makers and practitioners find out what happens in academia. For me, the missing link between the two is knowledge brokering.

In 2018, as part of the Children's Rights European Academic Network [CREAN], we organized a conference in Geneva on the impact of children's rights education and research on policy development where we addressed three broader questions. First, we looked at the needs for policy-makers to rely on robust scientific knowledge to develop evidence-based policies that can implement the children's rights normative framework. A second point was about how academia can ensure that its education and research programmes sufficiently resonate with contemporary social and political debates and have sustainable impact. The third point was about knowledge brokering, which we felt is important to facilitate the two-way transfer of scientific knowledge into operational policies and of social problems to academia.

I like to think of knowledge brokering as an autonomous space that not only brings theory and practice together, but also allows theory and practice to each do their own job properly. You cannot simply blame academics for being too academic. Of course, we are, being academic is what we are paid for. My job as an academic is to train future professionals, but also to make sure that someone will be sufficiently prepared to stand in my shoes to train also a next generation of professionals. If I am all the time busy influencing policy-makers and practitioners, who will be teaching and coaching the PhD researchers who can take up academic positions in children's rights after me? On the other hand, if you work for an NGO as a child and youth worker, it is great if you take time to be reflexive, but you should of course also make sure that you do your job properly. Kids out there are waiting for you. You must be available, listen to them carefully, and take their opinions into account, engage with the children and young people with whom you work. You cannot be constantly reflexive and tell them: 'Hey guys, today I can't be with you because I have things to read, I must keep up with the latest literature on child participation.'

It is here that I situate the need to develop more and stronger intermediate platforms between academia and practice. I would say, we can't have enough knowledge brokering platforms that are well equipped, from an autonomous third position, both to translate research findings to the field and to translate demands and ideas from the field to academia.

References

Children's Rights European Academic Network (CREAN) https://www.crean-network.org/

De Saussure, S. (2017) 'Quelle protection pour les enfants des contrevenants lors de la détermination de la peine? État des lieux au Canada'. In: Desrosiers, J., Garcia, M. and Sylvestre, M.-È. (eds), *Réformer le droit criminel au Canada [Criminal Law Reform in Canada]*, pp. 433–458, Montréal, Québec: Éditions Yvon Blais.

Fraser, N. (2009) *Scales of Justice: Reimagining political space in a globalizing world.* New York: Columbia University Press.

Hanson, K. (2014) '"Killed by charity" – Towards interdisciplinary children's rights studies', *Childhood* 21(4): 441–446.

Hanson, K. (2016) 'Children's participation and agency when they don't "do the right thing"', *Childhood* 23(4): 471–475.

Hanson, K. (2019) 'Societal impact of academic childhood and children's rights research: Sooner or later?' *Childhood* 26(4): 409–413.

Hanson, K. (2022) 'Reinventing children's rights', *Childhood* 29(2): 149–156.

Hanson, K. (2023) 'Children's representation in the transnational mirror maze', in Sandin, B., Josefsson, J., Hanson, K. and Balagopalan, S. (eds), *The Politics of Children's Rights and Representation*, pp. 181–201, Cham: Springer International Publishing.

Hanson, K. and Molima, C. (2019) 'Getting Tambo out of limbo: Exploring alternative legal frameworks that are more sensitive to the agency of children and young people in armed conflict', in Drumbl, M.A. and Barrett, D.C. (eds), *Research Handbook on Child Soldiers*, pp. 110–131, Cheltenham: Edward Elgar.

Hanson, K. and Nieuwenhuys, O. (eds) (2012) *Reconceptualizing Children's Rights in International Development*, Cambridge: Cambridge University Press.

Hanson, K. and Nieuwenhuys, O. (2020) 'A child-centered approach to children's rights law living rights and translations', in Todres, J. and King, S.M. (eds), *The Oxford Handbook of Children's Rights Law*, pp. 100–118, New York: Oxford University Press. https://doi.org/10.1093/oxfordhb/9780190097608.013.6

Horii, H. (2022) *Child Marriage, Rights and Choice: Rethinking agency in international human rights.* London: Routledge.

International Conference on Penal Abolition (ICOPA) https://actionicopa.org/

Poretti, M. (2019) 'Rights, participatory spaces and the daily fabric of children and young people's voices in Switzerland', *Children's Geographies* 17(4): 467–479.

Reynolds, P., Nieuwenhuys, O. and Hanson, K. (2006) 'Refractions of children's rights in development practice: A view from anthropology – Introduction', *Childhood* 13(3): 291–302. https://doi.org/10.1177/0907568206067476

Sandin, B., Josefsson, J., Hanson, K. and Balagopalan, S. (eds) (2023) *The Politics of Children's Rights and Representation*, Cham: Springer International Publishing.

Smith, C. and Greene, S. (2014) *Key Thinkers in Childhood Studies*, Bristol: Policy Press.

PART FOUR

Thinking forward

CHAPTER 23
Thinking forward: an introduction

All of the contributors throughout the book have raised issues and dilemmas, described and discussed good and bad practice, conditions for success and failure, questions over terminology, ethics, funding, and priorities. All of these contributions, based on practice experience, and reflection over some years, provide material and means for thinking ahead, based on current circumstances, future opportunities, and possibilities. The contributions have been compiled to provide food for thought to help shape future work. Key issues throughout have concerned participation terminology, both directly and in issues of cross-cultural translation, and how meanings are expressed in language, practice, and performance.

This part of the book aims to particularly highlight practical issues and approaches that are changing and consolidating practice: as with contributions allocated to previous parts, the processes of thinking forward are generally evident throughout. One hallmark of good practice has always been the process of reflection, including consideration of context, diversity, marginalization, discrimination, and ethics, along with safeguarding. How to put some of these concerns into practice has been an ongoing concern. How to reach the most marginalized; how to include, on the ground, in a practical way, children and young people who are not used to being included; or how to facilitate or contain those who are used to being dominant. How to deal with mental health issues, trauma, and experiences of conflict, abuse, and violence; how to ensure practices are embedded within communities, and both sustainable but also able to cope with change.

These and many other practical considerations have to be the basis of thinking forward, but alongside the conceptual and theoretical bases, recognizing that different cosmologies explain things in different ways, and that the concept of participation, the word, the term, is contested and slippery. We may know what we intend and want to do, but sometimes describing this is difficult, and getting consensus and understanding across language can also be difficult (particularly where there are different expectations of a person's role and behaviour based on their age, gender, disability, ethnicity, and other claimed or ascribed identities). The location of power must also be considered – who has the funds, how do they disburse them, and on what conditions – within families, communities, and states.

The importance of change has become very relevant and apparent over the years of the global pandemic. The lives of children and young people changed, often dramatically. For example, school closures in places changed the lives of girls, not only in terms of domestic work expectations but also increased gender violence and pregnancy (personal review of unpublished research). The pandemic provided new reasons to invest in children's and young people's participation, and organizations. Contributors in this book (see Deepak Chapter 4, Glencorse Chapter 21, Prelis Chapter 19, on Ebola) noted how mechanisms established to deal with some situations subsequently helped during an Ebola crisis. While many contributors spoke about sustainability in community-led work, and child and youth-led work, the importance of developing agile structures that can respond to change becomes very clear during occasions such as the pandemic. The theme in Part Four concerns challenges and opportunities across child and youth rights and meaningful participation.

Mike Wessells (Chapter 24) discusses work in central Africa, particularly around conflict experiences and conflict transformation, and the vital importance of a contextual approach that involves also learning about and understanding local cosmologies. He describes developing processes of ethnography and from that a more culturally grounded approach, that looks to integration of traditional and external, in this case Western, models of practice; finding what works best for what problems and issues. He looks at assumptions and listening gaps in the development of community-led and managed work, and ethical issues.

Beniamino Cislaghi (Chapter 25) describes his work at Tostan, discussing ethical processes, theoretical approaches, and issues in identity; after he went through his transcript, he elected to reformat his interview content more explicitly around five issues and dilemmas he sees emerging from his practice and experience.

Claire O'Kane (Chapter 26) provides a range of examples from practice focused in particular on work on peacebuilding, and issues in the use of adult researchers. She looks at frameworks for practice and particularly at practical factors that contribute to the development and implementation of successful work including the use of participation practice standards. She also looks at the context of children's rights and human rights.

Olga Nieuwenhuys (Chapter 27) looks at her practice work in research and teaching, and the development (along with Karl Hanson, see Chapter 22) of tripartite concepts of living rights, translation, and social justice as a framework for considering children's rights in practice. She looks at questions of why children should want to participate, but also recognizing that children can and do take action, and are taking actions that generally are not seen in that way, for example, unaccompanied minors moving as refugees, children leaving home to escape abuse.

Kavita Ratna (Chapter 28), through a transcript of a short presentation to a Rejuvenate webinar in 2022, talks about children's own demands to be treated as citizens in India, and to be seen as part of the solution not part of the problem. She raises a range of questions related to this, in terms of adult–child relationships and particularly around the duties of adults.

One of the issues raised not only in this part of the book, but throughout, implicitly and explicitly, is the problem of organizations developing, designing, and implementing interventions that pay minimal attention to children's agency; the fact that children do make decisions and take actions. It is a concept that (as practitioners and academics have pointed out here) may be difficult to explain, and so could act as a barrier. Moving forward has to be done in a way that works across communities and practice, academia and practitioners, and local contexts.

CHAPTER 24

Supporting youth agency, decision-making, and action in community-led child protection

Mike Wessells

Background

My interest in youth participation stems from personal experience during Vietnam war protests in the 1960s, when the US was involved in a horrible war that damaged the lives of many civilians and was not only unjustified but also quite immoral. One of the things that struck me was the power of young people.

If I fast forward, a couple of decades I was visiting a refugee camp in Jordan. Dialoguing with Palestinians about the situation there, I stepped aside because most of the discussions were with adults, but there were a lot of youth gathered and quite interested in talking. I sat with them for a couple of days. They taught me a lot about Palestinian history, politics, identity, cultural practices. They showed me the power of youth in that context, really outstripping the term 'participation' as it is usually used. In fact, they were engaged in deep agency and leadership. I saw immediately that I had a lot to learn from them, and the perspectives they were sharing with me were deeper and richer than I was getting from adults. The adults often thought that they could speak for the youth and the children. It was apparent they really could not; there was something about the power of speaking with one's own voice.

It was also about the social positioning of the girls and boys, and the depth of what they could share by virtue of those different positionings. They put a lot of pressure on me; they said there is a lot you can do that we cannot do. They really put it on me to go back to try to work with US Senators and Congress people, and maybe align with different groups to try to be active. They wanted me to lobby for a just US foreign policy, oriented away from hegemonic support for Israel, and more balanced and historically informed support, which I did. It was really quite influential.

Jumping forward again, I have been involved in the psychology of peace and non-violent conflict transformation at least since the early 1980s. Getting young people involved in that has been very central. In the early

1990s, I was a full-time academician who did a lot of activism and youth engagement on the side. I was interested in deepening and expanding that. I got involved with an international NGO in Richmond, in central Virginia: the Christian Children's Fund (now) ChildFund. They were involved in supporting work with children and youth in Angola, where a talented, all Angolan team needed support in documenting what they were doing, also in evaluating and adapting their approach.

Angola: contextual learning

When I first visited in the early 1990s, the voices of young people were beginning to teach the Angolan team that they were partly on the right track, but there were things missing. With the aid of a US consultant they developed an approach that emphasized trauma healing and conceptualized trauma as the main problem. There is no doubt that trauma was an important problem.

One day, a 10-year-old girl came to Carlinda Monteiro, the technical head of the programme and said, 'The government's troops attacked our villages and destroyed our homes. They pulled my parents out into the street and I watched them get murdered.' Carlinda never encouraged people to talk about terrible things, but this girl wanted to talk. She said, 'the worst thing for me was that I had to run away before I could bury them'. Carlinda had the presence of mind to ask, 'why is this so important to you?' The girl said, 'where I live, if we don't perform the Obito, the burial rituals, the parents are not able to cross, to enter the realm of the ancestors and they are agitated, they cause lots of problems, they can cause even death or a variety of problems'. That got under our skin, as it was apparent that we needed to learn from young people, from their perspectives.

In that same context a boy soldier, age 15 or 14 (it was hard to tell, there was no birth registration in Angola at the time), said 'Carlinda, I can't sleep. I am troubled. I am agitated.' She asked, 'why can't you sleep?' He said, 'the man, the spirit of the man that I killed, comes up to me at night and asks me "why did you do that to me?"' That really indicated the strength of the particular cosmology that was guiding the experience and the action of the young people. She asked him, 'what would help you?' He said, 'Where I live, we have traditional healers who can do rituals that appease the angry spirits.'

All this indicated a need for a shift towards a more contextual approach. It was clear that children's own voices and experiences were key in enabling this shift. It was clear in this case that the trauma focus, which was very Western in orientation, made no contact with the traditional cosmology that was dominant in the rural areas. Carlinda got the strength and courage to say, 'I know little or nothing about these cosmologies', even if she herself had a grandmother from a rural area who herself held such beliefs. Carlinda dropped everything and asked if I would accompany her on a journey for ethnographic learning. For the next year or two, when I visited we would work during the day until about 5:30 p.m., have dinner, and from 6 o'clock to about midnight, she would get her ethnographic notes and we would dialogue about what we were learning. What were some of the gaps? What were the variations? How could we use what we were learning about local beliefs to strengthen programming? The good news is ultimately she and her team put children's voices and lived experiences at a much more central level, and found a locally appropriate way to mix local approaches that use traditional healing and spiritual understandings alongside Western approaches. It was basically enabling local communities to pick and choose how they wanted to do things. It was very nice and did not amount to us coming in and imposing trauma perspectives, or cultural perspectives. It was sort of sharing what other communities were talking about. This experience had a big impact on my thinking and approach.

Integrating traditional and Western approaches

Carlinda realized that we needed to give our Angolan teams training on how to learn about local cultural beliefs and practices. She hired Dr Alcinda Honwana, a Mozambican social anthropologist, to train our teams. The teams did ethnographic work in their respective provinces, because there are lots of ethnic groups and linguistic variations. Sometimes, Christianity and outside influences interweaved with indigenous understandings. When Carlinda wanted to integrate the more culturally grounded work, one thing she wanted to do was to make sure that the Western ideas were not thrown out. I supported this too.

As one example, one day in a remote, war-affected area, I was talking with the traditional chief, and there was a young boy, probably four years of age, sitting without speaking, interacting or playing. Other children of the same age were speaking, interacting, and playing with each other. Eventually, I asked the chief the boy's name and 'Does he ever interact with other people?' He doesn't that much; he doesn't speak. 'Has he ever spoken?' Yes, there was a time when he spoke. 'When was the last time that he spoke?' The chief thought for a moment, confirmed with someone else, and they agreed that he had spoken to his family before the village had been attacked, a couple of years ago. He was two years of age; he did not have extensive language development, but he could say typical two-word sentences. Since the village had been attacked and his mother murdered in front of his eyes, he had not spoken. The chief showed no understanding of the psychological or emotional connection there. So, I shared some ideas about why such children might be uncommunicative, and he took an interest. This episode reminded me of the value of sharing knowledge across different cultural systems.

Recognizing this point, Carlinda developed participatory trainings where people could learn together across cultural systems. She would ask questions such as 'what does a child need to be healthy?' In response, people would say 'love', 'care', 'education', 'support', and 'friends', among other things. Out of that, they created an ecological framework around the child and then identified who does those things.

Carlinda and her team also learned about gaps. For example, she asked initially what are the traditional supports for children? People answered that some come from the grandma, the healer, the chief, the herbalist and all these different things. Then she would describe certain situations where she would ask them: what are things traditional practices don't heal? People pointed out that for a broken arm, you should go to the Western health post for that, but if you have spirits talking with you, you definitely want to go to the traditional healer.

Carlinda gave examples of how Western knowledge could potentially be helpful, then asked local people whether they wanted to focus entirely on indigenous, traditional practices or would they also be open to learning outside ways. The examples explored how to heal children, and early care for children. At the time, under-5 mortality rates were very high, due in large part to chronic malnutrition and the fact that mothers did not know to interact with children and provide stimulation. After Carlinda had given these examples, the participants picked and chose what they wanted to learn about, and were interested in. The important thing is that the areas were not imposed by outsiders. Rather than marching in as 'experts', Carlinda and her team took a more humble approach of learning where local people were in their thinking and starting with a focus on their priorities. Over the years, this grounded, respectful, participatory approach has stuck with me.

Assumptions and listening gaps

I work primarily in the field of child protection, also in mental health and psychosocial support. Particularly in child protection, we have a listening gap – we do not take time to listen to and learn about people's lived experiences or to learn about the strengths and assets that they have that could be used to address particular harms to children. In part this gap arises because child protection workers tend to view local people as some of the perpetrators of harms against children. Even though the field understands that families and communities do the heavy lifting in child protection and well-being, there has been a reluctance to start with their own perspectives. Local people are often demonized and viewed as part of the problem. I do not agree. My view is that in every society, the US included, you can find families that horribly abuse children. But these are a minority, and it makes little sense to throw families out of the window as protectors of children. The vast majority of families at least intend to provide a rich, caring, loving environment for children, and we should be learning from them.

A critical lesson is the importance of learning from local people. The most important thing is to be humble and realize whatever context you are trying to work in, you are an outsider. I have worked in Sierra Leone for over

25 years now. But the more I learned, the more I know that I don't know. Sierra Leoneans are the experts on their society, culture, historic context, and the strengths, adversities, challenges, and coping skills. Since they will know it far better than I ever will, it is highly important to start with open listening and empathy. In the child protection sector, open listening and empathy are often limited by our tendencies to judge and impose our own categories. For example, when someone says that sometimes children do heavy work, we leap to the conclusion that there is a problem of child labour. This can be a big mistake since what people call 'heavy work' might not overlap with Western outsider categories. Often, older boys are expected to help with farming, which is necessary for the survival of families and can be done in ways that do not pull children out of school. It is important to understand how families and children themselves view particular activities that are glossed as 'heavy work'.

To learn about children's lived experiences and perspectives, it is valuable to ask questions that are not judgemental and that enable learning. Relevant tools can include rapid ethnography, and narrative methods for older children. With young children, we use games such as body mapping to learn about their perspectives. You can sit with a group of 10 girls, age 6–9, for example. First they draw a figure on the sand or a big sheet of paper and make it a game by asking questions such as 'what's the name of the girl?' The children then colour her hair, give her nice clothes, and a name. We then ask 'What do the eyes see that they like?' The children typically say things like, 'She sees her mother coming home and she is very happy'. Next we ask 'What do the eyes see that they don't like?' The children may say, 'The eyes see the father hitting the mother and they don't like that'. Or they say, 'The eyes see a child who is really sick and does not have enough food, and the girl is sad about it'. We repeat the process with ears and body parts. Asking about different body parts is useful in enabling learning about where people get beaten or are being punished. This approach also gives clues about somatization, or issues or episodes of mental health. All is done in the context of a game with a lot of care not to be talking about individual children's bad experiences.

This game is a powerful tool of learning, and it often discloses issues such as intimate partner violence and child beating that adults seldom discuss. For example, when we did this in the urban slums in Mombasa, Kenya, adults never mentioned dead foetuses on the beach, which were numerous in particular areas as women often did self-abortion at the beach because they lacked access to health care. Young children always mentioned the foetuses, which had a significant psychological impact on the young people. Children also mentioned fathers hitting the mothers and how upsetting that was, whereas adults nearly never mentioned this.

If you are interested in child protection and children's worlds, you have to start with the perspectives of children themselves and then take a developmental approach. The views, situation, experiences, harms, and protective factors are very different for adolescents than for younger children. There are big differences between children under five, or between six and ten, and for older children. Children's views vary tremendously by gender, making it important to keep in mind the power dynamics, social roles, and inequalities between men and women, and the discrimination against girls and women. It's also crucial to think about the social positioning of children, recognizing the importance of social class and factors such as poverty level, disability, and caste that limit people's status and can heighten their protection risks. You cannot just assume that there is an Indian context or an Afghan context. There are hundreds of thousands of micro-contexts buried within these. The micro-contexts are different for children that live and work in the streets, for sex workers, for kids in armed groups, and groups in gangs. You have to be humble and learn from local people and children themselves about their lived experiences.

The view that capturing children's voices is essential and that is what you do and that is the end of it, I think is exploitative, and not helpful. The approach I have been taught by children and by communities is that voice is meaningful only when it is coupled with a true agency. Meaning that in difficult stages, where you are dealing with autocratic societies, elder-dominated societies, adult-centred societies, children have to find the way to have power. You have to do it in a way that does not affect the power balance so much that it puts them at risk. Let me outline two situations I have experienced. One humanitarian and one longer term for development.

Example of successful work

An example of a more child-centred approach came from Afghanistan following US attacks against the Taliban in 2002. I was working in the north in Takhar and Kunduz provinces, which were not that infiltrated by Taliban at that point. The villages were very poor and have lots of child protection issues. I entered following the cultural script of meeting with the *Shura* (all men), talking with elder women, and following that, to children. We wanted ultimately to help communities engage in their own monitoring of, and take actions to correct, harms to children. What most agencies were doing at the time was setting up child protection or welfare committees.

What we did was engage girls and boys separately because of gender norms. They drew pictures of their villages and then identified places that were dangerous and where harms occurred. They also identified places and people that could help them. Afterwards, the question was how this information could be shared with the communities as a whole. The children were very interested in doing drama. So, they went through very respectful channels to the elders and asked if it was possible to do that. The elders agreed with the approach and taught them how to do it in a respectful manner.

One drama showed toddlers moving around in an area where there were uncovered old and unused wells. The toddlers sometimes fell into them and become seriously injured. Following this drama, there was a process of reflection in which numerous village people expressed their concern for the children's well-being and decided on the spot to cover up the old wells. Not waiting for NGOs or outside support, they gathered lumber and constructed covers for those wells. This is a great example of how young people's voices excited community action, and it reminds us that communities themselves can do much on their own to protect their children.

Ethical complexities

Of course, ethical complexities arise when one invites children to identify issues that affect their protection and well-being. For example, if a child identified a teacher who abuses children sexually, that was not going to be the kind of thing said in public. We never silenced a child, but wanted to make it clear that we wanted to help them in a manner that kept their situation confidential and posed no threat of reprisal by the perpetrator.

In learning how to do this, we were guided by advice from Imams, grandmothers, women who were dynamic leaders of local women's associations, and others. This was important because local people had many insights into the situations of children and families, and they understood well the contextual risks associated with reporting. Because we listened to and learned from Afghan colleagues, we developed a contextualized way of understanding and addressing ethical issues. This is quite different from the more usual process of managing ethical issues through an Institutional Review Board of institutions such as Columbia University. The latter is useful up to a point, but lacks context and also the ideas of children (e.g. adolescents) themselves. My view is that to do ethical work, you really have to listen and learn and engage with lots of different actors in the context on an ongoing basis, recognizing that new challenges and complexities will arise continuously.

Community-led work

My day job for the last 10 years has been enabling community-led child protection work in Sierra Leone, Kenya, and India. The approach differs from the more dominant, expert-driven approaches by NGOs, as it puts communities (including children and adolescents) in the driver's seat. This approach came out in an interagency learning initiative on community-based child protection mechanisms that began in 2008. Diverse agencies were involved, including UNICEF, Save the Children, Christian Children's Fund (for which I served as senior adviser on child protection), Plan International, and World Vision, among others.

The participating agencies often set up or facilitated child protection or child welfare committees to help monitor and address violations against children. These committees, formed usually at community level, had some strengths, but also presented challenges in areas such as sustainability, and there was a paucity of evidence regarding their effectiveness. We decided to conduct a global review of these committees, and I had the honour of being the technical lead. One key finding was that approaches that used child welfare committees typically had low levels of child participation. Usually, there was little learning from children and a light look at the context, as agencies tended to set up and facilitate committees using a standard checklist. The committees failed to ignite the tremendous energy and agency of community people and youth, and they seldom achieved a highly positive impact. For the most part, they are unsustainable as they fell apart or became dormant after the external funding had expired.

To address these limitations, we designed the next phase of action research to identify and use a community-led, owned, and managed approach in which children's voices would be front and centre. It would not be children driving the whole process, but children were to be at the centre rather than sitting at the margins. To test it out we selected two countries: Kenya and Sierra Leone, based on the context differences and UNICEF's willingness to support the process there. In both countries, we engaged deeply with community people and also with government stakeholders because we wanted the community process to be linked with the formal system, for purposes of support, sustainability, and because efforts to develop national child protection systems have often marginalized community voices.

To set the stage for the community-led work, we started with rapid ethnography of the kind I described. It involves learning from girls, boys, women, men, people who are positioned differently within their communities. Then, communities began a process of reflection about which harms to children they might want to address. They were supported by a facilitator, who did not guide them in a particular direction, but helped them to create a more inclusive process. To enable inclusivity, the facilitators asked communities a series of reflective questions. When you ask in a community in Sierra Leone, Kenya, or anywhere in sub-Saharan Africa, how they make a decision, they nearly always say, 'We had a big meeting in the chief's *baray* [traditional meeting place], and everybody comes so the whole community is involved'. Next, the facilitator might ask 'I see there is an 11-year-old blind girl lives in that hut, is that right?' After people confirm that the blind girl lives there, the facilitator asks 'Does she go to the meetings in the chief's *baray*?' The community members usually respond by saying that the girl cannot go to the meetings there. Then, the facilitator might ask, 'Are there families who are really poor?' Community people respond decisively that some families are so poor that they only eat one meal a day. When the facilitator asks, 'Do the poorest people go to the meetings in the *baray*?' people explain that the poorest people cannot go to the meetings because they have to do extra work to feed their families. Gradually, the community members realize that the meetings held in the chief's *baray* exclude various people.

Wanting to call attention to the social norms at work in discussions held in the *baray*, the facilitators next ask questions such as, 'Inside the *baray*, do women speak up?' When the community members explain that the men speak first and the women speak only if asked, the facilitator then asks, 'Do the children speak?' As the community members explain that it would not be respectful for children to just speak up, people begin to realize that this is a useful venue but one that does not likely enable extensive input from children and women.

These realizations lead the communities to start dialoguing on how they can create a more inclusive process. If they say they want to meet with the poorest of the poor, the question posed by the facilitator is, 'How could you meet with the poorest of the poor?' Through dialogue and the expression of different points of view, community members usually decide to go and visit the homes of the poorest people and talk with the children. Since such visits could raise ethical issues, the facilitator asks questions such as, 'Is that going to stigmatize them?' Or, 'Is that going to possibly stigmatize children who don't go to school?' This type of dialogue and reflection is a good process. Over the years, I have been impressed by the ability of community people to manage ethics issues in a sensitive manner.

In order to learn more from girls, many communities created small groups and spaces, in which girls discuss harms to children among themselves. The communities realized that girls will not say if older men are abusing them sexually out loud in the community, but are often willing to say this in a small group. The girls do that, and the boys do similarly in their own small groups, with their inputs sent back with no names, usually by an elder or a facilitator, so no particular girl or boy can be identified or tracked down by the perpetrator. This small group process has yielded rich insights into children's lived experiences. Among the harms identified by girls are being out of school, sexual abuse by teachers or uncles, or beatings for disobedience that were very painful and hurtful.

This process helped the communities to become more aware of the lived experiences and challenges faced by young people. More important, it triggered strong concerns over children's well-being. In fact, as communities learned more about the harms to their children, they began asking each other, 'What are we going to do about this?' This question embodies a powerful mixture of collective caring and collective responsibility to ensure the well-being of their children.

This question led into the next phase of the process, which focused on selecting a particular harm or harms to children to address. In this phase, the facilitator worked with communities to consider a range of possible harms to children and to decide collectively which one(s) to address through community-led action. In their discussions, communities sometimes focused on issues that seemed most severe, that is, that inflicted the greatest harm on children. Communities also considered 'gateway' harms that opened the door for children to experience additional harms. Because the point of selecting the harms was to address them in a manner that would reduce or prevent them, communities also considered which harms were feasible to address successfully. Importantly, children's voices become increasingly loud as these discussions continued over a span of several months, as people begin seeing that children and youth had valuable ideas about which issues were most important to address and how to address them. Community people were impressed that children were neither making accusations nor focusing only on the issues that affected them personally but were thinking about the well-being of their families and communities and about change.

In Sierra Leone, the communities chose to address the issue of teenage pregnancy, which frequently leads to school dropout, increased maternal mortality, and related problems. They chose to address the issue through a mixture of peer education about issues of pregnancy and reproductive health and life skills that could lead to good decision-making. Girls and boys were key actors in the community action to address teenage pregnancy. For example, girls and boys conducted street dramas followed by collective reflections and discussions. One drama showed a girl and a boy going to a video hall, drinking alcohol, feeling an attraction, and having unprotected sex that led to a pregnancy, school dropout by both children, and the girl moving out of her home because her family could not afford another mouth to feed. In the second part of this drama, the girl and the boy felt an attraction to each other, discussed their dream of completing their education and starting a family, and used contraceptives as a means of preventing a pregnancy that would force them to end their education. In the animated community discussions that followed the drama, people affirmed the importance of young people staying in school, and they expressed their appreciation for the children's good values and sense of responsibility. Ultimately, the dramas, peer education, and community discussions had an impact on reducing teenage pregnancy.

The insights and actions of children and young people were central to this achievement. In some respects, the children showed better insight than adults into how to achieve the change. I can use my own thinking as an example. As a child protection worker, I was (quietly) a bit disappointed when the communities decided to address teenage pregnancy. Knowing that nearly 40 per cent of the pregnancies came from sexual abuse by older men, I had hoped that communities would address the problems of sexual violence against girls. It turned out that the girls knew better than I did. The girls knew that if they had identified sexual violence against girls as the main issue, the elder men would likely have undermined the work on that issue. Although the elder men would not likely have bought into addressing sexual violence against girls, all the community members recognized teenage pregnancy as a problem that they needed to address. As the community addressed teenage pregnancy, the community became so watchful in preventing teenage pregnancies that men were no longer able to abuse the girls without facing serious repercussions.

It was the insight and leadership of children that enabled this important outcome. In this community-led process, it became clear that the girls and boys had special knowledge. They knew way more why girls became pregnant than adults did. Over time, communities came to see children and adolescents as lead actors, not as beneficiaries and people that should be seen but not heard. They saw them as caring, smart, and willing to work with parents, elders, and adults.

The agency and constructive repositioning of children that occurred in this process are quite different from what one often sees in NGO-led processes that encourage children's participation via children's groups or clubs that conduct children's projects. Such approaches feature adults allowing children to have agency in a confined space, with adults still calling the shots and acting as the key decision-makers. In contrast, the community-led approach described above unlocks the agency and creativity of children and young people, enabling them to become influential in their communities in addressing child protection issues that are of collective concern. An important question for all of us is, 'Are we doing enough to listen to children, recognize their agency and creativity, and enable them to guide us in supporting children's well-being?'

Funding

To support community-led work, we need to help donors to be more flexible and move away from pressing for quick results requiring preconceived interventions and working according to log-frames with pre-specified time frames. If communities are to take ownership of an approach, it has to be led by them. This requires working according to community time rather than to predetermined time schedules. When communities take ownership of the process, they design and mobilize community-led actions that fit the local context, build on the strengths, assets, and networks that are already present, and achieve sustainability. Sustainability is really important since for the average child protection project, the end of external funding leads the work and any positive outcomes for children to subside or even collapse. Sustainability is key not only for fulfilling the Sustainable Development Goals but also for supporting children across different phases of child development. Also, in an age of protracted armed conflicts and emergencies, it seems well advised to think in terms of 'the nexus' rather than regard humanitarian and development work as comprising separate realms. I sincerely hope that donors will become more interested in and supportive of community-led approaches, which in an era of localization, enable much greater power sharing with local communities.

Community-led approaches and participation

In the NGO world, there is extensive attention to participatory approaches, but much of it is light participation. In some cases, NGOs predefine an issue such as violence against children and get communities to help them address these issues. Although this is not a bad thing, how much better would it be if communities were self-reliant and did not depend on outside NGOs to define and lead the work on addressing child protection issues.

Within the global child protection sector, the dominant approach is more community-based approaches rather than community-led approaches, although both are included in the global *Child Protection Minimum Standards*. The difference is that most community-based approaches are partnership approaches, where the NGO decides what the issue is based on an assessment, the results of which are fed back to the community. They encourage people to partner with them and to implement the intervention that is indicated based on global standards such as the INSPIRE collection of intervention standards. Because the NGO defines the issue, leads the assessment, and guides the implementation and documentation of the intervention, communities are relegated to the back seat – they have limited agency and correspondingly limited ownership and sustainability. Usually, children's involvement is limited, and their participation is tightly guided and limited by adults. Often, NGOs engage mostly with children who are better off, and they do not take the time required to build the deep trust needed to reach and work with children such as those who live and work on the streets, engage in dangerous forms of labour, etc. In the child protection world, then, we have a long way to go to fulfilling children's agency and participation rights in a meaningful way. Community-led approaches offer a useful means of enabling greater participation, including by children who had often been marginalized.

The work being done globally on climate change illustrates the power of young people's voice, agency, and influence. It is time to do away with the older notions that 'children are to be seen but not heard' or that it is somehow unfair or too burdening to enable children and youth to grapple with the world's most intractable problems. These problems have already affected young people, regardless of whether we have encouraged their participation. Perhaps now more than ever, we need to recognize that the abilities of young people to develop creative solutions is one of our most important resources for developing well-being and a sustainable future.

References

Stark, L., Macfarlane, M., King, D., Lamin, D., Lilley, S. and Wessells, M. (2014) *A Community-driven Approach to Reducing Teenage Pregnancy in Sierra Leone: Midline evaluation*. London: Save the Children.

Wessells, M.G. (2015) 'Bottom-up approaches to strengthening child protection systems: Placing children, families, and communities at the center', *Child Abuse & Neglect: The International Journal* 43: 8–21. http://dx.doi.org/10.1016/j.chiabu.2015.04.006

Wessells, M.G. (2018) *A Guide for Supporting Community-led Child Protection Processes*. New York: Child Resilience Alliance.

Wessells, M.G. and Monteiro, C. (2000) 'Healing wounds of war in Angola: A community-based approach', in D. Donald, A. Dawes, and J. Louw (eds), *Addressing childhood adversity*, pp. 176–201. Cape Town: David Philip.

Wessells, M., Kostelny, K. and Ondoro, K. (2014) *A grounded view of community-based child protection mechanisms and their linkage with the wider child protection system in three urban and rural areas of Kenya: Summary and integrated analysis.* London: Save the Children.

CHAPTER 25

Humanizing child well-being interventions: the beginning of a journey

Beniamino Cislaghi

Background

After several years volunteering in non-formal education of children (as an educator, a trainer, and a national director), I began to work within the so-called international child protection system in 2009. I conducted a multi-year research for UNICEF that resulted in the book *Values Deliberations and Community Development* (Cislaghi et al., 2016) and did a PhD on gender and child protection (Cislaghi 2018a). Once I finished my PhD, I worked as a research director for the NGO Tostan in Senegal, an organization that includes child protection work in a larger approach of, as I like to call it, harmonious community development. Their work is carefully designed to facilitate collective empowerment that changes dynamics of dominance into dynamics of liberation, where everyone collaborates interdependently towards a collective goal of better community life. Their three-year Community Empowerment Programme, designed by Senegalese experts in consultation with community members, creates intergenerational dialogues that open new avenues of imagination and action for community members by fostering internal incentives to change through Freirian pedagogical strategies (see Gillespie and Melching, 2010). Today, most of my work is at the research/practice intersection between decolonial imagination, gender equality, and child protection. As an Associate Professor at the London School of Hygiene & Tropical Medicine, I teach and conduct research on ethics of international development, where important questions related to child participation frequently arise. As I look at the issues riddling child participation, five come to mind: the maturity dilemma; working for liberation in an oppressive system; performative social justice action and participation; responsibility and reciprocity in the human rights framework; and how the internal conditions of the implementer are the most unexpected factor of success.

The maturity dilemma

As part of my PhD, I spent some time in a village in West Africa. In the first village meeting, I spontaneously sat among people of my age. The elders told me to move and go to the children's section: I didn't have children of my own, so that was my place. As I stood there, a 30-year-old among 5- to 15-year-olds, I noticed these children were in a way more mature than me: some were carrying their siblings on their backs, others just came back from work with the cows or gathering wood, and all knew how to use medicinal herbs around the village. In that village I was, undisputedly, a child, and probably a fairly inept one. What would that child-like status, I wondered, allow me to do and not to do if I were not an outsider?

There I was, a weird-looking 30-year-old child. What judgements would people have made about my capacities? What freedoms and agency would I be granted? I was facing the maturity dilemma. At what point in a child's life can they make autonomous decisions about their life?

Children's capacities to make decisions surely evolve with age. Different children are granted different degrees of agency on their different life decisions, varying from 1) complete control; 2) control with adult supervision; 3) having a consultative role while an adult takes the final decision; and 4) passively accepting a decision that is forced upon them. As newcomers in a complex world of social interactions, children are granted agency when they demonstrate they can play by the rules of the older members, the adults. The more newborns, toddlers, children, and adolescents are (often inevitably because of psychological, social if not even biological reasons) in a dependency relation with adults (requiring their financial support, their social care, their advice, or their love, for instance), the less they can disenfranchise themselves from having to follow decisions that adults take for them. As they mature, children's decision-making boundaries are thus continuously renegotiated bi-dimensionally (using Gaventa's (2006) language, across visible and hidden power lines). On any given occasion, children and adults negotiate children's agency in: 1) setting the agenda of what decisions children can take, and 2) taking decisions over the points included in that agenda. For instance, a child might not be given the option of whether they should get dressed or not to go to school, but they might be allowed to choose what they want to wear. Or, as another example, they might not be given the option to get married or not when they turn 12 years, but they might be given the chance to participate in the decision of whom they should marry.

In their struggle for recognition and agency, children strive to gain greater control on their lives, moving across the cracks in the power system to increase their agentic boundaries. Here's a real-life example relevant to child protection work. Over my time as a researcher, I was involved with several studies on child marriage that eventually shaped an informal network of colleagues studying the practice across different countries in the world. Now, child marriage is a very complex phenomenon, and evidence shows that it's often associated with a plethora of negative health and development outcomes. A large amount of well-intentioned funding goes into eradicating it. In many instances, marriage is forced upon children, disproportionately girls, who would rather not get married. In that case a social protection system grounded on children's individual rights seems to me relatively easy to apply: the child protection system must protect these children from engaging in something they don't want to do. As for the processes to do so, I believe in conciliatory processes, rather than punitive ones; that is, processes that help parents and communities to understand the suffering that children are exposed to when forced or pressured into marriage and to reframe their local cultural narratives to help children be seen and humanized.

The opposite case, however, when children intentionally (and at times secretly from their parents) initiate actions that will result in their marriage, is more challenging. Several colleagues and I noticed a pattern, in Somalia, in Cameroon, in Cambodia, in Honduras, for instance, of adolescents who said they themselves wanted to get married. The reasons children provided varied: some, for instance, simply wanted to experience sex and, in a society where premarital sex was counter-normative, feared the sanctions that would come to them if they did so outside of marriage. Others wanted to escape abusive situations at home. Others again associated marriage with social prestige and wanted to obtain that. And others again were just in love. To force their parents to accept their marriage, some of these adolescents would elope with their partner for a couple of nights. Once back, the normative system that shamed families for premarital sex forced parents to accept and support their wedding.

What is an NGO to do in these cases? Who decides what is the best interest of the girl child, especially when different opinions, the child's, the parents', the national and international child protection systems', clash? When a girl wants to get married, and their parents and families agree, and possibly so does the national legislative and moral system, what questions, what ethical and moral questions, do international NGO staff members and grant-makers need to ask themselves to design purposeful interventions? Should the NGO accept child marriage and advocate for easier divorces and greater social protection for the vulnerable spouse? Should the NGO design behavioural change interventions that convince children and their families that child marriage is not a good thing? Should the NGO find ways to engineer a worldview in these societies that suggests premarital protected sex is desirable, but marriage is not? And, most importantly, when all these systems diverge as to what is, in fact, in the best interest of the child, what system of values can be used that can help actors across these systems decide?

There is, in other words, an elephant-sized can of worms in the child participation room that only few are willing to open: when, how, and what can a child decide?

When, how, and what can a child decide?

The shaping of purposeful and expansive child participation practices pivots around the unsolved question of, when do children become adults? The 18-year-old threshold used by international organizations is based on a legal document, the UNCRC. Clearly, a threshold is needed for administrative efficiency (for example, a state needs to have a one-size-fits-all to grant citizens the right to vote, drink, or drive) but the age at which the threshold should fall for allowing children to make different decisions and take different actions (voting, drinking, marrying, having sex) is disputable. This is why countries set an age of majority but grant people different rights at different ages. The maturity threshold could be 16, 21 or even 30 (as it was at a certain point in the Roman empire). Based on what criteria do we grant permission to a human to increasingly participate in the decisions affecting their life? Parents of more than one child might know this too well: one sibling might be responsible at age 9 already, so that they trust them to walk to school alone, while their older sibling was only allowed to do so at age 12. NGO work is somewhat caught in between the state's view on maturity, defining clear age cut-offs, and that of the communities that NGOs mean to help, where biological age counts less than social and psychological traits of maturity.

Surprisingly (or maybe not), science seems to be more on the side of communities than the state. The evidence about how children develop seems to suggest an uneven process that varies for different brain functions, so that nobody can be said to be thinking as 'a child' one day and as 'an adult' a week later. For instance, the prefrontal cortex of the brain, which is the part responsible for emotional control and future planning, generally doesn't complete its development until a human reaches 25 years of age (Arain et al., 2013). Other parts of the brain develop at different rates: while the part responsible for logical reasoning is largely formed at age 16, other parts continue their growth well into adulthood – including the capacity for self-restraint (see Icenogle et al. 2019). But, while these are biological averages, human brain development can present significant differences among different people. In other words, as far as we know, it's considerably challenging to identify a single marker of adulthood that can help set an age threshold to decide when a human being can be trusted to make important decisions about their life, such as whether to practise safe sex or not, when to get married, or what university course to follow.

Differences aren't only biological. Even more important (and concerning) for the purpose of our conversation are cultural differences. Evidence suggests that children living in cultures where they are trusted in early age with adult-like responsibilities exhibit earlier personality maturation: rites of passage that give children roles associated with adulthood (such as marriage, having children, having a job) increase the speed at which a child matures. But here's the catch: those rites are now largely delayed in industrialized settings (most of which are in the Global North) and high-income, highly educated, more culturally globalized families (independently of their country of residence).

If the research above is right, we might be living in a global system in which children in one industrialized country (say, for instance, where the NGO headquarters are) are maturing more slowly than children in the rural parts of another given country (where the NGO programmes are carried out). But to obtain a job in the echelon of international development, certain skills are required that can only be obtained through extensive education: a university degree or the knowledge of a second language, for instance. Is it fair then to apply cross-culturally frameworks of participation and agency that are shaped by the people who experience a maturity development very differently from that of the children for whom they are designing interventions? How are we to reconcile the paradox of individual and cultural differences of brain development in Western-led, outcome-driven, population-level, fast-paced interventions implemented in the non-Western world?

Working for liberation in an oppressive system

When I was working on child labour in Côte d'Ivoire, one day a mother told me her struggle. 'I know that my daughter shouldn't be working with me in the plantation, that she'd better go to school. But I have no means to survive otherwise. Our grandparents used to live with the produce of their cultivation, it was a simpler life; we had less things but that gave us more freedom. Now that we depend on the money we generate; we don't have the luxury of going to school anymore.'

Because of the paradox of having to design population interventions that accommodate individual differences, one might ask whether we are left with a choice between 1) colonial interventions that apply Western worldviews in non-Western contexts, and 2) complete inaction. It is tempting to reason in similar dualities. On the one hand one could consider epidemiological evidence alone: child marriage is bad because it harms children's physical health, and that alone justifies the design of behavioural change interventions to eradicate it. On the other hand you might have people advocating for withdrawal and inaction: let people be and mind our own business.

I believe a third, middle way exists, for which we possess many examples: intervention approaches that can wrestle with the complexities of decolonizing praxis by contextualizing action within the niche in which each child lives and thrives. These approaches are flexible, understand the conditions that shape a child's life and adapt to their life, striving to help them achieve lives that truly matter to them. Similar slow-paced, people-centred approaches, however, struggle to emerge as the appropriate norm in funding and implementation. Behind practical challenges (the need for long inception phases, the challenge of guaranteeing multi-year funding, the need for strategies to report on varying and unexpected community outcomes, *et cetera*), I believe there is an important conceptual reason why the system of incentives in the development machine is not letting go of outcome, process, and timing control.

This reason, and please allow me a complex narrative at this point, is rooted in an illusion that virtuous development action will generate exclusively positive results. We know that's impossible. Not only will different people have different ideas of what 'positive' means, but it's ontologically impossible for an intervention to not generate suffering of some kind. For two reasons. The first is that any action brings suffering of some sort. To make an example close to us: in the intent to nourish a child, a positive action, we buy food that – even with the most ethically traded – has generated suffering of some kind such as on the plant, the animals, the environment, the people who have harvested it. As an even more relevant example, child labour can deny children their right to go to school, play, and more generally experiment with life in important formative years. At the same time, however, it helps them contribute to the economic survival of their families, in conditions that might require them to do so. Child marriage can be harmful to a girl's health and well-being but might guarantee survival of her family. Our interventions are designed as they are because we value certain things, for example, the girl's health, over others, such as the family's survival through marriage.

The second reason is that these interventions take place within a global economic and social system that sustains itself through exploitation and violence. The international hyper-capitalist, hyper-colonial, hyper-materialistic order ultimately resists justice, equality, liberation, critical education, and political participation. As we operate within that system, we need to accept that our interventions will generate suffering of some sort. We can, however, decide consciously which suffering is aligned with the moral values of our institutions, as well as our own. We can, in other words, create pockets of moral compromise that we are comfortable with because they are grounded within a thoughtful and transparent system of values.

The conversation on what to do to help the world's children should thus begin identifying the values we intend to embody both as people and as institutions. Firstly, our institutions need to create practical and operationalizable value systems. Secondly, they need to create matrices to orient their action and interventions using those values, to make sure they operate within the moral boundaries and compromises that they are ready to accept.

I believe in the value of a theoretical framework that supports the creation of similar decolonial interventions, to which feminist gender theory and decolonial theories are central (see video in Lancet Commission on Gender and Global Health (2021)). This multidisciplinary framework brings together, among others, Freire's insights into conscientizing cooperation for mutual liberation, Arendt's and De Beauvoir's philosophical existentialism, Gramsci's understanding of hegemonic discourses, and Bandura's work on self-efficacy. It can be helpful in understanding how humans at the core of global power create hegemonic discourses that get exported to the periphery of the world (Arendt, 1958).

Liberatory existential categories can and indeed do flourish from the bottom up. Liberation doesn't need to be led by outsiders. I wrote a paper (Cislaghi, 2018b) on how people in a Senegalese village developed a new cognitive schema for women (that I dubbed the 'now-women'). People spoke about women as if they did something different: now women do this, now women say that. They embodied new cognitive schemas in their daily life and allowed that schema to replace what they held before as immutable for women. Now women spoke in meetings, had good ideas, could manage the finances of the household. Breaking cycles of violence that stop harmful repetition doesn't require changing worldviews from the outside in; rather, children and their families can change common schemas of oppression together, expanding their aspirational map together, moving their collective imagination in directions that are completely unexpected and surprising for the outside implementer.

Performative social justice action and participation

A third issue relates to the fact that decolonial participation practice can be enacted perfunctorily. Decolonial theory invites us to break black and white dichotomies, asking who is embodying a colonial mind, independently of the colour of their skin; that is, investigating what are the colonial attitudes and approaches that people are embodying as they design child protection interventions. Can the upper-class, Western educated elite from Nairobi represent a disempowered and exploited poor child living as a nomad, migrating from Somalia and living in northern Kenya?

We are wrestling with core questions of building movements of social justice that do not repeat the same greedy power-grabbing of the globally oppressing system that we have experienced since our birth. We are aware of the paradox of social justice: we know that, on the one hand, the majority of the people in the world are actively penalized by a system designed to subjugate them and that, at the same time there can be immense power in the performance of the victim narrative in a system that is morally committed to transform itself for greater social justice. Freire (1970) was very conscious of this paradox when he wrote that change can happen only if oppressors and oppressed work together, connect at an emotional, not only at a cognitive, level and liberate each other. He suggested that social struggles for justice will be victorious not because they will flip hierarchies in a broken system, but when they are able to reimagine this current system of violence to transform it into a system of care. In a system of care each person thinks about helping others; they are focused on their responsibility of care towards others at least as much as they think about their own rights. In similar systems, people trust that someone else will help them when they need it. However, this seems hard in the current approach to social justice, which feels more like a boxing match than a mutually caring dismantling of oppression.

Using a Hegelian paradox: how can the slave take care of the master if the slave is only trying to get rid of them and get more power for themselves?

Can children and adults, people of different genders, people of different skin colours, let go of the idea of power as a zero-sum game (requiring some sort of rebalancing), and operate in a system where we are all disempowered by our collective human oppression and can move towards a world where everyone will awaken to greater compassionate power? Unless the slave and the master work together to reject the system that they were complicit in creating, acknowledging the suffering that the system creates for each other, any new system that emerges from the rubble of revolution will be representing the same violence, the same hate, the same suffering.

True social justice requires a moral revolution

But of course, a moral revolution is necessary to change a system that incentivizes us to dehumanize each other in order to grab as much as we can in a fight for survival. In the current hegemonic moral system, where people feel unsafe (without health coverage, with a mortgage, isolated from others and nature, reliant upon money to survive, detached from death and in the illusion of eternal life), the accumulation of money and power seems the only means to guarantee material and psychological safety in the face of an unknown future. In Europe (and later the whole Western world) the disentanglement of spirit and matter that followed the Enlightenment failed to replace spiritual values with secular ones. The capitalist global order that rose in the 19th century with the Industrial Revolution gave birth to a dominant worldview in which having money counted more than being kind. Without the profound belief in an afterlife (or at least the social belief), the God of the dollar is the only one left to worship. This is not to say that religious systems are caring by constitution: there existed extremely religious historical capitalist figures and we are all aware of the moral deformities that Christian, Islamic, Buddhist, and Hinduist institutions (among others) showed the world in recent human history. Performing religion to create a hierarchy among humans is different from adopting a spiritual path that leads to compassion. The first can easily (and indeed in the past it did) become a violent colonial action to grab power, the latter is an open-hearted jump into the unknown.

Performative and real participation

Performative action in social justice frameworks gives rise to tokenistic participation efforts. Often spoken about as one, if not *the*, solution to the limitations of traditional international development efforts, child participation is at times only performed to obtain funding and support, rather than fully integrated across the whole intervention cycle from grant-making to long-term evaluations. Part of the reason for performative approaches to child participation is that, taken seriously, implementing child participatory approaches requires wrestling with important ethical questions that have practical relevance. Some of these, for instance, include: what does 'participation' mean in the first place? How does children's agency change across contexts and ages, and with that their capacity to take decisions? Who should decide when is good for a child to participate and to what extent? How can somebody assess which decisions should be left to children, which decisions should be taken for them, and what options exist in between these two extremes? How does the current system of incentives in international development (dominated by outcome-driven interventions, pay-per-delivery funding, unrealistically fast behavioural change expectations, to cite three) contribute to, if not even reward, performative participatory approaches? What moral, legal, social, psychological, even spiritual frameworks are available to policy-makers and activists to guide their decisions?

Child participation activities are often designed under the belief that children should be empowered to say no to their parents who force children to comply with harmful practices, such as child marriage, FGC, labour. That's done under the belief that some people, often the implementers, have a clear and indisputable idea of what is in the best interest of the child. What is to be done, however, when parents are forcing children into a given action for their own good? Serious complexities arise when adults (whose frontal cortex is fully formed) force children (whose capacity to plan for the future is limited) to undertake certain actions because they genuinely believe these actions will guarantee their survival and help them succeed later in life. In a village surrounded by hyenas, ensuring that children do not leave alone might save their life. Uncritical participatory child protection approaches see expansion of children's agency as their ultimate goal. That's largely because those interventions focus on hard final outcomes that can be reported to donors. They might aim to rebalance child/elder relationships that have been shaped by generations of social interactions. These relationships might be both, non-dualistically helpful and harmful. Instead of helping the 'slave' and the 'master' work together to understand how their relationships of power are contributing to hold in place a system of suffering, interventions are often unwittingly designed to flip the existing power balance. Similar interventions have one raw outcome in mind (for example, expanding children's agency to resist their parents' decisions), a one-size-fits-all approach that, in reality, only fits specific situations.

The 'International Development Machine' is often a complex juggernaut of policies and implicit values that rushes and hurries, grinding interventions to finance its own survival. To care truly about children requires a slowing down, a refusal of incentives and matrices of success that are based on financial survival and hard outcomes, embracing a truly collaborative process that might result in the reduced possibility to work with the most outcome-based and top-down financing bodies. Truly participatory approaches work with children to unlock imagination of what could be different in their lives and who we need to work with to make it happen in a conciliatory way.

That action, to care for children while letting go of outcome anxiety, is difficult because of the power imbalances in the development machines.

Even in the rare situations where enlightened donors are mindful of their power to ask local NGOs to develop their own agendas, these NGOs have been socialized in a world where satisfying the donor ensures their own survival. Similarly, academics are pressured by a system of incentives that requires them to publish and get funding. In these complex and harmful power agendas, the children are dehumanized, commodified into means to an end, be it grants or papers. To continue these important conversations, we need a renewed market-independent group engaging with similar ethical questions. That is something that I and others are now working to establish.

Responsibility and reciprocity in the human rights framework

A few years ago, I was sitting at night under the West African sky with a man and his elder mother. They were feeding the cows coming back from grazing. We were talking about human rights, and they were sharing their wisdom. They liked human rights, but, they said, something was missing: the responsibility that we hold to each other, to help each other live a life of dignity. That cannot be done by receiving only. If we all receive, who is giving?

Because large amounts of money and power are absorbed and controlled by institutions in the Global 'Core', many interventions are designed and implemented using uncritical Western human rights approaches that foster strong individualistic worldviews. Don't get me wrong, I am a fan of human rights. The human rights discourse can be very powerful and has the potential of setting a baseline under which nobody should have to live, guaranteeing a threshold of dignity that every human should enjoy. Yet, the current approach to human rights is often individualistic, in stark contrast with social life that is ontologically relational. Individuals have both entitlements and responsibilities towards each other. One's human rights cannot be attained without the responsibility of the community towards that person. One might have a human right to clean water, yet they also have the responsibility to not waste it. One might have a human right to free speech, yet they also have the responsibility to not abuse it in ways that intend to harm others. Entitlements are important safeguards of dignity, but need to be used with pro-social intentions that aim at the greater good of self and the other living beings, non-human animals, and the world at large included. We have built an international governance system with aspirational intents and processes for protecting people's human rights, but still we struggle with systems to hold people accountable for their reciprocal responsibilities: it's easy to design interventions and policies that intervene when someone's right is breached, but it's much more complex to design and implement accountability systems for those not aligning their actions with the moral responsibilities that can ensure a balanced global system and non-violent relationships of care.

The work of the NGO Tostan that I studied during my PhD shines a light on practical approaches that embody a balanced rights/responsibility approach (see Cislaghi, 2018a). Their work aims to elevate community members in their wholeness. Not rebalancing unequal power dynamics that disadvantage one group by giving greater power to this one group, but helping members of the community as a whole recognize their complicity in an unhelpful status quo that generated suffering for some, if not all.

I mentioned above that interventions lack reciprocity. There is an adultist arrogance in believing that there is nothing we can learn from children themselves. That interventions are unidirectional. Decolonizing child participation activities requires humility to understand that there is much that can be learned in the generative cross-cultural interaction that interventions can facilitate. Development only happens as part of a reciprocal interdependent relationship, when it becomes a place of conversation where together people of different cultures can reimagine this global system of oppression to break the cycles of violence that bind us across time and space.

The internal conditions of the implementer are the most neglected factor of success

Effective child participation requires implementers to have 1) critical knowledge, 2) psychological equilibrium, and 3) right moral intention. If international development actors' subconscious is dominated by feelings of inadequacy, or they are worried about ensuring they have health insurance, or money to pay college fees, their intention will be easily, and, don't get me wrong, very understandably, corrupted, masquerading self-survival as aid. If the implementers (and the donors) carry unresolved fears and delusional knowledge, they might do all they can to implement rule-abiding actions, even when these are contrary to the moral principles that should direct ethical decolonial work. Conversely, if implementers have a genuine motivation to help children, then they won't be distracted by the seducing hallucination of running after financial resources to ensure the survival of their institution or the funding of their job. When they will need to choose between following the desires of a founding institution or government or those of children and their families, they will be able to align their action with their value matrix and act ethically.

Let me explain this more. One of the most innovative thinkers on child protection I have met, Dr Mathpati, introduced me to the following matrix of Dharma Sankar, which I simplified for the purpose of this conversation, derived from the Mahabharata (see video in Ranjan (2020) for more information). Note this is my own crude simplified interpretation of a piece of millennia-old wisdom. Anyone interested should watch the video and read more knowledgeable sources on it.

In one's action ...	Rules are respected	Rules are **not** respected
Principles are respected	1. The good human	4. The hero
Principles are **not** respected	3. The bureaucrat	2. The destroyer

The principles, the 'dharma', are all about helping the other. Almost always, the dharma demands oneself to help others even when doing so comes at a cost for oneself.

When the rules and the principles are aligned (quadrant 1), there is little to no moral conflict. When a social, economic, and political system is so well designed (which is rare) that one's material advantage comes with helping others too, virtuous action flows naturally. This is not to say that some might still prefer to break the rules to achieve greater power and resources, but in a perfect system there would be no need for that.

When one's actions break both the rules and the moral principles guiding pro-social intentions (quadrant 2) one takes on the role of the destroyer. They are completely self-absorbed, reacting to internal trauma, exclusively seeking self-realization and material gain in their job.

Similarly (in quadrant 3), when one respects the rules of a given system when it requires sacrifice of pro-social moral principles, people (at times, unwittingly) safely defend their position in ways that make them untouchable: if the rule is respected, the fault is not with the self, but with the system. It's the role of the existential bourgeois, the self-invested bureaucrat who protects their position, power, and resources, even at the cost of sacrificing pro-social moral intention.

Finally, when a person takes on the risk of breaking away from the rules to follow their aspiration for greater good (quadrant 4), they expose themselves to potentially losing their own gain to follow a superior system of internal moral values – even when it costs them their job, reputation, or resources. Colonial international development work often sits in the quadrant 3, where following the rules imposed by powerholding and resource-controlling institutions is more seducing than the opposite: refusing compromise with a system of exploitation in order to achieve meaningful moral action that helps children and their families live lives that profoundly matter to them.

In practice, moving from quadrants 3 to 4 requires us to wrestle with questions such as: how long an inception phase is being allowed in a grant? How long is the engagement with community planned for? How stringently are the grant outcomes defining the intervention success? What is the role of children and their family in designing the grant and the intervention, and then evaluating it? How are the personnel of the donor or implementing organization taking responsibility for unintended outcomes directly with the populations involved?

The vision for a way out and forward

I believe we need the following things. First, we need to establish new norms of acceptable intervention design and grant-making, or we will continuously replicate a capitalist and colonial system of arrogant oppression. Second, we need an anti-academic space of knowledge generation that can crack the Western wall of knowledge and develop new research methods that allow the queering of what we hold as good and true through new generative imaginative worldviews. Third, we need a holistic school of child protection and rights, a place where workers in this space can gather with the purpose of exploring new visions of how they can act in the industry by liberating themselves of their own greed, delusions, and fears. Fourth, we need to break siloed approaches to child protection and rights, and cultivate inter-departmental child-led strategies for that care for children's desires, and wrestle with the complexity of defining children's agentic boundaries. Fifth, we need people-oriented solutions (rather than problem-oriented) to foster a moral revolution within the international development industry. Sixth, we need to create institutional value matrices that can help us understand which compromises institutions are ready to make and why. And seventh, we need to embark on an uneasy spiritual humanizing journey to uncover the suffering that this system is creating and take responsibility for it.

References

Arain, M., Haque, M., Johal, L., Mathur, P., Nel, W., Rais, A., Sandhu, R. and Sharma, S. (2013) 'Maturation of the adolescent brain', *Neuropsychiatric Disease and Treatment* 9: 449–461. https://doi.org/10.2147/NDT.S39776

Arendt, H. (1958) *The Human Condition*. Chicago: University of Chicago Press.

Bandura, A. (1977) *Social Learning Theory*. Englewood Cliffs, NJ: Prentice Hall.

de Beauvoir, S. (1972 [1949]) *The Second Sex*. Harmondsworth: Penguin.

Cislaghi, B. (2018a) *Human Rights and Community-led Development: Lessons from Tostan*. Edinburgh: Edinburgh University Press. https://doi.org/10.3366/edinburgh/9781474419796.001.0001

Cislaghi, B. (2018b) 'The story of the "now-women": Changing gender norms in rural West Africa', *Development in Practice* 28(2): 257–268. https://doi.org/10.1080/09614524.2018.1420139

Cislaghi, B. (2019) *The Potential of a Community led Approach to Change Harmful Gender Norms in Low and Middle Income Countries*. London: ALiGN, ODI.

Cislaghi, B., Gillespie, D. and Mackie, G. (2016) *Values Deliberation and Collective Action: Community empowerment in rural Senegal*. Cham: Palgrave Macmillan. https://doi.org/10.1007/978-3-319-33756-2

Freire, P. (1970) *Pedagogy of the Oppressed*. New York: Seabury Press.

Gaventa, J. (2006). Finding the Spaces for Change: A Power Analysis. IDS Bulletin (Brighton. 1984), 37(6), 23–33. https://doi.org/10.1111/j.1759-5436.2006.tb00320.x

Gillespie, D. and Melching, M. (2010) 'The transformative power of democracy and human rights in nonformal education: The case of Tostan'. *Adult Education Quarterly* 60(5): 477–498.

Gramsci, A. *(1971) Selections from the Prison Notebooks of Antonio Gramsci*. New York: International Publishers.

Icenogle, G., Steinberg, L., Duell, N., Chein, J., Chang, L., Chaudhary, N., Di Giunta, L., Dodge, K. A., Fanti, K. A., Lansford, J. E., Oburu, P., Pastorelli, C., Skinner, A.T., Sorbring, E., Tapanya, S., Uribe Tirado, L.M., Alampay, L.P., Al-Hassan, S.M., Takash, H.M.S. and Bacchini, D. (2019) 'Adolescents' cognitive capacity reaches adult levels prior to their psychosocial maturity: Evidence for a "maturity gap" in a multinational, cross-sectional sample'. *Law and Human Behavior* 43(1): 69–85. https://doi.org/10.1037/lhb0000315

Lancet Commission on Gender and Global Health (2021) 'LCGGH: A journey into the messy nexus of agency, international justice and global health' [video]. YouTube, 31 March. https://www.youtube.com/watch?v=9WqSLf7AdQg

Ranjan, R. (2020) 'Business Sutra: 2 × 2 Leadership Matrix from Ramayana & Mahabaratha by Devdutt Pattanaik' [video]. YouTube, 8 April. https://www.youtube.com/watch?v=JJePaDnMrkk

CHAPTER 26

Reflections on children's participation practice: looking back and forward

Claire O'Kane

Background

I came into child rights work through volunteering with a local NGO Butterflies Programme of Street and Working Children in India, headed by Rita Panicker. My first time volunteering with them, for five months, was in 1995. The working children were very organized and the whole organization was based on a participatory approach. At this time, I got involved in some participatory research within the organization. The organization was kind of ahead of its time. It was already working from a rights-based approach before the broader rights-based work took off in international child rights NGOs a few years later. The way of working in Butterflies all made sense to me. It was like finding this is what makes sense, to really focus on rights, to listen to children, to find out the solution.

Butterflies had a children's council that was the basis of all their decision-making. The children were organized at that time at a working children's union, and they had a working children's newspaper group, a theatre group, a health cooperative, a credit union. It was very organized and all about collective work and children's own analysis of the problem.

Later, I returned to work with them; I volunteered for them for almost three years in the late 1990s and then I worked for Save the Children for a number of years. In the last eight years I have worked as a freelance child rights consultant, involved in a number of participatory research and participatory evaluation processes. Actually, thinking about some child rights situation analysis [CRSA] that I have been involved in, that is also a good example of participatory research. Even though it is an analysis of something, there is still a lot of the same principles of participatory research in undertaking good situation analysis with children and young people. I think that supporting participatory CRSA is a practical example whereby children's views and analysis do directly influence programmes or strategic planning. A few years ago, I was involved in supporting Save the Children Cambodia to implement a CRSA, and we worked with youth facilitators as part of our team. We had a whole series of consultations for analysis processes with children, involving young people in the broader final analysis workshop to bring together the findings.

In the last year and a half, I have been involved in supporting Kindernothilfe, a German child-focused organization. I have also been mentoring their staff and partners to implement participatory CRSAs, involving children in consultations and in the analysis. I have been involved in other types of participatory research on kinship care in East Africa, West and Central Africa, as well as with Syrian refugees in Jordan. I also supported a participatory evaluation on children's and youth participation in peacebuilding in Nepal, Colombia, and eastern Democratic Republic of Congo supporting evaluation teams involving children and youth representatives. Plus, I have been involved in participatory research and advocacy with and by working children in countries across Asia, Africa, the Middle East, and Latin America.

Factors for successful participation

Whether it is participatory research or analysis or evaluation, a lot of the enabling or hindering factors are quite similar. The main enabling factor is making space for a process, which needs time and preparation. Preparation of adults is particularly important if the participatory work is organizationally something that adults are not used to doing. If necessary get adults on board to understand what children and young people's participation is about, to look at some of the ethical principles and ways of working. Really focusing on children is not easy, because adults have more power and children can sometimes feel obligated to take part. It is important to break down what it really means in practice to give children and young people a choice on how much they want to engage, and what kinds of processes are needed to make it interesting and relevant for children and young people, who need to claim and share the power with adults.

The focus on power is key, recognizing different contexts. In most contexts, children and young people really have little free time, and adults also have little free time. Yet time is needed for quality participation. Thus, it can be helpful to engage children and youth over a longer period of time, to identify which are the pockets of time that children are available, when youth are available, and when adults are available to support them. Often, those times are different. Children and young people may be more available after school and weekends. How do you work with those pockets of time and have organizations with more flexible human resource policies to allow their staff to use some evenings and weekends to work with children and young people and to get time off during the week to compensate? Such logistic and administrative flexibility can also make a difference to quality participation processes.

When planning participatory processes, look ahead; if you say you are working with children in rural areas, what do you know about the agricultural seasons? Which times are family members engaged in sowing or harvesting? Are there certain times of the year when children and families are more or less available to be involved in research? Also should exam times be avoided if they are at exam age? All very practical details, but they can make a real difference to the success or failure of a participatory initiative.

If an organization plans to start a project in two months, how do you build in time for initial preparations to consult young people, to consult families, to have more chances to get it right? That is what we find is the difference. If you find time for good preparations, listening to children and families at the initial planning stage, this can enable everything else to be successful. If organizations jump in, that is when we face challenges and a lot of other hurdles, because they have not planned it in a way that fits the context. One of the things is that if they are planning two months for participatory research, consider whether it may be better to actually carry out the research over six months? And even if the research is going to take two months, work out which are the right two months to do it. Good processes often take time, particularly in terms of inclusion, to reach and get children and young people from marginalized backgrounds involved. If organizations are in a hurry, they tend to work with children and young people that are more confident and it is not often inclusive. But if you have time to actually really see which young people are interested and which ones need more support or encouragement to get engaged, this gives more chances to involve more than the usual suspects.

Time is crucial and linked to that it is necessary to recognize that children are different. You might need to adapt the process and methodology to different age groups or gender or other diversity factors, such as if children or youth are working or not working. There must be a readiness to adapt. Sometimes adults think children have a view on something and then they expect all children to have similar views. For example, when asking children their views on children's work it is not surprising that the views of children and young people are completely diverse, because if researchers ask adults about their working life, they are going to have completely different views depending on if they are in a job they like, if they have a good boss. Adults are often surprised that children have different views; but why would you be surprised? People are different, so why would they have the same views?

One thing, particularly when working with young people in countries where there are strong social and gender norms, is enabling spaces for research activities to be done in gender-separate groups so, girls, boys, and young people with other gender identities can express in their own context. Young people can also come together and compare their results so they get to reflect on what is similar and what is different and why. Similarly with age; we might have separate groups with 8- to 12-year-olds and then 13- to 17-year-olds, with separate gender groups. Children and young people can also look at their findings to identify what is similar for different age groups and also to see what may be different, as their priorities may be completely different based on age. Also, the ways in which they choose to express themselves, the kinds of formats of communication are often different among younger children. During the process of analysis with young people as researchers it is helpful to encourage them to see the importance of separating findings – to see is there a difference in what young boys and girls say, or among younger or older, or children with disabilities? Encourage young researchers to see what are the different factors we have to look out for and how do we constantly reflect on differences and similarities and ask questions about why that difference is there.

Some adults say: we don't know how to do this participatory research with young people, we need someone to come and do it. But we can encourage them to learn and to try it. Anyone who is willing to prepare and to learn, often they can do it, and [with] mentoring for adults they can support young people themselves.

The other thing that helps is working collaboratively with small groups. Within a number of different participatory research or evaluations we had small teams of child and youth, or child and adult local research or evaluation teams. Children and adults collaborate with one another, recognizing that children and young people have less time. Seeing which are the kinds of research activities that are most relevant for young people and which are the parts and processes that they don't have time for or are less interested in. For example, in the participatory research on kinship and care there were local research teams with children and adults as researchers. The child researchers were living with grandmothers, grandfathers, uncles, and other relatives. They were to work with some caregivers and some local staff. The children were trained and mentored as researchers and planned what they wanted to do. The girls organized participatory activities with the girls and the boys with the boys. But when it came to write up the findings from focus group activities (such as a body map activity on what children like and dislike about living in kinship care), they passed those body map findings to the adults to type up. Because with all that juggling of school and household chores and everything else, it was something that was too much of a chore to do. However, when it came to the analysis workshop, the child researchers, together with the adult researchers, were actively involved in analysing the findings.

When developing participatory research, in the planning process, how do we give power to children and young people to influence what the research is about? What methods did they use? How to be involved in analysis? But also to think about what tasks they can give to adults so that adults can take some of the burden. It is a constant challenge to find the right balance for children and youth to get opportunities, but not overburden them. Recognize that they are studying and often combining work and other activities.

During the initial stages it is also important to discuss child safeguarding, the protective role that adults need to take on to sensitively respond and make relevant referrals if children disclose abuse or other forms of harm. It is important that the child knows who is the adult safeguarding focal point they can talk to if they feel unsafe or have experienced harm, so the adult takes responsibility for responding to disclosures.

In the participatory evaluation of child and youth participation in peace-building, the child safeguarding element was really strong in planning. It has been really helpful to work with older youth and children together. It provided a lot more freedom and really good collaboration because the youth have more freedom of movement, more access to mobile phones and to digital technologies. The older youth were able to mentor and support child members of the evaluation team. Also some of the older youth aged 22–26 years were able to take on the child safeguarding responsibility and accompaniment for children.

Adult researchers

When NGOs want to start participatory research, if they have the choice between involving really experienced researchers who haven't got experience in collaborating with children as researchers, and working with younger researchers in their 20s or 30s who are more open to collaborating with children as researchers, I encourage that they go with the younger ones that are more open and to provide mentoring.

Once they get involved in a process, the adult researchers are often surprised at how capable children are in planning, facilitating research activities and in analysing the findings. But sometimes you get adults who think that they know it all and that adults know best. They create barriers to implementing participatory research because they don't value it.

A lot of the good practice in participatory research with and by children and young people was influenced by good PRA [Participatory Rural Appraisal or Participatory Rapid Appraisal] work from the 1980s and 1990s. Tools and lessons learned from PRA have been effective to empower children with interactive participatory tools, for example visual mapping and ranking tools, and to empower the adults to accompany children using creative participatory tools. Through use of such tools, children often have visual results of their key analysis findings that they can use to advocate on their issues. When children present their visuals, such as a body mapping of what children like and dislike about living in kinship care, it is so clearly their work and their own findings that their views are more likely to be taken seriously.

How we move forward

Working on rights and injustice issues, whether it is social or environmental, the only way ahead for me is to have some intersectoral cross-linking of women's rights, children's rights, environment, climate justice, minority rights, and land rights. It seems that for years, we have all been working in silos of child rights, women's rights, and environmental rights.

I wonder what are the different processes to bring representatives like children's activists and children researchers together with women activist researchers, environmental activist researchers, and those working on the rights of various minorities? I expect that a lot of the barriers and the enablers are the same for any group that is trying to speak up and address injustice.

We need to return to the original Paulo Freire kind of work to check that we are actually challenging power issues, using methods that come from those people who are most affected by oppression and injustice, and enabling representatives to get an audience with policy-makers and practitioners on matters that concern them.

It would be strategic to support collaborative research among representatives of different generational rights groups. It could be helpful, for example to have a series of events or a journal series to promote more collaborative research for intergenerational social and climate justice concerns, while also continuing to support child and youth-led initiatives.

Funding priorities

There needs to be more direct funding to youth organizations and for children's groups, children's organizations. They've got their own issues that they want to research, but often they are not registered, or now more and more donors only provide big funding because of the admin issues of providing a small grant. There needs to be more small grants, for both research and actions. Because it is frustrating if young people engage in research and do not have funds to implement actions and advocacy to amplify the influence from the evidence they have generated.

There could be more grants to support linkages between children's and youth research, especially for participatory action research and to fund platforms for policy and practice dialogue among child/youth researchers and influential decision-makers. It is important to have platforms where they can come together to have constructive dialogue on the findings and recommendations, as without such dialogue platforms, the initiatives are failing to be more successful.

It would also be strategic to support regional networks of child and youth researchers and advocates. When you bring together children and youth who have been involved in participatory research and action processes they can share their knowledge, competences, and skills. They can form a resource group, and they could mentor and support the expansion of resource groups in their countries.

It would also be very interesting to see if there is any way to certify, to provide certificates to recognize the skills that a young person has when they have been actively involved as a researcher. While agencies I have been part of have provided child and youth researchers with certificates, it would be good if the certificates were from a recognized professional institute.

Sometimes, you have people who only have six years of education, but they are amazing researchers. How do you recognize that? Something that links with their education and professional skill training systems. When we were working with child researchers in the kinship care study, we held the participatory kinship care analysis workshop in West Africa at the same time as a high-level Save the Children managers meeting so that the young researchers could share their results and influence programme developments and potential other funding. When one of the 15-year-old boys introduced himself, he said, 'I am a researcher'. Through his involvement in the research, it was his identity, he completely identified himself as a researcher, and rightly so, as he had done so much, the planning, facilitation of research activities, and the analysis, and he had gained so many skills. We gave him a certificate, but it is not the same as that country officially recognizing these real skills he has.

Frameworks for ethical and effective participatory research and practice

The whole study on diverse childhoods has been really influential; the social construction of childhoods, recognizing children as actors who both influence and are influenced by their wider socio-cultural political context. The study of childhoods has influenced the methodology and importance of participatory research, and the funds available to implement it.

There is a compendium on ethical research involving children, ERIC [Ethical Research Involving Children], by UNICEF with an Australian university. They brought together a lot of case studies and guidance, plus they have a website for updates and learning.

Back in 2005, Save the Children developed seven practice standards. General Comment No. 12 on the child's right to be heard by the Committee on the Rights of the Child (2009) has expanded and built upon Save the Children's standards to develop nine basic requirements for effective and ethical participation of children. These requirements are for participation to be: i) transparent and informative, ii) voluntary, iii) respectful, iv) relevant, v) child-friendly, vi) inclusive, vii) supported by training, viii) safe and sensitive to risks, and ix) accountable. I have been using and encouraging others to use these requirements as a planning tool, with whoever is involved, with children and adults, right from the outset. What are we going to do to ensure participation is transparent and informative? What do we need to do to make it voluntary? What do we need to do to make it relevant and respectful and safe and inclusive? Actually using the requirements as a planning tool has really made a difference.

For example, in the research with working children, or in this CRSA, the children and adults involved used the basic requirements to go down into detailed planning. The requirements can also be used as a tool for monitoring and evaluation. For example, children who were involved in the process, as well as adults, can evaluate to what extent the nine basic requirements were met.

In terms of youth, participation, and peacebuilding, the other framework that was influential was the UN Security Council Resolution 2250 that legitimized and supported youth participation in peacebuilding.

In national contexts there are other frameworks, such as national policies or strategies that support child and youth participation.

Rights and approaches

In child and youth organizations I think it is strategic to use the child rights-based approach to ensure that adults really see children as legitimate actors in their own right. But I also think there needs to be an integrated, human-centred, diversity focus. Somehow when many people consider the term human rights they often think that it is about adults, but even the Universal Declaration of Human Rights is about children. How do we bring children back to human rights? There has to be a human-centred approach that actually recognizes and automatically includes children as legitimate actors, while also recognizing and celebrating diversity, whether it is gender or age or sexuality or ethnicity. It is necessary to give those most affected the chance to speak up and ensure that different perspectives are heard and valued.

I wonder if the climate justice movement is a way in, with the child and youth activism inspired by Greta Thunberg and the media coverage that it got. That is not a child's issue. It is everybody's issue, but that might be an angle, an entry point to widen the debate and to look at that necessity to create inter-group linkages.

We need more and more focus on intergenerational dialogue. It goes again to the social norms, how do we use the media, social media, influential people, young people themselves to really amplify, celebrate, and showcase the perspectives and agency of children and youth and the value of intergenerational collaboration on social justice and climate justice issues?

References

Powell, M., Taylor, N., Anderson, D. and Fitzgerald, R. (2013) *Ethical Research Involving Children*. Florence: UNICEF Office of Research – Innocenti.

Save the Children (2005) *Practice Standards in Children's Participation*. London: Save the Children.

UN Committee on the Rights of the Child (2009) *General Comment No. 12: The right of the child to be heard*. Geneva: UNCRC.

CHAPTER 27
'Living rights' or why working children know about their rights

Olga Nieuwenhuys

Background

I started working on the topic of child labour in 1978, when I was included in a team of researchers from the University of Amsterdam that went to Kerala, South India to research labour and poverty. The team included two men, who found it quite evident that they should study male workers, and two women, one of whom, as a feminist, thought that women should research other women. I disliked the idea of being forced to studying women because of my gender, so I decided to focus on working children.

At that time, working children had hardly been the focus of anthropology. I started preparing by reading documents about child labour at the International Institute of Social History in Amsterdam. They were all about anti-child labour campaigns in Europe, the USA, and a few other regions and spoke mostly of children working in industries, mines, and plantations. But when I came to the village in Kerala where I was to do fieldwork, the first thing I noticed was that the child labour I had been reading about was quite absent. I had to make a choice, go home and say, 'Sorry I was mistaken', or say, 'I did not find what was supposed to be there, why not? What is going on here?' I chose the latter, which is, I believe, what all researchers should do.

I therefore started by piecing together what work meant for the village children. One of the first obstacles was that parents and children had quite divergent views. Parents thought that their children were burdens, who did little else than hanging around, just being annoying or 'up to mischief'. But when I managed, with difficulty, to speak to them separately away from parents, children told me another story. They worked very hard the whole day and had a lot of schoolwork too. That was one of the first moments in which I realized the importance of listening to the voices of the children. Being a foreign woman, and the first white person that the children had ever seen in their lives, made this listening particularly challenging. An added difficulty was a cultural one: people of low status, such as working children, were not supposed to talk about their difficulties to elders or guests. It was considered a sign of disrespect. I therefore trained young female graduates from the village, of which there were exactly three, to conduct interviews with the children, and this provided insights that I discussed in detail in my book *Children's Lifeworlds* (Nieuwenhuys, 1993).

Over the years I have often felt that, until the 1990s, the voices of children had been absent from most studies on children in the developing world. I tend to have a more nuanced opinion today. Looking again at anthropological texts, and particularly old monographs, I noticed that the children did have a voice, but one that the anthropologist filtered through his or her own assumptions about the 'Other'. These assumptions reflected not only ideas of local parents and communities about the insignificant economic role of children, but even more clearly colonial conceptualizations that worked in tandem to define their work away. The most common kind of work that children perform takes place under the supervision of relatives and neighbours, and is not considered harmful or exploitative even today. It is also not considered a source of profits and linked to the global political economy and geopolitical interests. In that sense, children's work is not taken seriously (see Nieuwenhuys, 1993).

In 1990 the University of Amsterdam launched a new Institute of Development Studies, InDRA [Institute for Development Research Amsterdam], with Joke Schrijvers as its director. Quite innovatively, the Institute adopted a bottom-up approach and chose three focus areas: women, children, and the environment. I was put in charge of obtaining funds for research projects on street children. We formed a small team with João Bosco Feres, Madeleine Vreeburg, and Henk van Beers, and succeeded in getting funds from the Minister for Development Cooperation of the Netherlands for a project called *Child Welfare for the Urban Poor*. The aim of the project was to train the local staff of NGOs who worked directly with street children on a day-to-day basis, to use participatory action research [PAR] to better understand their needs.

João Bosco Feres had been involved in Brazil's popular movements which had promoted the newly adopted Statute for children, *O Estatuto da Crainça e do Adolescente* (that is, the Children and Adolescents Statute, 1990). The Statute was particularly innovative in that it defined children and adolescents as subjects of rights, in other words as human beings capable of understanding and exercising their rights. This would be the starting point of our views on how the children of the urban poor could participate in developing welfare interventions. In the end, we managed to get funding for two research projects, one in Bangalore, India and the other in Addis Ababa, Ethiopia (for Ethiopia see Nieuwenhuys, 2001).

Based on these experiences with PAR, I taught for many years a course on children's participation in international development at the University of Amsterdam. The main idea was to train students, many of whom would often be working for NGOs in their later careers, to reflect and experiment with the ideas and methods we developed in the projects. As students had a very diverse background, in pedagogy, visual sciences, anthropology, politics, medicine, etc., and came from different countries, and had generally already volunteered in projects for children in the developing world, the interactive approach of the course and the way theory, research methods, and practice were interwoven, worked rather well.

Public funding for children in development in the Netherlands is completely in the hands of NGOs, who often have a missionary background and maintain strong connections with Christian churches, both Catholic and Protestant, particularly in the countries where they work. The religious dimension makes them adopt distinct approaches to the poor that differ quite significantly from public welfare policies. Though this is not the place to discuss this, it is noteworthy that support for working children's organizations like ENDA in Senegal or MANTHOC in Peru came from these Dutch and other European 'faith-based' NGOs. In spite of their progressive principles, trade unions vehemently oppose these organizations and see them as attempts at undermining workers' rights and to legalize child labour. Trade unions have also refused to talk with the working children, claiming that, despite their personal experiences, they would be too young to understand what is really at stake. This widespread belief, that experts without personal experience would be more knowledgeable about the issues that people experience in their daily life than the people themselves, has often had problematic if not catastrophic results. Also for children. This formed the background of my collaboration with Karl Hanson in reconceptualizing children's rights as *living rights*.

Living rights theory

The starting point of the theory is that also children's own experiences shape what their rights are and become in the social world. These experiences of rights born out of struggles may clash with those of experts whose rights conceptualizations fit the agendas of donors, politicians, or economic agents (Nieuwenhuys and Hanson, 2023). The starting idea resulted from discussions between Karl Hanson (see Chapter 22), a lawyer, and me, an anthropologist, a few years after the adoption and ratification of the UNCRC in 1989. At the time I felt a dissonance about the wordings of the Convention and the day-to-day experiences of working and street children among whom I was doing research. I was inclined to believe that children's rights were a Western invention, hardly relevant for the rest of the world (see Nieuwenhuys, 1998). Karl Hanson's position was that I had misunderstood the nature of law. He believed that rights 'on paper' are dead and can only come to life if needed, felt as legitimate, and supported by people who are ready to stand up in their defence. That is how we started building the living rights theory nearly 30 years ago.

The basic idea is actually very simple. No intervention can succeed, as I said, without adjustments and negotiation. For example, if you open a home for children, you cannot ignore their aspirations and needs, which may range from helping their families to maintaining friendships with other children or adults who live on the streets. Countless projects with lofty ideals of realizing what donors see as an ideal childhood for street and working children have had to deal with the children's conflicting conceptions of their rights (see for examples Nieuwenhuys, 2001). The gap between donors' intentions and the children's actual understanding of their rights is the main reason why the adjustments that ensue are rarely documented or researched. As I maintain [below], this research would reveal that the children are in command. Let me give some examples.

I have supervised quite a few students at the University of Amsterdam in carrying out individual research projects for their Master's thesis in International Development Studies in the framework of the living rights theory. Francesca Nicora did her fieldwork in Calais among the children in the 'jungle' who try to get to the UK and are being *de facto* denied access to schooling because the French state says that they are only passing. In reality, most children stay for a half year or a year and are offered little else than occasional educational activities by mostly untrained English volunteers. Denying *de facto* access to schooling serves the French state purpose of deterring 'illegal' migration. Nicora's research question was whether the children have a sense of their right to education and, if so, how do they seek to realize it in spite of being denied access to schools. She found that the children were teaching each other, were insisting on being given books and taught language courses, and complained that they were unable to follow a proper curriculum. In sum, when states infringe on children's rights for political goals, they are unaware that the children experience this infringement as a children's rights abuse.

Another student, Rick Schoenmaekers, went to a refugee camp in northern Ethiopia, where a Norwegian humanitarian organization was offering young refugees from Eritrea what they claimed were professional courses, among others as cooks. Many youngsters flocked to the camp from Eritrea in the hope to gain a professional training that would enable them to leave for Europe to earn a living. But even though the courses on offer were publicized as leading to an officially recognized diploma, they were of poor quality and useless in Europe. They were essentially meant to help the youngsters find local jobs, to prevent them from migrating to Europe. This is another example of how experts may attempt to misuse children's rights to serve their political agendas. But here also, the youngsters were not that easily fooled and decided en masse to leave the courses and embark on a dangerous journey to Europe where they hoped their rights would at last gain recognition. In other words, children's rights are alive because the children concerned keep them alive and need them to achieve a sense of dignity and fulfilment.

This brings me to the third example, Adriana Parejo Parador's research on living rights from the perspective of the right to dignity. Parador studied an organization in Bolivia that was not linked to the movement of working children but adopted a similar philosophy. The organization's main goal was to support working children who were suffering from stigmatization, because of the combined impact of the stereotyping of anti-child labour campaigning, exploitation at work, and negative experiences in school. The working children were helped to deploy activities that made them proud of who they were, what they were doing, and what they were capable of. Rather than seeing themselves as despicable failures, they learned to be proud of being able to do what more privileged children could not: support their mothers and younger siblings, combine work and school, pay for their fees and necessities, etc. I suppose that there are quite a lot of similar organizations in the world that adopt this social work type of approach in which they seek to build self-confidence, encourage children to speak out, and let them feel that they should be taken seriously. I have no concrete examples, but I imagine that in the field of refugees, a politically very sensitive issue, there are organizations doing that kind of work as well. We should not underestimate what a feeling of not being taken seriously or being looked down upon can generate in children and youngsters.

I feel that in the past the focus has been too much on participatory techniques, as if the obstacles to being listened to would be the main problem. But experts come from another class than the children they claim to help and whose rights they believe to understand even better than the children themselves. As experts say to these children, 'speak up', they may not be aware that children don't feel confident because they know that those who tell them so look down on who they are, how they look and speak, how their parents bring them up, what they are doing for a living. They know all too well that class and racial prejudice make experts unwilling and unable to accept the children as they are. They suffer from what has been termed the 'white saviour complex'. The living rights theory is also about liberating human rights from their instrumentalization by the rich and powerful at the top of society.

It is important to stop starting from the top and work bottom-up, with the most marginalized children, because they are the ones who have the highest stakes in their rights. One needs to have experienced injustice to be able to understand what social justice is, also when one is a child. The paradox is that this understanding does not readily translate into a language of rights that can be understood by those who yield power over the children. This is why the living rights theory purposefully leaves the conceptualization of what children's rights are open to debate.

Even if in the developing world children are a very prominent part of poor communities, their say in community matters is far from guaranteed. Local leaders, funding organizations, staff of organizations, and parents, tend to instrumentalize children's rights and decide for them how they should be interpreted. This lack of influence affects the quality of interventions. Of course, community workers interacting with children may know what the latter want and seek to take that as far as possible into consideration to draw them in, to make them participate. But it is never a peaceful process as conflict may arise between the children wanting their own needs and expectations to be recognized and other actors, including experts in children's rights whose agenda may not necessarily coincide with the children's. In successful interventions you see a continuous process of adjustment and compromise, which is also part of what makes rights 'living'.

We live in a period in which children's rights, and also other human rights, are under pressure. Looking at the rights of displaced people and asylum seekers, the UNCRC seems to be often either ignored, distorted, or challenged by the receiving countries. On the other hand, however, there is also a noticeable awareness about human rights among displaced people, including children, who often seem quite well informed and come to the UK, the EU or the US to make use of these rights.

The stories of those who leave their homes and migrate, taking unimaginable risks, speak of a heavy violation of their human rights in their countries of origin, made the more unacceptable in that it jeopardizes their children's futures, for instance by harming their right to education. In this respect the so-called 'refugee crisis' can also be seen as a clash between conflicting ideas about what human rights are. For Western governments human rights are still conceived as a cold-war political instrument that guarantees freedoms such as the freedom of expression and sexual orientation to people from 'unfree' countries. For the displaced and asylum seekers, they are part of the struggles of people against poverty, environmental degradation, and the lack of opportunities. These conflicting ideas are also very much at work in clashes between children and young people and those who claim to know what is good for them. These conflicts reveal that the power to decide once and for all what children's (and human) rights are, cannot be monopolized. Importantly, children cannot be excluded from deciding what their rights are, for doing so would nullify the very idea that they have rights, since human rights imply necessarily that humans can understand and exercise these rights. This also implies that children do not have the final say in deciding what their rights are. As said, these rights are and will remain the unstable result of a continuous process of adaptation and negotiation in which many actors are involved.

Promoting living rights

I think, first, that experts at all levels and the public at large need to be educated in understanding and appreciating that children are aware of their rights already. Taking them to be ignorant of their rights or unable to understand what they are is a dangerous, wrong starting position. The obstacles standing in children's way to realize their rights may be more formidable than normally believed and point at the existence of deep injustices in society, including laws that make it impossible for children to get access to services or get protection.

I would, second, involve those who work directly with children, to hear what they have to say. They are also often people who are not listened to but have a lot of practical experience. Try to understand what worked. Are there any ideas? Perhaps these people can start talking with the children and collecting their ideas and start bringing about what may seem like small changes. One of my students was doing research in a home for unaccompanied asylum-seeking minors in the Netherlands, and tried to bring the children together to talk about the food they were served. It seemed to her a very harmless activity. To her surprise, the management prohibited the student from continuing the experiment. Children's food is apparently a very sensitive issue that endangers the way food subsidies are distributed, who profits from buying bad quality food, and who suffers the consequences. A living rights approach is better suited than the conventional one to recognize the right of children to contest the injustices of food quality and distribution.

In short, if we, as adults or experts, become humbler and start from the premise that children struggle for their rights already, we can start building a better future together and rejuvenate our understanding of children's rights.

References

Hanson, K. and Nieuwenhuys, O. (eds) (2013) *Reconceptualizing Children's Rights in International Development: Living rights, social justice, translations*. Cambridge: Cambridge University Press.

Nieuwenhuys, O. (1993) *Children's Lifeworlds: Gender, welfare and labour in the developing world*. London: Routledge.

Nieuwenhuys, O. (1998) 'Global childhood and the politics of contempt', *Alternatives* 23(3): 267–289.

Nieuwenhuys, O. (2001) 'By the sweat of their brow? Street children, NGOs and children's rights in Addis Ababa', *Africa* 71(4): 539–557.

Nieuwenhuys, O. and Hanson, K. (2023) 'Living rights theory: An ontological perspective', in: S. Balagopalan, J. Wall and K. Wells (eds), *Handbook of Theories in Childhood Studies*. London: Bloomsbury.

Van Daalen, E., Hanson, K. and Nieuwenhuys, O. (2016) 'Children's rights as living rights: The case of street children and a new law in Yogyakarta, Indonesia', *The International Journal of Children's Rights* 24(4): 803–825.

CHAPTER 28

How ready are we to partner with young people?

Kavita Ratna

This is an edited transcript of Kavita Ratna's Rejuvenate presentation of September 2022, about a 'call to action' from vulnerable children and young people in India.

I would like to actually speak from the point of view of very vulnerable young people, not in colleges, not in schools – but of those outside these realms, and what is it that they have taught us in terms of uncertainty and in terms of our call for action.

I will just take two very quick examples. One is of this group of working adolescents in my country from 15 states, and they have been part of a very long movement. Very recently, they came up with some of their demands, many of which are not unusual or even unknown: safe occupations, quality education, livelihood with dignity, food security. But in the middle of all of those is that core demand 'see us as citizens today' which is actually the new addition in terms of a rights framework because all other demands may also be served within a welfare approach.

Another group of young people, about 2,500 of them, including young adults, were looking at the issues related to age of consent, marriage, child marriage, forced marriage, and they came up with a whole list of issues. Again, many things are not unknown to us. But what came across very strongly for us is the issue of personhood, agency, sexuality, self-determination, and looking at all of their demands as part of their entitlements.

Now, where does this leave us? What are the implications for us? Because when I say, as I am now speaking here, as an adult (many of you are very young, and probably you will be then on the other side of this conversation); but as adults, what are the implications of these demands within a children's rights framework? These imply that we adults are actually looking at 'sharing of power'. We are actually looking at being challenged and questioned. And these are very difficult arenas.

The minute we start talking about children's rights and participation, it is not an abdication of our duty, but actually an expansion in the scope of our duty. Like they say that it is easier to protect a bird inside a cage, the minute you want the bird to fly, then you have to make the whole world safe, which is the kind of challenge we would then be dealing with as adults.

And there is the issue of the right to self-determination, which is really the core of the rights discourse, both for children, for adults, and for human rights, per se. The right to self-determination is the least understood of all rights in my understanding. Also by children and young people themselves. They do not have any structures to exercise this right. They do not even have an understanding that this is a right. They do not have the mechanisms to hold anybody accountable, including us. And invariably, they end up depending on self-appointed advocates many times, also like us.

So if we are really looking at the challenges that we face, how do we gain clarity? How do we support children's participation, especially organized children, because that is when they actually gain a voice and agency; and how can we make sure of including the most marginalized, who are not part of the mainstream. Then how do we look at the resilience and the strength of those who are the most marginalized?

One thing I see is change and uncertainty are a part of our life. Then the question is how do we strengthen inner resilience and external resilience of the young people? And how do we make sure that what we do with or for children is not actually disempowering them in terms of giving them aid or support which takes away the support systems they already have in place to face problems because they are surviving anyway without us. So how can we make sure our intervention actually does not take away their resilience but builds on that?

There are also a whole set of issues related to 'projects'. As a lot of projects are donor driven, fund driven, event driven – how do we retain the integrity of what we are doing? For instance, a lot of the conversations we have had with young people have raised expectations. How do we go about that, and what is the ethical obligation we have for them, and with them – in terms of the processes that have already been unleashed? In all the studies that we have done, how do we continue our commitment to the processes under way and how to set in mechanisms to ensure that the processes continue as intended?

I have now been working in this field for about 32 years and all of these challenges remain to some degree or the other. As adults, what has been challenging is understanding 'childhood'; how do we even view childhood or youth and how does their developmental continuum play out? How do we try and find ways in which our innate need to protect children does not come in the way of their participation? How do we ensure that their risk-taking, which is very integral to growing, is supported by some security that they can fall back on, if required? How do we understand that young people coexist in multiple realities? Then how do we understand their multiple layers of personhoods and how do we help them to build up the strengths that lie within them?

How do we constantly bring their concerns to the centre? It is so easy for us to get hijacked into different agendas because we have so many pressing agendas of our own! How do we ensure that we keep coming back to children's primary concerns? And how do we look at ways and means of 'not' manufacturing consent? Because there are so many implicit and explicit ways of doing that.

When we are looking at working with children who are navigating so many uncertainties surrounding them, how do we help them do so from a place of strength? And I think very crucially, how does our engagement with them change the rules of the game and not compel them to 'play' by the rules set by adults in the adult world? There are so many examples where we do the opposite: when we wish to have them take part in a workshop, we want them to behave like adults, speak like adults, use the communication medium like adults. The challenge for us is how do we learn to listen to them – when they speak their way? And how can we create a level playing ground for them where their integrity and their strengths find space?

To do all of this, how do we build our own capacities? How do we even begin to understand the 'rights' framework and how do we even begin to understand our ethical accountability? One child actually told us 'the problem with you adults, is that you forget that you were also children once, and what you experienced'.

Our children also keep saying 'we are part of the solution, not the problem'. I think my most important point in terms of a 'call for action' is how do we ensure that we adults too are part of the solution and not the problem?

Children in communities and intergenerational justice

Andy West, Vicky Johnson, and Tessa Lewin

This conclusion provides a summary of the issues arising from the contributions to the book. A major point emerging from the discussions and interviews is that participatory practice towards child rights is very much alive and well, and while terminology and conceptualization are going through experiential review, a process of rejuvenation is happening. Additionally, successful methods are being put into place for intergenerational involvement in community development, bringing together beliefs and approaches from South and North. This work involves enabling children's engagement in donor decision-making, and even in the raising of difficult questions about what decisions can be made by which children and young people.

We then go on to consider several of the analytical points raised by contributors across this book, which essentially revolve around dimensions of power; for example, local norms, adultism, who speaks for whom, and difficult issues such as children in the justice system, as well as a discussion of living rights and social movements.

Practice since the 1990s has engaged with a range of approaches and innovations to address these issues, as the contributions in this book explore and exemplify. The underlying problem rests with the inherent ambiguities in the word participation, making it an essentially contested concept, particularly in relation to cultural perceptions of childhood that do not envision children as having a voice or involvement in decision-making and action, and that look to intergenerational hierarchies as the social norm. The use of the term participation might also be seen as a means of developing practice for children's and young people's emancipation, decision-making, and action, without being seen as explicitly challenging social norms, and as making change through intergenerational and other partnerships. A pragmatic use of terminology was highlighted as being necessary by contributors such as Swatee Deepak (Chapter 4) in order to use terms that are generally understood.

The contributions address the ambiguities of participation through their experiences of providing a range of practice arenas and approaches, thinking about and discussing the process issues and dilemmas in achieving ethical practice that adheres to commitments of recognizing children's rights in terms of what some refer to, for example, as citizenship (e.g. Cockburn, Chapter 7) and others as children's agency (see Beazley, Chapter 13).

The main arenas of practice of child and youth participation

Before the General Comment in 2009 laid out various settings for the child's right to be heard, training packages offered and undertaken on children's rights generally noted the importance of participation throughout services and practice to fulfil the rights encompassed in the UNCRC. Yet participation practice in reality varied, depending on organizations' and practitioners' interests, views, and interpretation of the term. In some areas of work, participation was seen as particularly applicable and taken up as aspects of the existing work of children's organizations, for example, who were already involved in community development, or developing practice for children in areas such as education and health. Organizations began looking at ways of engaging children and incorporating some forms of participation in matters of concern to children, their rights as well as the communities in which they live, although there was also resistance. Staff in some children's organizations regarded concepts and practice of rights, and particularly participation (except for children's involvement in recreation and education), as alien to the communities and places where they worked (West, 2007). Where they did see participation potential, it was often likely to be organized by adults, for example children trained to work as peer educators, or children trained in running water stands (see Hart, Chapter 2). Water and sanitation work by NGOs, widespread in many countries, provides an example of divides in how children's participation was viewed (see also Ivan-Smith, Chapter 3). Some staff involved in water technology, such as planning, designing, routing and laying pipes, water and sanitation, saw no reason for children's and young people's involvement in, for example, deciding the location of water stands, pipe routes or any other aspect of their work. But when water stand drainage became blocked, they blamed children acting as stand supervisors rather than the adults who were actually at fault (personal experience, South/East Asia).

European 'developed' countries often looked to mirror images of some adult participation or democracy, such as committees and councils, in particular through what they saw should be children's main location outside the family: schools. Schools were also often used as a base for selecting members of children's and young people's community councils paralleling the local government. Both of these forms generally raised questions of how elections and selections were run, and issues of representation (see below). Braxton (Chapter 18) discusses related issues and how these were overcome.

In countries in the South, development organizations, particularly those focused on children and young people, looked to involve them in various aspects of community work. The sectoralization of many organizations meant that, for example, community development involving children may follow one approach, such as consultation, while health practices another, often focusing on peer-to-peer or peer education processes for topics such as sanitation and illness prevention work, and HIV and AIDS awareness. As in Northern countries, development education practices, largely based around schools, tended to practise participation through school councils. Community work is also undertaken in the North and Trevisan (Chapter 16) points to the ideal for multidisciplinary approaches to take account of context, and issues of dealing with publicity.

While terminology of 'rights' was difficult in some countries, certain issues were also sensitive. For example, in places where abuse was perceived as a Western or Northern problem, rights-based child protection work, in terms of protection from abuse and violence, was difficult initially, although trafficking might be acknowledged in these contexts, often with a focus on legal aspects. Children and young people *working* were not necessarily seen as having a problem: local staff in some INGOs and NGOs were known to employ child domestic workers themselves, while much of children's work was an everyday occurrence (see Nieuwenhuys, Chapter 27, and Blagbrough, Chapter 6). Children and young people in street situations, usually also working, were (and still are) often difficult topics in countries where the main public perception was that the children had wilfully run off for an easy life, wasting time on the streets and abusing substances. (Practice with children working and in street situations is raised by many contributors, for example, Beazley, Chapter 13, Ofosu-Kusi and Mizen, Chapter 11, Nieuwenhuys, Chapter 27, O'Kane, Chapter 26, Ratna, Chapter 28.) As with issues of teenage pregnancy, the problem of abuse as a root cause was not initially seen as an explanation or issue to address. The importance of a holistic approach to children's lives and for joined up, or intersectoral working across agencies, organizations, and government departments has been stressed by several of the contributors to this book.

One other key arena for children's and young people's participation is in periods of emergency and post-emergency, including conflict, peace-building, and disasters. Prelis (Chapter 19) discusses policy and practice work around conflict, also Shrestha (Chapter 12), Bah (Chapter 20), and O'Kane (Chapter 26); participation work with children and young people in and after humanitarian disasters is also of prime importance (West and Theis, 2007; West, 2015).

Children's and young people's spaces

The General Comment of 2009 highlighted a range of places where children could participate. Ideas of 'mainstreaming' children's and young people's participation in development and related practice had been promoted before then, the basis being that children had a right to be heard with regards to any and all services they used, and places they lived and worked. This could be and was seen as children's participation where they are, and so as well as families and communities, this would also include alternative care such as foster care and institutions, and include places where they spent much time such as schools, and the broader realm of towns and cities. But when the question of *which* children is taken up then this must also look at children in other circumstances, who may not fit the local conventional pathlines, such as girls pregnant outside marriage, and particularly children who are marginalized, such as children in detention, children who are working, children who are homeless, and children in street situations.

A central tenet of many contributors has been about enabling spaces for children and young people. In practice, these have ranged from the particular, for example in girl-led projects, for girls to meet, discuss, and plan (see for example Deepak, Chapter 4, and Bah, Chapter 20), to the attempts to develop child-friendly cities (see Hart, Chapter 2, but also Ofosu-Kusi and Mizen, Chapter 11), and the development of ranges of indicators and processes to enable this. The circumstantial differences are significant: for example, child-led, youth-led, girl-led spaces and projects might be seen as components of child-friendly cities, whereas some spaces are targeted at particular age groups, gender groups, sexualities, or ethnicities for reasons of their exclusion, discrimination, or marginalization in 'places for all'.

A conventional place for children to be found is school, and perhaps since many child-oriented development organizations had education programmes, children's participation in schools has been attempted in various ways. As noted above approaches to children's participation in schools have often imported adult ideas and methods, replicating committees, councils, and other structures; and many also replicate adult problems of excluding various groups. For example, school structures of children's participation may easily do this by enabling the most articulate, those able to and who do attend regularly, those with confidence, who are not poor, and those seen as positioned to serve as exemplars of the school. These processes can easily exclude those who are marginalized, who face discrimination in the community and often in the school itself, those unable to attend on a regular basis, and those of low social status. Such problems emerge in the Global North and Global South, where time is not available to undertake participatory processes, where funding is not available, and where different agendas and perceptions are in play about who and what best represents the student population and the school.

On the other hand, school-related issues, as taken up by contributors here (see Braxton, Chapter 18), may follow different processes, and include students organizing for policy change, for social justice, and for inclusion. School provides a space for these activities, and in examples in this volume, include being active around discrimination, justice, and education issues. The range of possible outcomes, intended and unintended possibilities in schools alone, indicate the complexities of participation processes and how disagreements over tokenistic, decorative, and meaningful participation come about.

One of the main problems with schools as a basis for children's and young people's participation not only in education but as processes for involvement in community and local governance, is not only which children are engaged and elected within the school, but what of those who do not attend, are formally or informally excluded, or are in custodial detention.

Children's clubs in communities (see Hart, Chapter 2) have been seen and used as ways for children to raise issues, deciding on and taking action, and in some places as means for their involvement in local decision-making, and a pathway to having a voice in local governances. These have also been used by development organizations as a way of ensuring children's and young people's views and participation in organizational planning and work, at least at local level. Many such clubs are initially facilitated with the intention, and subsequent reality, of becoming child and youth-led; that is, run by children and young people themselves.

Child and youth-led and marginalized groups

Some of the most successful organizations that are child and youth-led, are run by those who are marginalized, excluded, and/or working. From necessity, they have found their own ways of organizing and supporting themselves with or often without support and resources from adults. The street and working children's movements in South America, Africa, and parts of Asia have been cited in this volume, and there are others, some well-known, some not, located in particular cities. These organizations have had to deal with the question of age: children grow older, become young people, and then adults. If the organization is to remain child- or youth-led then the leaders at some point must relinquish their leadership and power to a younger generation.

Such movements are not limited to the Global South where children and youth in street situations are often more visible in comparison to the many homeless children and youth in the Global North, for example in the UK, who come into the light occasionally. Children and youth in street situations and working around the world often find themselves in conflict with the law, and fear authorities who may also be violent and sexually abusive to them. Children and youth in conflict with the law in the Global North also experience marginalization and discrimination. A youth-run organization in the US (Nowlan and Jones, Chapter 15) shows how the practice of participation around justice issues is needed both North and South, in different manifestations.

Places for children and youth such as street situations, custody, and detention may also be linked to institutional care. Many children and youth who leave alternative care such as 'orphanages' become street-connected or come into conflict with the law, in both the Global North and South. Children with impoverished parent or parents, children who are in street situations or come out from detention are often placed in such institutions. Although the numbers of children in 'orphanages' in many countries are very high, only a small percentage are 'double' or even 'single' orphans, having lost both or one parent. Many of these, often large, institutions have children placed there by parents (single or couple parents) because they cannot afford school fees or just the costs of raising them and think children will be better off there. Institutions also collect children to fill spaces. Apart from questions of quality of care, many children become stigmatized and marginalized through such placement. Some experience violence and abuse there. At question here is also children's involvement in decision-making on the move to the institution, involvement in decision-making within the institution, and how and when they can and should leave, and what aftercare and support is provided. Child- and youth-led groups and organizations of those living in or who have lived in institutional or alternative care have also developed in both North and South, including those facilitated and supported by adult-run organizations.

Child protection

Recognition of the extent of violence and abuse experienced by children and young people in the South as well as the North, and of marginalized groups, especially street-connected and working children (also both South and North, such as the UK), has brought a focus on the types of systems needed to enable the protection and development of vulnerable and abused children. This applies equally to those falling outside conventional spaces, such as being out of school, in conflict with the law, in street situations, and working as carers for parents and other family members. In Northern countries with supposedly developed child protection systems, approaches focused on participation of children and young people within the system; in Southern countries, approaches often focused on the development of community-based systems, as discussed by many contributors in all parts of the book. Approaches to child protection in the community are discussed by several contributors (see for example, Ondoro, Chapter 5, Admassu, Chapter 9, and Wessells, Chapter 24) and the importance of partnerships and networks to bring together organizations in the field raised by, for example Admassu (Chapter 9) and Marriam (Chapter 10).

Communities and intergenerationality

Attempts at engaging children in protection work through forming local Child Protection Committees that would include some children, and involving children and young people in any type of community development work through consultation or other means were initiated by the early 2000s. Processes and methodologies were developed, but as contributors to this volume make clear, the main learning from these attempts concerned the need for time for engagement; as well as the need for adaptation and revision (see Admassu, Chapter 9 and Wessells, Chapter 24). Interviewees stressed the importance of developing any mechanisms from within the community, and not bringing in ready-made tools from outside. They emphasize that existing leaders and local people of all ages should identify the purpose, problems, methods, and resolutions themselves. They point out that such development from within takes a lot of time and transparent engagement, with all the implications for funding and donors that such 'slow' and 'undefined' strategies that are not pre-planned and costed entail.

Similar insights are heard from contributors throughout, that organizations bringing in ready-made models of practice, especially those which rely on the provision of resources and an NGO presence for their operation, and those set to pre-timed project proposal and funding goals, will not be sustainable, and will not work after the organization's and sponsor's departure. Even a year or two of support is found to be insufficient to shape and embed long-term change if it is externally driven. There are also questions over the ethical applicability of externally devised interventions.

This point concerns not only local perceptions but local methods and practices, taking account of existing structures, and relationships, hierarchies, and beliefs. The inadequacy of externally driven community practice is shown particularly in comparison with approaches described throughout that focus on slow and open engagement and also incorporate local and external strategies, but most importantly, which are based on local decision-making.

Although these practices are defined as community-based, and seek to involve adult men and women in identifying problems and resolutions, the purpose is to seek out issues that concern children and young people. This requires children's direct engagement in the process, because problems they experience are not readily recognized by, identified by, and/or remain hidden from or even denied by older people. At issue here is a core, intergenerational problem of power, as raised by contributors, that problems need to be if not identified by, then agreed by adults in positions of authority, and this can be a major barrier if they do not recognize the problems raised by children and young people, because there would be no action taken. The processes involving children identifying and raising problems they experience would be futile. In many places it was found that, essentially, if the adults were not involved in the processes of identifying problems, and the power remained with adults and elders who then did not publicly recognize the problem and so would not commit to be part of any solution, there would be no response. Children and young people might identify problems, and solutions, but generally are without access to power to implement across a community. The difficulties of solely child-led identification of problems and solutions, and the failures of adult-led processes to identify children's circumstances, have been recognized and so led to the development of intergenerational methodologies, as described in this book.

Local focus: power, context, and diversity in populations and purpose

These protection-based interventions encompassing engagement of the whole community intergenerationally do not mean that child-led and youth-led practices and organizations have no role to play, but rather highlight the importance of seeing and undertaking work in context. Wessells (Chapter 24) looks at the importance of integrating traditional cosmologies through ethnographic approaches. The general location of power resides with adults, and often adults of particular status and identity, especially men who are sufficiently prosperous, connected, not disabled, not marginalized, perhaps of a specific ethnic group, and other particular identities. The roles of all adults in a location may be brought into play in interventions within bounded communities for the protection of children and young people but different social, cultural, environmental, political, and material contexts can highlight a variety of specific issues, offering ranges of different possibilities for and requiring diversities of children's and young people's engagement. For example, children's and young people's opportunities and requirements for work vary by environment, social, and political context, as well as age and family income.

One point emerging emphatically from the protection interventions involving whole communities is that they should be locally led (as noted by contributors throughout). This might be seen as part of an explicit shift towards locally led, child-led, girl-led, youth-led practices. This could include child clubs in communities, and mechanisms for influencing community leadership, local governance, and local and even national government and policy. Often such 'led' terms have not been debated, nor explicitly contested, yet they have been used over many years without always having the same emphasis and meaning in practice.

The community interventions discussed by contributors, involving not only local decision-making but local identification of problems, indicate the potential multiplicity of meanings associated with the term 'locally led'. Difficulties emerge from interventions seeking to resolve, for example, problems of abuse, violence, or early pregnancy, and from bringing not only suggested mechanisms and methods but even these concepts in from outside. This does not mean that the problems are not known about or recognized locally, but that to make change, the participation of children and young people must be within the context of adults also engaging, and local intergenerational identification of problem and resolution.

Similarly, concepts such as child-led and youth-led solutions have been the goal for many projects and processes, yet they are not always accompanied by the same long-term attempts at engagement nor start from, for example, local identification and agreement of purpose and processes to work. Some have, with all similar intentions, instead relied on training in rights and methodologies to follow, essentially brought in from outside. For example, some projects have used mechanisms such as children's committees, children's councils, and children's parliaments, which are methodologies based on practice and familiar in some parts of the world, but which need adaptation elsewhere. Or a different process is needed whereby children and young people are part of defining strategies. The question of methodology includes *which* children are involved in identifying issues and solutions as well as methods, if they are not to simply reproduce existing hierarchies and patterns of discrimination and so exclude parts of the children and youth population.

Being local concerns an understanding of context, those who live in that context, local power, and the particular groups involved. This includes not only children and young people but questions of which children and young people, the associated difficulties of representation of views and voice, and issues of prevailing social norms and customs. Who speaks for who? Or just for themselves? Alongside these questions contributors also raise the ethical issues involved in interventions, including accountability and the role of funding (see below). Many of these questions and issues emerged in engaging with children's and young people's concerns in a community, but these may also be associated with any spaces where children are.

Research

One other place or space where children and young people are found is in research. Children and youth are involved as research subjects, but also have been recruited, facilitated, or encouraged to do their own research. Hence their involvement in research may run from answering questions, and drawing diagrams to designing, planning, and running their own research, including devising the overall purpose and questions.

The degree of children's and youth involvement in research has raised questions over what 'participatory' research might be. This raises familiar issues of which children are included, what aspects they are involved in, how much power they have to decide questions, and what happens after. For example, institutional care has been the location of much research, including children doing their own research. But ultimately, where institutions have power, and particularly where they fund children's schooling or education, children may not want to challenge problems they experience, because being thrown out of the institution will mean they cannot take examinations.

These issues raise not only ethical considerations, but also questions of power and money, if unexpected problems emerge that cannot be addressed within the available budgets. Where taking action in an institutional care setting, for example, would actually require re-housing and supporting large numbers of children over a long period of time, research may have to be stopped due to practical (temporal/financial) constraints. The ethical processes of safeguarding may be intended to plan ahead, but in such cases might then preclude research going ahead, because responses to issues raised could not be met. A further issue in terms of children's and young people's participation relates to what constitutes their 'best interests'; for example, if children live in institutional care where they experience violence and report this during research, they may request that nothing be done because they want to finish school and think this is in their best interest, rather than being thrown out of the institution (for reporting abuse) and then being unable to continue education without a place to live and fees paid. In places without a functioning and funded child protection system, such situations may arise: proposed research projects may not always be able to envision these sorts of problems.

Ethics and accountability

Contemporary research protocols, certainly those run through universities and increasingly through (I) NGOs, need to pass ethical requirements and checks. In some cases protocols have prevented research with children going ahead because of notions that effectively deny children's agency, see them as unable to give consent, and are concerned about their safeguarding and protection if they are involved. However, practical work with children and young people is necessary in a variety of fields, and children's rights to making decisions and taking action on matters of concern to them means that this sort of participation is also necessary. Ethical considerations arise throughout participation practice, and are not limited to research. 'Ethical building blocks' have been applied and debated throughout the 1990s and onwards (Johnson et al., 1998). Many practitioner professions have turned their attention to formulating ethical codes. The practice standards for participation, published in 2004 and subsequently incorporated in the General Comment of 2009, provide a guide not only for research but also for other practice (see O'Kane, Chapter 26).

Linked to this is the question of accountability. In some projects this is often spoken of in terms of accountability to the managing or facilitating organization and/or to the funding agencies concerned. Yet there is a need to address accountability to children and young people and formulate how this is to be undertaken in practice (see Shrestha, Chapter 12 and Glencorse, Chapter 21). Alongside this is the question of intergenerational accountability; that is, to the community.

Funding and funders

Accountability remains a concern for many funders, ensuring spending is used properly and as intended. But this also raises issues where there are constraints on project goals and practice, or where the processes of participation practice (decisions on goals are intended to come from children and young people) are difficult to incorporate when outcomes and indicators must be defined before funds are made available. Navigating the involvement of funding bodies is an issue raised by a number of contributors, and clearly significant are innovative forms of practice that make use of children's and young people's participation from the outset (see Ondoro, Chapter 5 and Wessells, Chapter 24).

Main themes, dilemmas, decisions, and moving forward in participation practice with children and young people

As with all participation practice, some or even many children and young people may not have the interest or the time to be involved in various aspects of work pursued by organizations and services, such as designing and writing up research, deciding funding applications, and so on. Children and young people are not homogeneous groups, so in order to realize rights there needs to be engagement across a diverse spectrum. This entails a continual process of understanding contexts, especially of time and place, changes that are happening, and different sectors of communities and governments, and will bring complex dilemmas as indicated above.

These sorts of complex dilemmas may emerge across children's and young people's participation, largely because children's rights and their empowerment and emancipation are not a reality. Which decisions are actually permitted and approved to be made, and which are not? Who sets the boundaries, and on what grounds? Who designs and owns projects – adults, organizations, donors, funders, children, youth? Where is the power located? Contributors to this volume raised a number of central themes and concerns that regularly appear in child and youth participation practice. From all of the arenas of practice alluded to, described, discussed, and analysed by the contributors, various main issues emerge that help to provide areas for analysis of projects and point to the future.

Local social norms and intergenerational approaches

In considering the different spaces and places for children's and young people's participation, a key basis is the local social norms. For example, expected behaviours of children and young people at different ages, and gender have been seen as a key context for development of participation along with norms of respect for elderly, public respect, and the position of men in particular, and the location of power, both formal and informal. Children and youth are generally not used to having voice and are not expected to be heard. Integrating local perspectives and incoming practice are approaches considered by contributors (see Wessells, Chapter 24).

Such issues of local social norms and power show how children's and young people's participation, in the sense of defining issues, problems, and solutions, may be of no consequence without being located in an intergenerational process. This process needs to overcome social norms and develop methodologies where adults recognize the problems children experience, and adults will themselves engage in the solutions identified. For example, where teenage pregnancy stems from abuse and power of older men or teachers, children find it difficult to raise and identify perpetrators, and local methods of engagement are necessary. This is in contrast to more formal strategies in some countries, where a child or adult is expected to report abuse. This assumes that the reporting will generate action, although this does not always happen, and when it does, it may not be in a way the child would prefer.

Responsibilities and rights

As many contributors identified, the exercise of rights may also be associated with responsibilities. There is a question over how 'responsibilities' have been perceived: for many supporters of traditional norms, this has been interpreted as children knowing their place, and not having rights to be consulted, make decisions, or take action, particularly that would challenge existing situations.

At the inception of the UNCRC, a focus was on promoting children's rights, particularly to being heard, through information and training, and the question of responsibilities may not have been so much discussed, since this might also be expressed as children's responsibility to be 'seen and not heard', and therefore remain powerless. It seems that variations of this expression are found in so many languages.

Greater recognition of children's and young people's rights, and their relationship with conventions on human rights, which also apply to them, have brought renewed focus on responsibilities. At issue are also questions on diversity, marginalization, discrimination, and exclusion, which challenge the exercise in practice of both rights and responsibility, as well as agency and empowerment, and suggest how particular targeting and projects on participation are necessary (see Ivan-Smith, Chapter 3 on tagging).

Yet in this discussion on responsibilities, it is also important not to devolve all responsibility onto children: if children and young people are expected to exercise responsibilities and duties alongside their rights, then so too are adults, including responsibilities to recognize children's and young people's rights, evolving capacities and for adults to put these responsibilities into practice.

Adultism

The problems of where power lies intergenerationally and in social norms also raise questions of marginalization and discrimination within communities and societies. Can these be overcome through intergenerational working? Some groups of children and youth, the focus of 'targeted participation' or who form their own organizations because of their circumstances of marginalization, may not see the possibility of working together but rather act more as a social movement. Some children and youth speak of adultism (see Nowlan and Jones, Chapter 15), but then some adults agree with this perspective and are prepared to support and work alongside them in what might be identified as another form of intergenerational collaboration. The issues of marginalization and discrimination raise the question of which children and youth are involved in organizations, projects, and processes.

Which children: who speaks for whom?

In projects open to all children and young people social norms may work against diversity, and the most articulate or conventional identities of children and youth may be dominant, to the exclusion of some groups. The development of targeting by projects and funders aims to enable the involvement of marginalized, or less powerful, groups in raising issues, working together or for other purposes. Although poverty is clearly a major factor, other social norms, and the identities, status, and experiences of children and their families, are as important and reveal huge intersectional diversity.

The problems then emerge, as highlighted throughout the book, of who speaks for whom? There are two key issues involved: children are not a homogeneous group but since they are often categorized implicitly as 'not adults' on grounds of age and capacity, their diversity of experience and views are not taken into account.

Recognizing the extent of diversity means that it is difficult for one child or young person to be the representative of even a particular segment or identity. Age alone makes a significant difference to a child's experience and the expectations of others in their communities, for example of how girls and boys are conventionally expected to behave at different ages.

Yet one of the problems throughout many participation processes is that children are homogenized: they are often seen as 'other' in social processes because they are not adults, and social systems and structures are designed and operated by and with adults in mind. While children and youth are generally expected to develop along particular, locally constructed pathways, there are some marginalized and discriminated against who will not be on those pathways, and so when children are selected by adults or peers or self-select to speak about 'children's' issues and concerns, there is an underlying question of who speaks for whom (see Hanson, Chapter 22).

Some projects, as noted in this volume, attempt to bring together children from different backgrounds, for example aiming to engage different classes (see Rizzini, Chapter 14). These may have potential to challenge practices in adult society and suggest scope for change. The need to start the work from the bottom up, not top-down, is stressed (Nieuwenhuys, Chapter 27).

While different societies and cultures have different expectations of children and young people, these expectations also shift over time: change is a key context and one which all projects and practitioners working with and for children and young people are effectively part of and engaging in. This may also be linked to the purpose of the participation.

Purpose and process: dilemmas, decision, and moving forwards

Given the breadth of meaning associated with the term participation, the purpose of projects involving children and young people can vary. Although the right to be heard is central to the General Comment and is the basis of children's participation in the varied places and spaces noted, the practice of participation, in terms of decision-making and action, brings a range of benefits for children and young people, their families and communities.

The benefits of participation for children, young people, communities, organizations, and society have emerged through evaluations over the years. They include a range of outcomes for children's and young people's personal benefit, including self-development in knowledge and capacities, increased self-esteem, increased self-confidence, improved performance at school, and social engagement. Various organizational benefits have been identified by involving children and young people through consultation and other means to achieve better targeting and performance. Social benefits have included the identification and resolution of problems and greater community cohesion. This means that the purposes of participation might be for the benefits of children and young people themselves, as well as families and communities.

These elements and purposes of participation might be related to the need for recognition of children's and youth agency, and to their empowerment; in order for children to raise their ideas and to have a voice in decision-making, they need to be empowered to do so, because social norms generally act against this.

Other purposes of 'participation' revolve around rights, particularly the right to be heard and involved in matters of concern to children, to make relevant decisions and take action, which might also be related to questions of citizenship. If children's participation benefits them and their communities, provided they are empowered to do so, and they have rights, then their agency and rights and participation are also components of their citizenship. (See Ivan-Smith, Chapter 3, on 'citizen engagement' as active terminology.)

The question of the purpose of participation is linked to ongoing matters of process: how the practice is conducted, supplemented by the need for ethical approaches and accountability. These matters draw in funders and funding bodies, because awareness of the purposes and processes of participatory practice with children and young people, the time it takes, the potential for their involvement from the outset, working across generations as necessary, must also take on difficult issues if it is to move forward. Such issues occur throughout policy, service, and other provision in human life, including ethical assessments on capacities and circumstances: the grounds of age and constructions of childhood make them more complex with children and young people.

Difficult issues – justice

The questions of rights and responsibilities, empowerment, citizenship, and agency, that should apply to all children and young people also raise difficult issues as highlighted by contributors (see Hanson, Chapter 22). In some areas, children's participation and right to make decisions is applauded and approved: in other areas, there are difficulties as noted, for example, in questions of consent, questions of justice, and questions of decision-making over one's own body. In many of these the notion of the child's best interest being decided by a parent, guardian, or particular authority is argued to take precedence.

These complicated questions, however, could be applicable to adults, and are not limited to children and young people. These may be difficult issues, but the practice of discussing, evaluating, and resolving them is something that goes on, or should go on at all ages, and in all identities.

Living rights, translation, and social justice

The need to take up particular questions and look at how they operate in practice is an aspect of the living rights articulated by contributors (Hanson, Chapter 22 and Nieuwenhuys, Chapter 27) in this book, along with the notion of translation. How are rights actually used, supported, and negotiated, how they are seen and taken up. The purpose of rights and participation might be seen as achieving social justice both for children and across generations; that is, while recognizing individuals as citizens, ensuring that the mechanisms that function against the citizenship of some are overcome, such as practices of marginalization and discrimination, withholding power, or using power to exclude, impoverish or otherwise diminish them. Child and youth participation might be a way of overcoming those barriers and invigorating social justice.

In that way child and youth participation becomes a social movement comprising individuals of particular ages, claiming their rights to have their views, opinions, needs, perspectives, and circumstances taken into account in community and government decision-making. Claiming rights to be involved in decision-making would need someone to operate or be taken up inter-generationally. It also means participation needs to take account of the diversity of children and young people; and in turn they would need to look to their responsibilities towards each other, and to older humans and to communities and the environment. That is itself then making the word 'participation' do a lot, but without necessarily 'paying it more' as Humpty Dumpty would say (see West 1996). Is it the right term?

'Participation', children and young people, and the future

Recognizing that 'participation' as practised in projects and situations described here is not simple; that it cannot be abbreviated down and it does not affect children and young people only, raises questions as to whether it is the best term to describe and encompass what is meant. There are key intergenerational aspects, from issues of adultism, to the strong commitment shown by all contributors along with many others, to children's and young people's rights and citizenship, forms of emancipation and their decision-making and action. The diversity of lives in terms of capacities and how they fit with prevailing social norms, and the struggle for inclusion of those that fall outside those norms, applies to individuals and groups, to citizens, of all ages, genders, disabilities, sexualities, ethnicities, and other constructed, claimed, or given identities. Age is one dimension that inevitably changes for everyone who lives long enough; within particular or across different groups age can always be used as the basis of power by adults, even if only within a particular group. Many adults, having experienced constraints (seen and not heard) and even age-based oppression as a child are reluctant or unwilling to give up the status and power over children as they grow up.

The need for children's and young people's participation rights is partly because of that diversity, as well as the location of power. Adults have power, but not all adults. Children and young people have rights, but not all are able to realize them because of marginalization and discrimination. Some children and young people are more powerful than others. Some children and young people form their own organizations to support each other and attempt to claim their rights: this process is known as participation. Other groups are facilitated in activities and organizations to do the same: to identify problems and solutions; this process is known as participation. Yet others are facilitated to do that in conjunction with adult groups and leaders; this process also is known as participation. Children and young people going on strike; marching; taking decisions and actions on issues such as climate change, violence at school; this also is known as participation. Children's involvement in family court decision-making; this is also known as participation. Children as consumers is almost certainly seen as their participation by commercial companies. And so on.

The term is difficult because of its ambiguities in English and in other direct translations of this word. Rizzini (Chapter 14) notes how it is *protagonismo* that resonates in South America, 'referring to children and young people's place and roles in society as active citizens' (see also Taft, 2019). This is partly reflective of the notion of children's agency preferred by some contributors, but goes beyond that, while terms such as empowerment and emancipation have what might be seen as contentious histories. Rather than attempt to find a utilitarian replacement, it might be preferable to focus on children's citizenship, and acknowledge that, and engage with, the potential debate on what children should and should not be allowed to decide does actually apply across society. What universal marker exists of a particular degree of maturity that can be applied to all ages, for all individuals? If all are citizens, and all have rights and responsibilities, those responsibilities extend to those in power ensuring social justice that is not their personal perspective of social justice, but one that includes rights and views and opinions across the population equally including children and young people. The process of rejuvenation required is recognizing and engaging citizenship and its complexities, perhaps as a social movement particularly involving and even led by children and young people, since all the issues of concern to them are frequently amplified versions of issues of concern across the population. Intergenerational social justice for all.

References

Johnson, V. and West, A. (2018) *Children's Participation in Global Contexts: Going beyond voice*, London: Routledge.

Johnson, V., Ivan-Smith, E., Gordon, G., Pridmore, P. and Scott, P. (eds) (1998) *Stepping Forward: Children and young people's participation in the development process*. London: Intermediate Technology Publications.

Johnson, V., Lewin, T. and Cannon, M. (2020) *Learning from a Living Archive: Rejuvenating child and youth rights and participation*, REJUVENATE Working Paper 1, Brighton: Institute of Development Studies. https://doi.org/10.19088/REJUVENATE.2020.001

Taft, J.K. (2019) 'Continually redefining protagonismo: The Peruvian movement of working children and political change, 1976–2015', *Latin American Perspectives* 46(5): 90–110. https://doi.org/10.1177/0094582X17736037

West, A. (1996) *But what is it? Critique of undefined participation*. Leeds: Save the Children.

West, A. (2004) 'Children and participation: meanings, motives and purpose', in: West, A. and Crimmens, D. (eds), *Having Their Say: Young people and participation – European experiences*, pp. 14–26. Lyme Regis: Russell House Publishing.

West, A. (2007) 'Power relationships and adult resistance to children's participation', *Children, Youth and Environments* 17(1): 123–135.

West, A. and Theis, J. (2007) *The Participation of Children and Young People in Emergencies: A guide for relief agencies, based largely on experiences in the Asian tsunami response*. Bangkok: UNICEF.

West, A. (2015) *Putting Children at the Heart of the World Humanitarian Summit*. New York: ChildFund Alliance, Plan International, Save the Children, SOS Children's Villages International, War Child, World Vision International.

Index

Note: Page numbers followed by "n" refer to notes.

www.ingramcontent.com/pod-product-compliance
Lightning Source LLC
Chambersburg PA
CBHW051256020426
42333CB00026B/3229